PROBATION AND POLICE:

Peace Officers In Conflict In Keeping The Peace

by

Dr. E. Scott Ryan

ISBN-0-935633-23-5

Library of Congress Catalog Card Number: 2001088688

Published by
Anchor Communications
Lancaster, VA 22503
www.goanchor.com

ABOUT THE AUTHOR

E. Scott Ryan, or "Ted", earned his Ph.D. from the Rockefeller Graduate School of Criminal Justice. He held the first Woodrow Wilson Fellowship in Criminal Justice Conflict Research, and was the first Visiting Fellow at the United States Department of Justice. He has served as Charter and Emeritus Chair of the American Board of Forensic Counselors, and Dr. Ryan is currently president of the Forensic Analysts and Case Managers Association (FACMA). In addition to seven book and monograph publications in criminology, Professor Ryan's studies have been internationally published in peer review journals of psychology, philosophy, forensics, education, theology and political science. Ted, who holds a tenured Full Professorship in the State University System of Pennsylvania at Mansfield, has published numerous articles on Freemasonry, survival swimming and metaphysics. He is author of the internationally acclaimed The Theology of Crime, in reference to which a Theology of Crime case study seminar series was introduced at Cornell University. In addition he's written A Forensic Counseling Approach To Prevent Adult And Juvenile Criminality in The New Millennium, which is the first book to be published on the subject, and one that is being hailed as an important new seminal work in reformulating criminological treatment. Both are available from Anchor Communications as part of the Dr. Ryan Series in Forensics, Criminology, Psychology and Freemasonry. (www.goanchor.com)

From The Editor

This book represents the only national study ever conducted on probation-police interaction and conflict. The data was obtained and analyzed on a systematic basis, in presenting field research information on operational conflict and contact, personal dissensus, organizational conflict and perceptual distortion, and three particular conflict adaptation styles. The implications of this study effect both research and administration in probation and police agencies.

Kenneth D. Roberts, Pres.
Anchor Communications

FOREWORD

It is gratifying to read informative material relating to my background in criminal justice in having served as a former Senior Pennsylvania State Parole Agent and in various other positions in both law enforcement and corrections at the state and county level.

The findings of Dr. Ryan validate my personal experiences with the interactions and attitudes between the probation/parole officers and the police community. Sometimes they held diametrical adaptation positions in the sharing of information and in the treatment and attitudes toward the offender. These differences, indicated by Dr. Ryan, also occur within the individual parole/probation agents in their orientation. As parole agent, I personally gravitated toward the police adaptation style, rather than a proponent of the parole/probation style. Other colleagues were middle-of-the road, i.e. neither strongly police nor parole/probation in orientation. All of these findings were supported by detailed statistical data from Dr. Ryan's research for his book.

The role of a parole/probation officer is unique since they have a dual function of protecting society and "rehabilitating" the offender. The term rehabilitation was gradually substituted by the words "reorientation." Experience seemed to indicate that attempts at rehabilitation were fruitless, instead the approach was reorientation of the offender to society. When the offender was released from prison or placed on probation, it was felt that a parole agent could only facilitate behavioral changes or adjustments to society. The desire for rehabilitation had to come from within the offender, and the agent could only offer the opportunity and tools that would foster acceptable personality and character changes.

Dr. Ryan's conclusions and assumptions are solidly supported by in depth research data that is quantified and qualified by tables of comparative statistical information garnered from past studies and field survey interviews. As a past practitioner in parole/probation and presently the police law enforcement field, I can attest to the validity of his findings through actual related experiences.

Of particular interest to this reader is Chapter VII relating to Conflict Adaptation Assessments of police and parole/probation officers style through measurements of attitude and job interactions, not only between themselves but also their offender "clients." The data drawn by Dr. Ryan from a series of interviews in Conflict Adaptation gives credence to my personal impressions and attitudes due to my fortunate experience in both areas of criminal justice. I am consequently more appreciative of the difference in parole/probation and the police adaptation styles, and I unequivocally concur with findings by Dr. Ryan.

I vividly recall the discussions between fellow parole agents and their attitudes towards the police and their offender caseload. There was never any consensus among the agents, and each seemed to go their separate way I adaptation styles. Throughout my employment in the police arena of law enforcement, such discussions among each other rarely occurred.

However, in my present position as Chief Deputy Sheriff, I am experiencing very recent notable changes in attitudes. I have observed some advancement towards the improvement in interactions between parole/probation and police officers by their willingness to share information.

Previously, at our bi-monthly crime task force meetings, the participants were state and municipal police, sheriff's department and occasionally the FBI. Presently, the local state parole agent and the warden of our county correctional facility are included as members of the police community. This was unheard of when I was a parole agent where the sharing of information was minimal and occurred only on an individual basis with a one-on-one police contact. However, the lines of communication are gradually opening with an apparent increase in respect for the other's profession.

There is a technological movement in Pennsylvania through JNET (Justice Network) which will eventually include all state and local correctional facilities, state parole, county adult and juvenile probation, district justices (minor judiciary) and court administrators' offices. This technology , which is in a pilot program stage, will enable these agencies to interface by computer and retrieve information from the Pennsylvania State Police Central Repository and the FBI, in the same manner as all the police departments through the Commonwealth are doing now.

This book comprises a unique research-based approach to understanding the dynamic interactions of two areas of the criminal justice system. It's clearly written, and it has a wealth of information grounded in the vast experience of the participants in Dr. Ryan's research. Frankly, it could be considered a guidebook to understanding what appears to be a dichotomy of approach to each other and the offender by these criminal justice entities of parole/probation and the police. Hopefully, Dr. Ryan's efforts will lead to a spirit of mutual acceptance and cooperation.

Harold J. Rowan

Chief Harold Rowan presently serves on an Advisory Subcommittee of the Pennsylvania Commission on Crime and Delinquency (PCCD). He received "Agent of the Year" commendation as a senior Parole Agent with the Pennsylvania Board of Probation and Parole. He has also served as a Policy Specialist for the Pennsylvania Inspector General's Office, and as a County Administrator in the District Attorney's Office. He is currently a Chief Deputy Sheriff, who sits on numerous justice system boards, in obtaining and administering grant funding for technological innovations in the criminal justice system.

Foreword

This book is essential for not only probation administrators, such as myself, but for criminal justice students who plan to pursue a career in the criminal justice system. It presents the facts of contact and conflict without any polemics. There are similarities between probation and police officers to the extent that they are both peace officers, but there are significant differences as well. Dr. Ryan's book describes, delineates and even measures those differences according to their organizational dimensions and personal dynamics.

In my twenty five years of working my way up through the probation ranks to the position of Chief Probation Officer, I've experienced an increased emphasis on the peace officer role of probation officers. That intensive supervision and intermediate punishment orientation, which is presented in Dr. Ryan's conflict adaptation classification, is neither that of traditional police law enforcement nor probation social casework. This book will inform veteran probation and police officers, among others, as well as acquaint students with what they will face as entering professionals in the profession of criminal justice. Furthermore, it does so with scientific documentation that provides a systemic guide for probation officers, correction managers, police administrators, judicial administrators, and criminal justice researchers and planners.

Robert McCullough
County Chief Adult Probation and Parole Association of Pennsylvania

Foreword

This one of a kind national study is essential for research, development and administration in the criminal justice system. It examines and documents the personal and organizational variables involved in criminal justice agency interaction. Police and Probation are the two front line criminal justice agencies that police and protect our communities. There is much more involved on the personal and organizational levels than meets the eye of not only the average citizen, but of police and probation officers themselves. Dr. Ryan's study probes broadly and deeply into all that's involved; and he does so in a scientific but personal, organizational but non-bureaucratic, scholarly but practical, analytic and conceptual but exact and precise manner. Frankly, I don't see how anyone in research and development and planning, as to police and probation matters, can be without this systemic study.

As a former Coordinator of a Masters Degree Program for in-service police and correctional managers, among other criminal justice professionals, I can attest to the value of this book as a resource and reference at both the graduate and undergraduate levels. Further, it is also quite useful for both pre-service students and in-service practitioners in conjunction with a training academy or educational institution at both introductory and higher levels of instruction. Although the demands put upon police officers can be immediate and case loads put upon probation officers can be heavy, this study can help police and probation better coordinate their interaction and collaborate in policing and protecting their communities. It also presents an example to others of what the best system research and analysis in criminal justice is all about.

James Chapman
Professor Emeritus of Criminal Justice at SUNY Corning
Director of The Southern Tier Law Enforcement Academy and Crime Lab at Corning, NY

ABSTRACT

This study consists of analyses of various dimensions of conflict between police and probation officers and their respective agencies in the criminal justice system. The data for the study were obtained from police and probation respondents to a field survey instrument in Nassau County, New York; Albuquerque, New Mexico; and San Jose, California. The study sites and the survey instrumentation are described with attached appendices containing pre-testing data.

The research is based upon findings about conflict determined from laboratory testing held at a conference at the School of Criminal Justice in Albany, New York. The conference demonstrated that conflicts were evident between police and probation involving four general dimensions of conflict – dissensus, esteem and status discrepancy, differential operational interests, and perceptual distortions. However, the specific nature and extent of operational and attitudinal conflicts (and their relationships to each other) in the field was not established. In the field research, these relationships were studied and the situations of contact as well as the demographic characteristics associated with conflict were examined.

The following measures were developed for this research effort: operational conflict scale, political – legal conservatism scale, status and esteem items, police prerogative scale and probation autonomy scale. In addition to the use of a structured questionnaire, a series of interviews were conducted based upon a conflict adaptation typology formulated during the study. These interviews elicited illustrative information concerning styles of inter-agency and officer-client interaction among sub-groups of police and probation officers classified according to three conflict adaptations.

The information from the field research is presented under four chapter headings:

1. operational conflict and contact (police interaction with probation);
2. dissensus (dealing with political – legal conservatism and status and esteem differentials);
3. organizational conflict and perceptual distortion (based upon the police prerogative and probation autonomy scales);
4. conflict adaptation styles (presenting the interview findings based upon three conflict adaptation types: police adaptation, probation adaptation, and moderator – neither police nor probation – adaptation).

This study extended the analysis of conflict between police and probation officers and their agencies into the world beyond laboratory – in order to clarify the nature and extent of conflict, to specify the dimensions (attitudinal, demographic and contact) related to conflict, and to develop further methods of conflict analysis. The information in this study is meant to contribute to the systems emphasis in criminal justice research and organization.

TABLE OF CONTENTS

LIST OF TABLES

Chapter 5

CHAPTER 1

INTRODUCTION AND BACKGROUND

For many years, there has been an increasing emphasis toward viewing criminal justice agencies (police, the courts, probation, etc.) as part of a unified system of criminal justice. The work of the President's Crime Commission,[1] the studies of the American Bar,[2] and the continuing focus on systems analysis[3] all tend to formulate a perception of the criminal justice apparatus as a single system.

The National Advisory Commission on Criminal Justice Standards and Goals presents the system model as envisioning "interdependent and interrelated agencies and programs that will provide a coordinated and consistent response to crime."[4] This conception has some obvious merits. It recognizes, for example, some commonality of objectives and a degree of interdependence among a set of agencies that share allegiance to superordinate goals such as the control and reduction of crime. Furthermore, the very fact that persons are processed from the status of suspect through that of parolee necessitates some linking among the agencies. In addition, this system concept serves to orient and order research and organizational development.

To this end, requests for more joint work, coordination, integration, collaboration, and merging of functions and agencies in the criminal justice system are frequently heard.[5] Suggestions for establishing liaisons that assume a broad criminal justice focus and make more salient the larger system rather than traditional agency concerns are strongly recommended.[6]

As stated by the National Advisory Commission on Criminal Justice Standards and Goals. "This is but another way of saying that no element of the criminal justice system completely discharges its responsibility simply by achieving its own immediate objective."[7] These perceptions have the advantage of forcing each agent and agency in the system to view their role and functions as part of the whole, thereby facilitating the surfacing and identification of obstacles to the completion of common tasks.

However, this system view can also pose conceptual and operational problems – foremost among which is the tendency to oversimplify the problems of interrelationship. System complexity among criminal justice agencies has been well documented,[8] and it is quite apparent that although the various agencies of the system work together, their formal relationship is amorphous, largely because they are structurally independent."[9] Therefore, while at one level it is possible to say that both police and probation are part of the same system of criminal justice and both are working toward common ends, "it is equally important to view them as discrete agencies, with objectives and techniques that are distinct and sometimes contradictory in purpose or methods."[10]

Conflict Issues

The problems of conflict inherent in criminal justice are not unique. A considerable body of literature has developed, particularly in recent years, about this phenomenon at the interpersonal, group and organizational levels. Although the substantive basis of conflict varies from system to system, the same processes have been identified and studied in many settings.[11] Also, a variety of strategies to cope with them have been suggested.[12]

From these studies of conflict, several aspects about this characteristic of man and his organizations have been identified. There are occasions where conflict can mean destruction, a loss of resources, and the failure to achieve personal or organizational goals. On the other hand, conflict can have integrating results on individuals and systems. It can lead to increased personal motivation and through the development of new forms of cooperative interaction increase organizational productivity.[13] From this perspective, conflict is seen as necessary to growth and constructive transactions among people and among organizations. Accordingly, the goal becomes, not the elimination of all conflict between systems, but, rather, the eradication of that conflict which is clearly and importantly dysfunctional.[14]

Conflict may occur because of differences in functions and objectives of specific agencies, or it may emanate from sources not directly related to agency objectives and tastes. If there are identifiable variations in beliefs and values between persons in criminal justice agencies, such differences may form the basis of conflict related to, yet different from, that arising from different agency roles. If intrasystem conflict does emanate from different sources and occurs on different levels, then it is important to identify these sources so that we can better know where conflict is, and, thus, better analyze its effects.

The Albany Conference

An attempt to study systematically some aspects of these problems was undertaken at a conference in May of 1969 at the School of Criminal Justice in Albany.* The setting of this conference and the research procedures and findings will be presented in some detail since the conference served to identify issues which became the major topics of the current study. The following statement best describes the rationale for the conference:

> The police and corrections are the two elements of the criminal justice system that are farthest apart, both in the sequence of their operations and, very often, in their attitudes toward crime and criminal offenders. Yet police and corrections serve critical functions in society's response to crime. And cooperation between police and correctional personnel is essential if the criminal justice system is to operate effectively.

---

*Responsible for planning the conference and serving as faculty were: Warner Burke, Institute of Applied Behavioral Science, National Training Laboratories; Harvey Hornstein, Department of Social Psychology, Columbia University; Alvin Cohn, Director, Probation Management Institutes, National Council on Crime and Delinquency; Charles McCloskey, Deputy Director, New York Division of Local Police; Robert Sullivan, Director of Training, Division of Probation, New York Department of Correction; and Vincent O'Leary and Donald Newman, School of Criminal Justice, State University of New York at Albany.

A four-day experimental meeting was organized which brought together in teams thirty-one police and probation officials from eight New England and Northeastern cities. The program was co-sponsored by the National Council on Crime and Delinquency, the International Association of Chiefs of Police, and the New York Department of Correction and Division of Local Police.* The purpose of this meeting was to attempt to identify the types of conflict which existed at the interface of two segments of the criminal justice system – in this case police and probation agencies. The goal was to increase understanding of the nature of conflicts at this point in the system and identify strategies which might better cope with them. Presumably, the techniques of study used and the resolution strategies suggested would have applicability to other points of conflict within the spectrum of criminal justice – police versus courts, prison versus parole or prosecutor versus police.

The participants were mature public officials; all were over forty years of age, with considerable experience in the criminal justice field. All were fairly well educated; all had at least some college experience. Probation executives were slightly older and had attained a higher level of education.* On the other hand, police officials tended to have been employed longer by their present agencies than did the probation officials. Almost all of the police had been with their current employers more than fifteen years while a significant number of the probation officials more recently jointed their present organization. This is less a commentary on differences in individuals and more on the differences in practice between two fields. Lateral transfer occurs much more frequently between agencies in the probation field than between police departments. It is a rare instance when a police official rises to ranks as high as all of these participants had attained without a substantial length of service in an agency.

Four general dimensions of conflict – dissensus, esteem and status discrepancy, differential operational interests, and perceptual distortions – were selected for analysis at the conference.[16] These classifications were not conceived as being mutually exclusive. Rather, they can best be thought of as different perspectives on the phenomenon of discord rather than as distinct categories.

Attitude scales were adapted and constructed to tap feelings concerning legal processes, approaches toward the offender, tolerance of deviance, faith-in-people, status and esteem perceptions, feelings of community-acceptability, organizational and perceptual conflict.[17] Although the number of participants was small, many of the differences found in questionnaire results were substantial. More importantly, the direction of the difference of opinion found between the two groups was very consistent. The difference appeared especially important in view of the relatively high level of education and rank of the participants. It was suspected that the disagreements between police and probation officials found here would be further accentuated among personnel at lower levels of their organizational hierarchies. The data yielded clues for further research and suggested methods of conflict resolution which might possibly have a chance of being effective. Furthermore, the Albany Conference established the basis for a further delineation of attitudinal and demographic variables associated with the subprocesses of interaction and conflict.[18]

Findings Derived From the Albany Conference

At the Albany Conference, an attempt was made to sample opinions of police and probation officials around issues which would likely affect the character of their interactions and yet would transcend essentially parochial concerns. Specific instruments were utilized which sought to tap value differences between groups with respect to: attitude about legal developments, views concerning approaches to the control of crime and offenders, tolerance of deviance and faith-in-people. Instruments were also used which were designed to measure differences in perceptions of role status and esteem, and conceptions of appropriate role behavior in police-probation interactions.

The first type of conflict examined was that which arises out of differences in the needs and values among members or groups of members within a system.[19] This type of conflict is basically ideological and rooted in differences in beliefs and norms. It may arise over the question of what is right or wrong, or over differences in methods of achieving goals. Conflict based on dissensus requires the interaction of groups each of whom are highly motivated to keep the core of their own set of values intact. Its source does not lie in immediate issues, although they may affect its intensity, but in the pre-existing beliefs of the participants.[20]

Probation and police officials are part of a system that requires increasing interdependence and interaction.[21] In such situations, if differences in important values exist between them, the probabilities are high that disputes will occur between members of each group whenever issues affecting both are at stake. Often the issue appears simple to reconcile until the covert underpinnings of the conflict are understood.[22] For example, it is not uncommon for the head of a probation agency who has been recruited from a different region which is believed to represent sharply variant political and cultural values to encounter problems with a police department over routine operational issues while a "native" administrator can follow precisely the same course with little or no conflict.[23]

To tap these dimensions, one scale was developed that measured favorable or liberal sentiments toward current legal developments. It was constructed through adapting questions prepared in other settings by Banton,[24] Bordua,[25] and at Boston University's Law Medicine Institute.[26] The data (presented in Table 1 in Appendix A)* indicated that probation officers scored much more positively toward liberal legal developments than did the police.

Another set of questions designed to measure relevant value differences between the groups tapped reactions to alternative approaches toward offenders (The questions and scores are presented in Table 2 in Appendix A.). Not surprisingly, probation officers demonstrated greater agreement with a treatment-oriented approach. Some of the greatest discrepancies were found between police and probation attitudes toward community treatment facilities; in general, probation officers favored such facilities and police were much more doubtful about their value.

A third scale, constructed to test tolerance of deviant behavior, yielded another measure of value differentials. In order to avoid answers which were too closely locked into occupational activities, questions were used in this scale which did not include operational issues likely to be encountered by police or probation officers in the course of their work. The questions were directed at more personal attitudes (The results are presented in Table 3 in Appendix A.). These questions were concerned with the following: homosexuality, hippie life styles, student demonstrators, welfare recipients and marijuana users. The probation officers displayed an overall more tolerant response to these groups of questions while the police responded negatively. The amount of disagreement varied by specific questions, but in all cases the probation officials' responses were consistently in the direction of greater toleration than were the police.

A fourth scale (contained in Table 4 in Appendix A) measured a generalized attitude described as "faith-in-people".[27] Skolnick and others indicate that an important difference between police and other groups would likely be found in their relative degree of faith in or suspicion of others.[28] The differences were not great but the police did reveal somewhat lower "faith-in-people" scores than the probation officials.

It is quite clear from the laboratory testing that the two groups tended to have a generalized difference in views, about law violators, deviants, and legal processes. These differences consistently manifested themselves in the responses to almost every question. As the item on community based treatment indicated, there was considerable disagreement between the two groups about desirable pathways to the goals of public protection and rehabilitation of offenders.[29]

A second major series of questions were then asked which tapped respondents' views about their roles and the status attached to their jobs. Three sets of questions were asked of the participants. The first (presented in Table 5 in Appendix A) dealt with status perceptions and was adapted primarily from the work Banton.[30] The second set of questions centered around the possibility of role transferability between the two fields (presented in Table 6 in Appendix A). A third scale was designed to test feelings of acceptability in the community. (Results are presented in Table 7 in Appendix A).

It was concluded from these laboratory scales that police and probation officials considered that the community accorded a higher status to the probation officer's task. Yet, the police gave many indications that they saw their jobs as fully professional and more demanding than the probation officer's. On the other hand, probation officials believed that there were greater differences between their job and a policeman's than perceived by police officials. The strains caused by differences in assessment of roles and selective status and esteem were fairly clearly evidenced.

A third major perspective on conflict between probation and police agencies was obtained by studying their conceptions of appropriate behaviors for each role in situations in which interaction took place between the two agencies. In specific terms, the question was asked, "How did representatives of the two groups behave as they shared responsibility for handling offenders and sought to serve their own organizational requirements in the process?" In order to measure these issues, a series of paragraph length statements about practical police and probation situations were presented to the two groups. They were asked to express their evaluation of a possible course of action. Table I-1 presents a summary of the vignettes and the mean responses to them by police and probation officers at the conference.

TABLE I-1
RESPONSES OF POLICE AND PROBATION OFFICERS
TO OPERATIONAL SITUATIONS,
ALBANY CONFERENCE

VIGNETTE SUMMARY	MEAN SCORES Police Score (N=15)	Probation Score (N-16)	Difference
1. Police requested revocation of probationer for rule violation when new crime can't be proved.	2.72*	4.06*	1.34
2. Probation department requests police chief to require policemen to report any probation violation	3.00	3.00	.00
3. Police contend probation department should be required to arrest probation violators.	2.20	4.33	2.13
4. Probation department refuses police department request for a list of names of persons on probation.	3.45	1.40	2.05
5. Probation department refuses police request to hold probationer in custody pending investigation.	2.63	2.00	.63
6. Police department requests 16-year-old youth be held in detention.	1.99	3.41	1.42
7. Police department wants information, which youth counselors may gather, shared with them.			
8. Police department believe it should be given right to make recommendations to judge.	2.72	4.53	1.81
9. Probation department will not allow probationers to act as informer for police.	3.90	3.60	.30
10. Probation department refuses police request for access to a probationer's case file.	4.45	2.60	1.85
11. It is proposed that police and probation agencies be combined into a single agency.	5.09	4.60	.49
12. Police department argues that a man with serious prior record should not receive probation.	3.18	5.00	1.82

*The higher the score the greater the disagreement with the viewpoint expressed (or action requested) in the vignette.
The scores range from 1.0 to 6.0.

There were obvious differences between the two groups. On the issue of arrest for probation violation, for example, probation officers indicated their strong feeling that the probation department is a treatment agency and should not make arrests at, whereas the police thought that probation officers should make arrests for probation violations. With respect to the matter of confidentiality, probation officers strongly opposed giving the police a blanket list of the names of probationers, while the police only slightly opposed such an action. Concerning the issue of recommendations to the judiciary, the police agreed somewhat, while probation officers disagreed, with the suggestion that the police department should be given the right to make recommendations directly to the court on whether specific individuals should be granted probation or not. Regarding the question of case file accessibility, there was disagreement regarding the probation officer's refusal to turn over his file for police use. While on the issue of risk taking, the police would refuse probation to a youngster because of its possible effect on others, whereas probation officers would grant it.

Value dissensus or discrepant role demands may explain some of the conflict between police and probation staffs, but a significant portion of the conflict which does exist also seems to be rooted more in the day-to-day job related demands placed on a policeman or probation officer. The frame of reference may be considered an operational one rather than individual. While probation and police officials have responsibility for executing tasks which at certain points intersect, conflicts arise as the two organizations concentrate on improving their specialized functions.[31]

The final major approach to the study of conflict which was explored at the conference centered on perceptual distortions which can prevent a clear understanding of the characteristics of other groups on whom one must ultimately depend for some support or resource. Distortions may arise from the lack of interaction between persons or organizations; more frequently they stem from the defective quality of the interaction which does occur. The important point is that, whatever their basis, they have enormous potential of becoming in themselves sources for creating and enlarging conflict.[32]

It is possible to scale several aspects of perceptual distortion in the interactions between police and probation officials at the experimental conference. The responses of police and probation officers as they attempted to estimate their own group's and the other group's responses to the twelve operational situations described above are summarized in Table I-1. Each participant was also asked to respond to the situations as he thought the average police officer and average probation officer would respond. Discrepancy or error scores were obtained by comparing these predictions with the actual responses of the two groups.

Thus, we have each police officers' own response (OP), and the mean response for all police $\overline{(OP)}$. Likewise, we have each probation officer's own response (OR), and the mean response for all probation officers $\overline{(OR)}$. The $\overline{OP}$ and $\overline{OR}$ values were presented in Table I-1. In addition, we have responses predicted or attributed to "the police" for each respondent (AP). When the respondent is a police officer, the response attributed to the police is designated as APP. When the respondent is a probation officer, the response attributed to police by probation officers is designated as APR. Finally, we have responses attributed to "probation officers" (AR), either by police (ARP) or by a probation officer (AR).

Discrepancies between these various measures were utilized as indices of several properties: prediction accuracy, actual and perceived conflict, and perceived distance between an individual's own answer and estimated group answers. Table I-2 demonstrates the use of one of these discrepancy measures. It describes the degree to which police and probation participants were able to predict the response of their own and opposite group to the twelve operational vignettes.

TABLE I-2

INACCURACY OF RESPONSES ON SITUATIONAL SCALE ATTRIBUTED TO ROLE INCUMBENTS BY POLICE AND PROBATION OFFICERS, ALBANY CONFERENCE

VIGNETTE SITUATIONS 1-12	MEAN ERRORS IN			
	POLICE (N=15) ATTRIBUTION TO:		PROBATION (N=16) ATTRIBUTION TO:	
	POLICE	PROBATION	POLICE	PROBATION
TOTAL OF MEAN	4.9	7.8	11.5	8.0
ERRORS	APP-OP	ARP-OR	APR-OP	ARR-04

The discrepancies were obtained on an individual respondent basis. For example, a police officer's response to an item (OP) was compared with the response he attributed to other police (APP). The discrepancy in absolute value was obtained $|APP\text{-}OP|$. The same value was obtained for each item, and the sum of these discrepancies served as the discrepancy score for the individual. For each subgroup of respondents, the mean discrepancy score was obtained. It is these values which are presented in Table I-2.

These findings emerged:

1) The most accurate predictions were made by the police anticipating the responses of other police officers (APP-OP=4.9).

2) The most inaccurate predictions were made by probation officials when they tried to estimate what the answers of police would be (APR-OP=11.5).

3) There was little difference between police and probation officials in their ability to predict how probation officers would respond (ARP-OR=7.8), (ARR-OR-8.0).

Another series of measures can be generated from these data relating to actual conflict and perceptions of conflict. These were differences in responses of police and probation officers to the operational situation vignettes. The actual conflict was indexed by obtaining the absolute difference for each item between own police $\overline{(OP)}$ and own probation responses $\overline{(OR)}$, and then summing these values for all 12 items. The actual conflict value between police and probation officers was 14.1 as may be seen in Table I-3. However, both police and probation officers believed even greater differences existed between the two groups, (APR-ARP), and probation officers perceived a greater discrepancy than did police officers.

TABLE I-3
ACTUAL AND PERCEIVED CONFLICT ON
SITUATION VEGNETTES

VIGNETTE SITUATIONS 1-12	MEAN DIFFERENCES IN:		
	ACTUAL CONFLICT	CONFLICT PERVEIVED BY:	
		POLICE (N=15)	PROBATION (N=16)
TOTAL MEAN DIFFERENCES	14.1	25.2	33.0
	OP-OR	APP-ARP	APR-ARR

The table shows that both groups overestimated the amount of conflict which actually existed between them. Probation officials presumably reflecting their greater distortion of police responses, were much more inaccurate about the amount of conflict which existed. After these data were revealed at the conference, some probation officials asserted that the police participants probably were unique and that their attitudes did not reflect typical police reactions. The police present vigorously denied this assessment and argued further that they had no idea who would be represented at the conference when they completed their estimates before coming to the conference. In fact, the representatives from various cities had generally never met before.[33]

While the analyses presented in Table I-2 and I-3 illustrate the nature of group or aggregate differences, still another and different discrepancy measure can be derived from responses of individual respondents. In this case, for each respondent one can examine the differences between his own answer, the answer he attributes to police, and the answer he attributes to probation. In this case of a police officer, it is possible to examine the difference between one's own response and the response attributed to police (OP-APP), and then calculate for all police the mean of these differences, i.e. with differences being treated in absolute terms. This mean is indexed as $\overline{\text{OP-APP}}$. The results of this analysis are summarized in Table I-4.

TABLE I-4

PERCEIVED DISTANCE BETWEEN OWN RESPONSES AND RESPONSES ATTRIBUTED TO INCUMBENTS

VIGNETTE SITUATIONS 1-12	MEAN OF DISTANCE SEEN BETWEEN:			
	OWN POLICE RESPONSE AND:		OWN PROBATION RESOIBSE AND:	
	ESTIMATED POLICE RESPONSE (N=15)	ESTIMATED PROBATION RESPONSE (N=15)	ESTIMATED POLICE RESPONSE (N=16)	ESTIMATED PROBATION RESPONSE (N=16)
TOTAL ESTIMATED DIFFERENCES	12.8	21.1	29.1	14.0

While both groups see some difference between their own response and those they attribute to members of their own occupational groups, they believe considerably more difference exists between their own response and those of the other occupational group. This latter finding is particularly marked for probation officers.

The differences in perception which have been demonstrated could have arisen from misunderstandings about value systems or they may have been the result of dysfunctions in the mechanisms which provide information to members of each system about the other. In either case, the probability was substantial that members of these two groups would inappropriately respond to each other by assuming conflicts which were much less than actually existed. This is a particularly costly kind of conflict which needs to be reduced in order to deal efficiently with those conflicts that are more reality based.[34]

A series of conclusions were drawn from the Albany Conference:

1) It was possible to identify and scale several types of conflict dimensions: dissensus, status and esteem stemming from role

functions, operational and perceptual.

2) Specific strategies needed to be developed to deal with specific types of conflicts.

3) There was a need to move from the laboratory setting to conduct further research in the field.

The purpose of the laboratory simulations of conflict between police and probation officers was to simplify reality: to provide some starting points as to identifiable and significant questions for further field research. The laboratory tests at Albany did confirm that the conflict classifications of Richard Walton – dissensus, esteem and status discrepancy, differential operational interests and perceptual distortions – were identifiable sources and objects of conflict among the conference participants representing their respective police and probation agencies.

The early conference findings served as a foundation and pilot for the dissertation research. Specifically, the following questions were raised for more detailed analysis in the field:

1) Is operational conflict related to the amount (as well as situation and location) of contact that exists between police and probation officers?

2) Which demographic variables (i.e. age, experience, religion, rank, ethnicity of officer, category of assignment, etc.) are related to conflict?

3) Are dissensus and status and esteem differentials associated with conflict?

4) Are there significant perceptual distortions along organizational conflict dimensions?

5) Are there identifiable conflict adaptation styles that affect the nature of agency and agent-client (offender) interaction?

This study is meant to contribute to the systems emphasis in criminal justice research and organization. While this emphasis is being widely encouraged, the problem of oversimplification based upon a scarcity of information remains. This study attempts to deal with this problem by providing information consisting of attitudinal, demographic and interaction dimensions that are related to police-probation conflict.

It was discovered at the Albany Conference that major differences and conflicts did exist between police and probation officials. However, the specific nature and extent of these operational and attitudinal conflicts (and their relationship to each other) in the field was not established. Furthermore, the situations of contact as well as the demographic characteristics associated with conflict remained unknown.

Accordingly, this study extended the analysis of conflict between police and probation officers and their agencies into the world beyond the laboratory – in order to clarify the nature and extent of conflict, to specify the dimensions (attitudinal, demographic and contact) related to conflict, and to develop further methods of conflict analysis.

After a series of interviews and pre-tests (described in detail in Chapter 3), the final study took place in Nassau County, New York; Albuquerque, New Mexico; and San Jose, California. (These study sites are described in further detail in Chapter 2.) The directors of the police and probation departments in these sites had agreed to lend their full cooperation to the study. In addition, it was felt that these three area sites—representing the Northeast, the Southwest and California—would provide a comprehensive national base for data collection and analysis.

NOTES

[1] President's Commission on Law Enforcement and the Administration of Justice, The Challenge of Crime in a Free Society, (Washington, D.C.: U. S. Government Printing Office, 1967), pp. 8-9.

[2] See American Bar Association Project on Standards for Criminal Justice, Standards Relating to the Administration of Criminal Justice) Chicago, Illinois: American Bar Association, Institute of Judicial Administration, 1974); Wayne LaFave, Arrest: The Decision to Take a Suspect into Custody (Boston: Little Brown and Co., 1965); Donald Newman, Conviction: The Determination of Guilt or Innocence Without Trial (Boston: Little Brown and Co., 1966); Lawrence Tiffany, Donald McIntyre, and Danial Rothenberg, Detection of Crime: Stopping and Questioning, Search and Seizure, Encouragement and Entrapment (Boston: Little Brown and Co., 1967).

[3] See Chris Argyris, Management and Organizational Development (New York: McGraw-Hill, 1971); C. Churchman, Systems and Management Annual (New York: Mason/Charter Publishers, 1975); Alvin W. Cohn, "Training in the Criminal Justice Nonsystem," Federal Probation 38, No. 2 (June 1974): 32-37; Ronald G. Havelock and Mary C. Havelock, Training for Change Agents (Ann Arbor, Michigan: Institute for Social Research, 1973); Frederick W. Howlett and Hunter Hurst, "A Systems Approach to Comprehensive Criminal Justice Planning," in Classes Conflict and Control, ed. By Jim Munro (Cincinnati: Anderson Pub. Co., 1976), pp. 539-550; Frederick R. Kellogg, "Organizing the Criminal Justice System: A Look at Operative Objectives," Federal Probation 40, No. 2 (June 1976); 50-55; Jay W. Lorsch and Alan Sheldon, "The Individual in the Organization: A Systems View," in Managing Group and Intergroup Relations, eds. Jay Lorsch and Paul Lawrence (Homewood, III.: Richard O. Irwin, 1972), pp. 161-182; Arlyn J. Melcher, General Systems and Organization Theory: Methodological Aspects (Kent State, Ohio: Center for Business and Economic Research, Kent State University, 1975); Jim L. Munro, "Towards A Theory of Criminal Justice Administration: A General Systems Perspective," in Classes, Conflict and Control ed. by Jim Munro (Cincinnati: Anderson Publishing Co., 1976), pp. 135-152; National Advisory Commission on Criminal Justice Standards and Goals, Criminal Justice System (Washington, D.C.: Gov't Printing Office, 1973); Anant R. Negandhi. Organizational Theory in an Open System (New York: Kennikat Press Corp, 1975); Everett M. Rogers and Rekha Agaraula-Rogers, Communication in Organizations (New York: The Free Press, 1976); Daniel L. Skoler, "Correctional Unification: Rhetoric, Reality, and Potential," Federal Probation 40, No. 1 (March 1976): 14-20; James C. Taylor, Technology and Planned Organizational Change (Ann Arbor, Michigan: Institute for Social Research, The University of Michigan, 1971), pp. 121-125; Ludwig von Bertalanffy, General System Theory (New York: George Braziller, Inc., 1968); Karl E. Weick, The Social Psychology of Organizing (Reading, Mass." Addison-Wesley Pub. Co., 1969), p. 108.

[4] National Advisory Commission on Criminal Justice Standards and Goals, Corrections (Washington, D.C.: Government Printing Office, January 23, 1973), p. 5.

[5] Preliminary Report of the Governor's Special Committee for Criminal Offenders (New York, NY: June, 1968); Final Report of the National Commission on the Causes and Prevention of Violence, "To Establish Justice, To Insure Domestic Tranquility" (Wash., D.C.: U.S. Government Printing Office, Dec. 1969), pp. 158-163; National Advisory Commission on Criminal Justice Standards and Goals, Corrections, pp. 6-7. 332-323; Police, pp. 73-75(Wash., D.C.: Government Printing Office, January 23, 1973).

[6] Vincent O'Leary and Edward Ryan, A Study of Conflict Resolution in Criminal Justice (a publication of the Probation Management Institute, administered by the National Council on Crime and Delinquency, Oct. 1969), pp. 25-26; National Advisory Commission on Criminal Justice Standards and Goals, Corrections (Wash., D.C.: Government Printing Office, Jan. 23, 1973), p. 8.

[7] National Advisory Commission on Criminal Justice Standards and Goals, Police (Wash., D.C.: Government Printing Office, January 23, 1973), p. 70.

[8] See Frank Remington et al., Criminal Justice Administration (Indianapolis: Bobbs-Merrill, 1969), pp. 3-47.

[9] See Vincent O'Leary and Donald Newman, "Conflict Resolution in Criminal Justice," Journal of Research in Crime and Delinquency (July 1970): p. 100

[10] Ibid., p. 5

[11] See Kenneth Boulding, "A Pure Theory of Conflict Applied to Organizations," in Power and Conflict in Organizations, eds. Robert Kahn and Elise Boulding (New York: Basic Books, 1964), pp. 136-145: Douglas Brown, The Human Nature of Organizations (New York: American Management Associations, 1973), pp. 65-67; Morton Deutsch, "The Effects of Cooperation and Competition upon Group Process," in Group Dynamics, eds. Dorwin Cartwright and Alvin Zander (New York: Harper & Row, 1968), pp. 461-482; Morton Deutsch, The Resolution of Conflict (New Haven: Yale University Press, 1973), pp. 351-359; John M. Dutton and Richard E. Walton, Interdepartmental Conflict and Cooperation: Two Contrasting Studies," Human Organization 25 (1966): 207-220; Robert Faris, "Interaction Levels and Intergroup Relations," in Intergroup Relations and Leadership, ed. by Muzafer Sherif (New York: Wiley and Sons, 1962), pp. 24-45; Ronald G. Havelock and Mary C. Havelock, Training for Change Agents (Ann Arbor, Michigan: Institute for Special Research, 1973), pp. 7-38; James W. Julian and Franklyn A. Perry, "Cooperation Contrasted with Intra-Group and Inter-Group Competition," in Small Group Communication, eds. Robert S. Cathcart and Larry A. Samavar (Dubuque, Iowa: William C. Brown Co., 1970), pp. 89-91; Colin Kessel, "Effects of Group Pressure and Commitment on Conflict Adaptability, and Cognitive Change," in Human Judgment and Social Interaction, eds. Leon Rappoport and David Summers (New York: Holt, Rinehart and Winston, 1973), pp. 296-303; Carl E. Kuhlman, Monroe J. Miller and Erol Bungor, "Interpersonal Conflict Reduction: The Effects of Language and Meaning," in Human Judgment and Social Interaction, eds. Leon Rappoport and David Summers (New York: Holt, Rinehart and Winston, 1973), pp. 229-237; Rensis Likert and Jane Likert, New Ways of Managing Conflict (New York: McGraw-Hill, 1976), pp. 11-44; Douglas McGregor, The Human Side of Enterprise (New York: McGraw-Hill Book Co., 1965); David C. Mortensen, "A Transactional Paradigm of Verbalized Social Conflict," in Perspectives on Communication in Social Conflict, eds. Gerald R. Miller and Herbert W. Simons (Englewood Cliffs, New Jersey: Prentice-Hall, Inc., 1974), pp. 90-124; John A. Seiler, "Diagnosing Interdepartmental Conflict," in Managing Group and Intergroup Relations, eds. Jay W. Lorsch and Paul R. Lawrence (Homewood, I11.: Richard D. Irwin, 1972), pp. 310-324; Herbert W. Simons, "The Carrott and Stick as Handmaidens of Persuasion in Conflict Situations," in Perspectives on Communication in Social Conflict, eds. Gerald R. Miller and Herbert W. Simons (Englewood Cliffs, New Jersey: Prentice-Hall, 1974), p. 178; Abraham Zaleznik, Gene W. Dalton, and Louis B. Barnes, Orientation and Conflict in Career (Boston: Harvard University Graduate School of Business Administration Division of Research, 1970).

[12] See John D. Adams, Organizational Development and Change (Wash., D.C.: National Training and Development Service, 1974); Chris Argyris, Integrating the Individual and the Organization (New York: John Wiley and Sons, 1964); Chris Argyris, Interpersonal Competence and Organizational Effectiveness (Homewood, I11." The Dorsey Press, 1962): Chris Argyris, Intervention Theory and Method (Reading, Mass.: Addison-Wesley, 1970); Dean C. Barnlund, and Franklyn S. Haiman, "A Philosophy and Method of Change," in Small Group Communication, eds. Robert S. Cathcart and Larry A. Samovar (Dubuque, Iowa: William C. Brown Co., 1970), pp. 206-215; Richard Beckhard, "The Confrontation Meeting," Harvard Business Review 45, No. 2 (1967): 149-153; Robert R. Blake, Jane Mouton and Herbert Shepard, "An Intergroup Problem-Solving Approach to Mergers," in Managing Intergroup Conflict in Industry, eds. R. Blake, J. Mouton and H. Shepard (Houston, Texas: Gulf Publishing Co., 1964), pp. 46-152; Robert R. Blake, Jane S. Mouton and Herbert Shepard, "Strategies for Improving Headquarters – Field Relations," in Managing Intergroup Conflict in Industry", eds, R. Blake, J. Mouton and H. Shepard (Houston, Texas: Gulf Pub. Co., 1964), pp. 114-121; Douglas Brown, The Human Nature of Organizations (New York: American Management Associations, 1973), pp. 65-67; Lester Coch and John French, Jr., "Overcoming Resistance to Change," in Group Dynamics, eds. Dorwin Cartwright and Alvin Zander (New York: Harper & Row, 1968), pp. 336-350; George Cvetkovich, "Small Group Dynamics in Extended Judgment Situations," in

Human Judgment and Social Interaction, eds. Leon Rappoport and David Summers (New York: Holt, Rinehart and Winston, 1978), pp. 315-335; Morton Deutsch, "Conflicts: Productive and Destructive," Journal of Social Issues 25 (1969): 7-41, Morton Deutsch, The Resolution of Conflict (New Haven, Yale University Press, 1973) chaps. 6, 8,12, 13; Roger Fisher, "Fractionating Conflict," in Conflict Resolution, ed. by Clagett Smith (Notre Dame, Indiana: University of Notre Dame Press, 1971), pp. 157-169; Neely Gardner, Group Leadership (Wash., D.C.: National Training and Development Service, 1974), pp. 32-33; Ralph M. Goldman, "A Theory of Conflict Processes and Organizational Offices," Journal of Conflict Resolution 10, No. 3 (Sept. 1966): 328-343; Ronald G. Havelock and Mary C. Havelock, Training for Change Agents (Ann Arbor, Michigan: Institute for Social Research, 1973), pp. 7-38; Murray Horwitz, "Managing Hostility in the Laboratory and the Refinery," in Power and Conflict in Organizations, eds. Robert Kahn and Elise Boulding (New York: Basic Books, 1964), pp. 77-94; Robert L. Kahn and Donald Wolfe, "Role Conflict in Organizations, in Power and Conflict in Organizations, eds. Robert Kahn and Elise Boulding (New York: Basic Books, 1964), pp. 115-126; Rensis Likert, The Human Organization. (New York: McGraw-Hill Book Co., 1967); Rensis Likert and Jane Likert, New Ways of Managing Conflict (New York: McGraw-Hill, 1976): A. J. Marrow, David G. Bowers, and S. E. Seashore, Management by Participation (New York: Harper & Row, 1967); David C. Mortensen, "A Transactional Paradigm of Verbalized Social Conflict," in Perspectives on Communication in Social Conflict, eds. Gerald R. Miller and Herbert W. Simons (Englewood Cliffs, New Jersey: Prentice-Hall, 1974), pp. 90-124; Eric H. Heilsen, "Understanding and Managing Intergroup Conflict," in Managing Group and Intergroup Relations, eds. Jay W. Lorsch and Paul R. Lawrence (Homewood, I11.: Richard D. Irwin, 1972), pp. 329-343; Stewart B. Shapiro, Management of Conflict (Los Angeles: Institute of Industrial Relations, University of California, 1973); Herbert A. Shepard, "Responses to Situations of Competition and Conflict," in Power and Conflict in Organizations, eds. Robert Kahn and Elise Boulding (New York: Basic Books, 1964), pp. 127-135; Muzafer Sherif and Carolyn W. Sherif, Intergroup Relations," in An Outline of Social Psychology, eds. Muzafer and Carolyn Sherif (New York: Harper and Bros., 1956), pp. 280-332; Kenneth W. Thomas, "Issues in Management of Conflict," in Management of Conflict, ed. by Stewart Shapiro (Los Angeles: Institute of Industrial Relations, University of California, 1973), pp. 9-11; Richard E. Walton, "Legal-Justice, Power Bargaining, and Social Science Intervention: Mechanisms for Settling Disputes," Institute for Research in the Behavioral, Economic and Management Sciences, Institute Paper No. 194, March 1968; Richard E. Walton, "Third Party Roles in Interdepartmental Conflict," Industrial Relations 7, No. 1 (Oct. 1967): 29-43; Karl E. Weick, The Social Psychology of Organizing (Reading, Mass.: Addison-Wesley Pub. Co., 1969), pp. 107-109; Gerald Zaltman, Robert Duncan and Jonny Holbeck, Innovations and Organizations (New York: John Wiley and Sons, 1973).

[13] See Chris Argyris, Management and Organizational Development (New York: McGraw-Hill, 1971), p. 157; Lewis Coser, The Functions of Social Conflict (New York: The Free Press, 1964), pp. 49-50; Morton Deutsch, The Resolution of Conflict (New Haven: Yale University Press, 1973), pp. 359-364; Edward Gross, "Symbiosis and Consensus As Integrative Factors in Small Groups," in Small Group Communication, eds. Robert S. Cathcart and Larry Samovar (Dubuque, Iowa: William C. Brown Co., 1970), pp. 63-71; Victor Harnack and Thorrel B. Fest, Group Discussion Theory and Technique (New York: Appleton Century Crofts, 1964), p. 176; Ronald G. Havelock and Mary C. Havelock, Training for Change of Agents (Ann Arbor, Michigan: Institute for Social Research, 1973), pp. 37-38; William S. Howell and Donald K. Smith, Discussion (New York: The Macmillan Co., 1956), p. 256; Daniel Katz, "Approaches to Managing Conflict," in Power and Conflict in Organizations, eds. Robert Kahn and Elise Boulding (New York: Basic Books, 1964), pp. 105-114; Clark Kerr, Labor and Management in Industrial Society (New York: Doubleday and Co., 1964), pp. 172-173; Donald Klein, "Some Notes on the Dynamics of Resistance to Change: The Defender Role," in Concepts For Social Change, ed. by G. Watson (Wash., D.C.: NTL Institute for Applied Behavioral Science, 1967), p. 30; Rensis Likert and Jane Likert, New Ways of Managing Conflict (New York: McGraw Hill, 1976), pp. 1-10; John L. Petelle, "The Role of Conflict in Discussion," in Small Group Communication, eds. Robert Cathcart and Larry Samovar (Dubuque, Iowa: William C. Brown Co., 1970), pp. 143-148; George Simmel, Conflict, trans. By Kurt H. Wolff (New York: The Free Press, 1955), pp. 43-49, 87-99; Herbert W. Simons, "The Carrot and Stick as Handmaidens of Persuasion in Conflict Situations," in Perspectives on Communication in Social Control, eds. Gerald R. Miller and Herbert W. Simons (Englewood Cliffs, New Jersey: Prentice-Hall, 1974), pp. 178-184; Herbert W.

Simons, "Prologue," in Perspectives on Communication in Social Control, eds. Gerald R. Miller and Herbert W. Simons (Englewood Cliffs, New Jersey: Prentice-Hall, 1974), pp. 3-8; Kenneth W. Thomas, "Issues in Management of Conflict," in Management of Conflict, ed. Stewart Shapiro (Los Angeles: Institute of Industrial Relations, University of California, 1973), p. 7; Victor A. Thompson, Bureaucracy and Innovation (University, Alabama: University of Alabama Press, 1967), pp. 16-17; Richard E. Walton, Interpersonal Peacemaking, (Reading, Mass.: Addison-Wesley Pub. Co., 1969), p. 145; Richard E. Walton and John M. Dutton, "Interdepartmental Conflict and Its Management: A General Model and Review," Krannert Graduate School of Industrial Administration, Purdue University, March 1968; Abraham Zaleznik and David Moment, The Dynamics of Interpersonal Behavior

[14] See Robert R. Blake, Jane S. Mouton and Herbert Shepard, "Using Third-Party Judgment to Resolve Intergroup Disputes," in Managing Intergroup Conflict in Industry, eds. R. Blake, H. Shepard, and J. Mouton (Houston, Texas: Gulf Publishing Co., 1964), pp. 50-57; Elise Boulding, "Further Reflections on Conflict Management," in Power and Conflict in Organizations, eds. Robert Kahn and Elise Boulding (New York: Basic Books, 1964), pp. 146-150; Morton Deutsch, "The Effects of Cooperation and Competition upon Group Process," in Group Dynamics, eds. Dorwin Cartwright and Alvin Zander (New York: Harper & Row, 1968), pp. 461-482; Ronald G. Havelock and Mary C. Havelock, Training for Change Agents (Ann Arbor, Michigan: Institute for Social Research, 1973), pp. 16-17; Rensis Likert and Jane Likert, New Ways of Managing Conflict (New York: McGraw-Hill, 1976), Chap. 4, pp. 59-69; Norman R. F. Maier, Problem Solving and Creativity: In Individuals and Groups (Belmont, Calif.: Brooks Cole Pub. Co., 1970): Robert D. Nye, Conflict Among Humans (New York: Springer Publishing Co., 1973); Stewart B. Shapiro, Management of Conflict (Los Angeles: Institute of Industrial Relations, Univ. of California, 1973); Kenneth W. Thomas, "Issues in Management of Conflict," in Management of Conflict, ed. Stewart Shapiro (Los Angeles: Institute of Industrial Relations, University of California, 1973), pp. 6-11; Richard E. Walton, Interpersonal Peacemaking: Confrontations and Third Party Consultation (Reading, Mass.: Addison-Wesley Pub. Co., 1969), pp. 144-146; Abraham Zaleznik and David Moment, The Dynamics of Interpersonal Behavior (New York: John Wiley and Sons, 1964), pp. 347-349.

[16] These classifications were suggested primarily by the work of Richard Walton of Harvard University who generously made available a substantial body of material.

[17] Vincent O'Leary and Edward Ryan, pp. 9-27.

[18] Vincent O'Leary and Donald J. Newman, p. 100.

[19] See Robert F. Bales, Personality and Interpersonal Behavior (New York: Holt, Rinehart and Winston, 1970), pp. 274-281; Douglas Brown, The Human Nature of Organizations (New York: American Management Associations, 1973), p. 15, 65; George Cvetkovich, "Small Group Dynamics in Extended Judgment Situations," in Human Judgment and Social Interaction, eds. Leon Rappoport and David Summers (New York: Holt, Rinehart and Winston, 1973), pp. 315-335; Morton Deutsch, The Resolution of Conflict (New Haven: Yale University, "The Cognitive Conflict Paradigm" in Human Judgement and Social Interaction, eds. Leon Rappoport and David Summers (New York: Holt, Rinehart and Winston, 1973), pp. 188-205; Kenneth R. Hammond and Berndt Brehmer, "Quasi-Rationality and Distrust: Implications for International Conflict," in Human Judgment and Social Interaction, eds. Leon Rappoport and David Summers (New York: Holt, Rinehart and Winston, 1973), pp. 338-391; Ronald G. Havelock and Mary C. Havelock, Training for Change Agents (Ann Arbor, Michigan: Institute for Social Research, 1973), pp. 10-15; Colin Kessel, "Effects of Group Pressure and Commitment on Conflict, Adaptability, and Cognitive Change," in Human Judgment and Social Interaction, eds. Leon Rappoport and David Summers (New York: Holt, Rinehart and Winston, 1973), pp. 235-236; Carl E. Kuhlman, Monroe J. Miller, and Erol Gungor, "Interpersonal Conflict Reduction: The Effects of Language and Meaning," in Human Judgment and Social Interaction, eds. Leon Rappoport and David Summers (New York: Holt, Rinehart and Winston, 1973) pp. 235-236; Henry McCarthy, "Some Situational Factors Improving Cognitive Conflict Reducation and Interpersonal Understanding," Journal of Conflict Resolution 21 (June 1977): 217-234; Serge Moscovici, Elizabeth Lage and Martine Naffrechoux, "Conflict in Three Person Groups: The Relationship Between Social

Influence and Cognitive Style," in Human Judgment and Social Interaction, eds. Leon Rappoport and David Summers (New York: Holt, Rinehart and Winston, 1973), pp. 311-314; Barbara F. Muney and Morton Deutsch, "The Effects of Role-Reversal During the Discussion of Opposing Viewpoints," Journal of Conflict Resolution 2 (Sept. 1968): 345-356; Milton Rokeach, Beliefs, Attitudes and Values, (San Francisco: Josey-Bass, 1970); Thomas C. Schelling, "Game Theory and the Study of Ethical Systems," Journal of Conflict Resolution 12, No. 1 (March 1968): 34-44; Muzafer Sherif and Carolyn Sherif, "Attitude Formation and Change," in An Outline of Social Psychology, eds. Muzafer and Sherif (New York: Harper and Bros., 1956), pp. 538-578; David A. Summers, "Conflict, Compromise and Belief Change in A Decision-Making Task," Journal of Conflict Resolution 12, No. 2 (June 1968): 215-221; Frederick J. Todd, Kenneth R. Hammond and Marilyn M. Wilkins, "Differential Effects of Ambiguous and Exact Feedback on Two-Person Conflict and Comprimise," Journal of Conflict Resolution 10, No. 1 (March 1968): 88-97; Gerald Zaltman, Robert Duncan and Jonny Holbek, Innovations and Organizations (New York: John Wiley and Sons, 1973), pp. 97-100.

[20] Vincent O'Leary and Edward Ryan, p. 7.

[21] National Advisory Commission on Criminal Justice Standards and Goals, Corrections (Washington, D.C.: Government Printing Office, January 23, 1973), p. 6.

[22] Chris Argyris, Management and Organizational Development (New York: McGraw-Hill Book Co., 1971), p. 175; Kenneth Boulding, "The Individual as A Party to Conflict," in Conflict and Defense, ed. by Kenneth Boulding (New York: Harper & Bros., 1962), pp. 80-104; Douglas Brown, The Human Nature of Organizations (New York: American Management Associations, 1973), p. 65; Morton Deutsch, The Resolution of Conflict (New Haven: Yale University Press, 1973), p. 364; Neely Gardner, Group Leadership (Washington, D.C.: National Training and Development Service, 1974), p. 33; Kenneth R. Hammond, "The Cognitive Conflict Paradigm," in Human Judgment and Social Interaction, eds. Leon Rappoport and David Summers (New York: Holt, Rinehart and Winston, 1973), p. 201; Ronald G. Havelock and Mary C. Havelock, Training for Change Agents, (Ann Arbor, Michigan: Institute for Social Research, 1973), p. 10; Carl E. Kuhlman, Monroe J. Miller, and Erol Gungor, "Interpersonal Conflict Reducation: The Effects of Language and Meaning," in Human Judgment and Social Interaction, eds. Leon Rappoport and David Summers (New York: Holt, Rinehart and Winston, 1973), p. 236; Rensis and Jane Likert, New Ways of Managing Conflict (New York: McGraw-Hill, 1976), p. 327; Jay W. Lorsch and Alan Sheldon, "The Individual in the Organization: A Systems View," in Managing Group and Intergroup Relations, eds. Jay W. Lorsch and Paul R. Lawrence (Homewood, I11." Richard D. Irwin, 1972), p. 180; Eric H. Neilson, "Understanding and Managing Intergroup Conflict," in Managing Group and Intergroup Relations, eds. Jay W. Lorsch and Paul R. Lawrence (Homewood, I11.: Richard D. Irwin, 1972), pp. 330-331; Robert D. Nye, Conflict Among Humans (New York: Springer Publishing Co., 1973), pp. 1-36; Everett M. Rogersand Rekha Agarwala-Rogers, Communication in Organizations (New York: The Free Press, 1976), p. 147; Robert Tannenbaum, "Management and the World of Work," in Innovations and Barriers in Conflict Resolution, ed. Stewart B. Shapiro (Los Angeles: Institute of Industrial Relations, University of California, 1973), p. 85; Richard E. Walton, Interpersonal Peacemaking (Reading, Mass.: Addison-Wesley Pub. Co., 1969), p. 144; Abraham Zaleznik and David Moment, The Dynamics of Interpersonal Behavior (New York: John Wiley and Sons, 1964), pp. 347-348; Gerald Zaltman, Robert Duncan and Jonny Hilbek, Innovations and Organizations (New York: John Wiley and Sons, 1973), p. 44.

[23] Vincent O'Leary and Edward Ryan, pp. 7-8.

[24] Michael Banton, The Policeman in the Community (New York: Basic Books, Inc., 1964).

[25] David Bordua, The Police: Six Sociological Essays (New York: John Wiley & Sons, 1967).

[26] Boston University Law-Medicine Institute: Training Center in Youth Development, "Report and Evaluation of Curriculum Development in the Police - - Community Relations Pilot Project," (Washington, D.C. :

Office of Juvenile Delinquency, Department of HEW, October, 1966).

[27] Morris Rosenberg, "Faith in People and Success Orientation" in The Language of Social Research, eds. Paul Lazarsfeld and Morris Rosenberg (New York: The Free Press, 1955), p. 160.

[28] Jerome Skolnick, Justice Without Trial (New York: John Wiley and Sons, 1967).

[29] Vincent O'Leary and Edward Ryan, p. 14.

[30] Michael Banton, Ibid.

[31] Vincent O'Leary and Edward Ryan, p. 29.

[32] Ibid., p. 30.

[33] Ibid., p. 34

[34] Ibid., p. 34

CHAPTER 2

DESCRIPTION OF STUDY SITES

The study sites were in Nassau County, New York, Albuquerque, New Mexico and San Jose, California. Nassau County was chosen after preliminary work had been completed with Bronx County and Manhattan County police and probation offices in New York City. Extensive interviews were conducted with police officials and police organizations in North Manhattan and with probation officers in the Adult Division in Manhattan and the Juvenile Division in the Bronx. After considerable field research and interviewing, it was decided that for the purpose of this study, conditions in New York City were such that it appeared to be less than suitable for the desired survey research. In addition to the uniqueness of New York, the five county jurisdiction within the City and the frantic pace in police officers, the virtual impossibility of getting either a probation officer out from under the files or of conversing with a police officer for more than a half-minute was totally frustrating.

Accordingly, Nassau County was chosen due to its proximity to New York City and its location within the New York Metropolitan area. All of the urban problems of New York City were present in Nassau County in a more modified form. The overcrowded, hectic, multi-jurisdiction, and amorphous uniqueness of New York City were absent. It was also believed that Nassau County would be more representative of the region in a national study.

Albuquerque and San Jose were included because of their participation as pilot cities for the research activities of the National Institute of Law Enforcement and Criminal Justice of the United States Department of Justice. The populations selected for this study (Nassau County, New York; San Jose, California; and Albuquerque, New Mexico) are described in the following table:

Characteristics of the Communities

TABLE II-1

REGIONAL POLICE AND PROBATION CENSUS DATA

LOCATION	CIVILIAN POPULA - TION	POLICE POPULA- TION	PROBATION POPULA- TION	AREA (SQU MILES	POLICE PER 100,000	PROBATION PER 100,000	POLICE PER 100,000	PROBATION PER MILE
NASSAU CO. NEW YORK	1,428,080	3,680	220	289	258	15	13	.8
SAN JOSE, CA	506,800	752	218	142	148	43	5	1.5
ALBUQUE-RQUE, NM	243,751	398	32	82	163	13	55	.4

*Nassau County has a unified police department serving the entire county.

It can be seen from the regional population data that although all three localities are developed ones, there are striking differences among them. Nassau County, New York represents a highly urbanized metropolitan area of the northeast directly adjacent to New York City. While New York City is unique in many respects, Nassau County is typical of many metropolitan urban-suburban areas of the country. It shares many major national urban crime problems due to its contiguous boundary with New York City, yet it is not as overwhelmed by them as is New York City. In addition, it has distinct crime problems of its own due to its huge 289 square mile area. The large size and population of Nassau County and its huge police department of 3,630 officers present a locality quite representative of the highly developed metropolitan region.

San Jose, California with a population of over a half-million people, could also be described as a metropolitan area. However, in addition to its California location, San Jose is different in that it is not contiguous to a national urban center. Although San Jose has a probation department approximately equal in size to that of Nassau County, its civilian and police populations are much smaller. Nassau's civilian population is three times as large as San Jose's, its area is twice as big and its police force is five times larger than San Jose's. In comparing San Jose to Nassau County, it is clear that while San Jose is a developed metropolitan region with a population of over a half-million people, it is not as highly congested nor as representative of major urban metropolitan conditions as is Nassau County.

Albuquerque, New Mexico might best be described as a metropolitan oasis of the southwest. It has a population of approximately a quarter of a million. The ratio of police per square mile and the number of police in relationship to the civilian population is very close to that of San Jose.

In contrasting the three regions, it can be stated that the study includes a major urban metropolitan region (Nassau), a middle-sized metropolitan area (San Jose), and a comparatively small metropolitan area (Albuquerque) that is quite representative of the southwest.

In addition to presenting different kinds of metropolitan areas from the northeast, the west coast, and the southwest, comparative police and probation population data are available. Police and probation ratios were computed by measuring the ratio of the number of officers according to the size of the civilian population and according to the area in square miles. It was discovered, as reported in Table II-1, that Nassau Count has more intensive policing than either San Jose or Albuquerque. In other words, in relation to the number of square miles to be covered and the number of the civilian population, there are twice as many police officers in Nassau than there are in San Jose or Albuquerque. However, in regard to probation coverage, San Jose shows more intensive use when compared to the population of the area served (Table II-1).

Characteristics of Police and Probation Officers in the Study Sites

The basic instrument employed in this study was a structured questionnaire. The instrument was distributed to the entire probation department in each of the three sites and to the day shift of the entire police department in Albuquerque and San Jose. In Nassau County, the day shift of every other police precinct was chosen. Contact was established with each department through its personnel division which distributed and collected the questionnaires. A cover sheet was attached to each questionnaire explaining the nature of the survey and requesting, on a completely voluntary basis, the signature of the respondent.

The rate of return was over 90% for both police and probation in each region with the exception of the San Jose Probation Department where the return rate was approximately 75%. The questionnaire was distributed by officers of the Personnel Department of each agency.

There were a total of 1,064 police and 393 probation respondents. In Nassau County there were 598 police respondents and 216 probation respondents. In Albuquerque, New Mexico, there were 180 police and 32 probation respondents. In San Jose, California, there were 286 police and 145 probation respondents. A description of the personal and job characteristics of respondents was obtained as part of the final survey instrument (Appendix C). More details about this instrument and the sampling design are contained in Chapter 3.

In Table II-2, certain personal characteristics of the respondents are presented, namely: age, ethnic group, religion, education and enrollment in job-related courses of study.

TABLE II-2

PERSONAL CHARACTERISTICS OF POLICE AND PROBATION OFFICERS BY SITE

PERSONAL CHARACTERISTICS	POLICE				PROBATION			
ITEM NUMBER	(598) Nassau	(180) Albu.	(286) S.J.	(1064) All	(216) Nassau	(32) Albu.	(145) S.J.	(393) All
1. AGE								
Younger (under 30)	33%	39%	43%	37%	43%	59%	32%	40%
Middle (30-44)	52%	50%	44%	49%	28%	13%	59%	38%
Older (over 44)	15%	11%	13%	14%	26%	29%	9%	20%
2. ETHNIC GROUP								
White	96%	76%	94%	92%	93%	50%	90%	88%
Black	3%	3%	0%	2%	4%	6%	3%	4%
Hispanic	1%	20%	4%	5%	0%	22%	7%	4%
3. RELIGION								
Protestant	23%	60%	53%	37%	26%	51%	57%	39%
Catholic	70%	40%	41%	57%	43%	45%	38%	41%
Jewish	2%	0%	1%	1%	20%	0%	4%	13%
4. EDUCATION								
High School	29%	20%	3%	20%	1%	16%	1%	2%
Some College	64%	74%	53%	63%				
College Degree	5%	5%	44%	16%	30%	45%	36%	33%
Graduate Work					67%	35%	60%	61%
5. JOB COURSES								
Yes	52%	71%	61%	58%	43%	42%	41%	46%
No	47%	28%	39%	42%	54%	58%	48%	52%

NOTES: Categories do not add up to 100% for all items. On some items there were considerable numbers of multiple and no responses.

The specific grouping of responses classified in the above categories is presented in Appendix C.

A review of the modal characteristics of police officers reveals the following attributes: white, middle aged (30 to 44 years), some college education and enrollment in job related courses. It should be noted that the San Jose police are distinguished by their large percentage of college graduates, 44% as compared to only 5% of college graduates among Nassau and Albuquerque police. Modal probation characteristics indicate white ethnicity, graduate schooling, and young ages (under 30).

In Table II-3, certain job descriptive characteristics of the respondents are presented, namely: years of experience, rank, nature of work and assignment, ethnic identity of offender population, personal conception of role (job image), and the types of staff in the opposite agency with whom contact is most likely to occur.

TABLE II-3
JOB CHARACTERISTICS OF POLICE
AND PROBATION OFFICERS

JOB CHARACTERISTICS	POLICE				PROBATION			
ITEM NUMBER Number	(598) Nassau	(180) Albu.	(286) S.J.	(1064) All	(216) Nassau	(32) Albu.	(145) S.J.	(393) All
l1. YEARS EXPERIENCE								
Low (Less than 6 years)	34%	39%	45%	38%	63%	77%	53%	61%
Middle (7-15 yrs)	36%	46%	36%	38%	27%	19%	43%	32%
High (More than 15 years)	29%	15%	19%	24%	7%	3%	4%	6%
11. RANK								
Low	76%	71%	67%	72%	51%	81%	41%	50%
Middle	16%	19%	24%	19%	35%	12%	55%	41%
High	7%	10%	9%	8%	8%	7%	4%	6%
12. NATURE OF WORK								
Supervisory	23%	26%	21%	23%	32%	30%	16%	26%
Field	66%	63%	74%	68%	43%	53%	69%	53%
Administrative	6%	6%	5%	6%	16%	17%	8%	13%

TABLE II-3

JOB CHARACTERISTICS OF POLICE AND PROBATION OFFICERS

JOB CHARACTERISTICS	POLICE				PROBATION			
ITEM NUMBER Number	(598) Nassau	(180) Albu.	(286) S.J.	(1064) All	(216) Nassau	(32) Albu.	(145) S.J.	(393) All
10. CATEGORY OF ASSIGNMENT								
Patrol	41%	45%	73%	50%				
Detective	20%	28%	4%	17%				
Headquarters	12%	17%	13%	13%				
Juvenile	6%	9%	10%	8%	19%	39%	37%	28%
Adult Probation					54%	58%	56%	55%
Family Court					9%	0%	7%	7%
9. SPECIALIZED ASSIGNMENT								
Morals	2%	14%	0%	4%				
Narcotics	6%	4%	2%	5%	14%	7%	4%	10%
Intake					8%	16%	20%	12%
7. JOB IMAGE								
Community Service	26%	29%	31%	27%	50%	37%	53%	50%
Law Enforcement	59%	62%	55%	59%	6%	6%	18%	10%
Both	5%	9%	9%	7%	33%	57%	29%	33%
6. TYPE OFFENDER								
White	40%	6%	28%	31%	50%	12%	46%	48%
Black	20%	3%	6%	18%	7%	0%	1%	4%
Hispanic	1%	39%	29%	15%	0%	88%	28%	18%

TABLE II-3 (Continued)

JOB CHARACTERISTICS	POLICE				PROBATION			
ITEM NUMBER	(598) Nassau	(180) Albu.	(286) S.J.	(1064) All	(216) Nassau	(32) Albu.	(145) S.J.	393) All
15. TYPE PROBATION OFFICER								
Adult	28%	32%	16%	26%				
(Family- Juvenile	10%	14%	34%	17%				
50-55								
15. TYPE PO POLICE OFFICER								
Juvenile					24%	0%	5%	15%
Detective					31%	39%	35%	33%
Lieutenant					2%	26%	25%	12%
Patrolman					18%	22%	8%	15%
Multiple					8%	13%	27%	15%

NOTES: Categories do not add up to 100% for all items. On some items there were considerable numbers of multiple and no responses.

The specific grouping of responses classified in the above categories is presented in Appendix C.

As compared to the modal characteristics of probation officers, the table shows that police officers tend to have more years experience, are more likely to be engaged in field work, and experience more contact with none-white offenders. The police officers are most likely to be assigned to patrol work, define their role as that of law enforcement rather than community services, and experience interaction with probation officers responsible for supervising adults.

Probation officers are less experienced and are most likely to be from the adult divisions. They interact primarily with detectives and they are more likely to define their role as community service or as a combination of law enforcement and community service than are the police.

It is interesting to note that while 36% of police and 30% of probation officers are not able to identify the primary ethnic group among the offenders they serve, probation officers are somewhat more likely than police to identify their clients as white.

Finally, as part of the survey instrument, a fairly detailed account of the amount and focus of police-probation interaction was obtained (Appendix C). In Table II-4, reported interactions of both a personal and job-related nature as well as the location, situation and numbers of persons involved in them are presented.

TABLE II-4

CHARACTERISTICS OF CONTACTS OF POLICE AND PROBATION OFFICERS

INTER-ROLE CONTACTS	POLICE				PROBATION			
ITEM NUMBER	(598) Nassau	(180) Albu.	(286) S.J.	(1064) All	(216) Nassau	(32) Albu.	(145) S.J.	(393) All
18. PERSONAL								
Low	78%	71%	58%	71%	32%	34%	28%	31%
Medium	15%	25%	29%	21%	30%	31%	36%	32%
High	6%	4%	12%	7%	36%	35%	36%	36%
13. JOB-RELATED								
Low	79%	74%	78%	78%	27%	7%	16%	21%
Medium	15%	20%	13%	15%	37%	48%	45%	41%
High	5%	6%	8%	6%	33%	42%	38%	35%
14. NUMBERS								
Low	63%	60%	62%	62%	21%	0%	9%	15%
Medium	10%	10%	10%	10%	8%	12%	11%	9%
High	26%	30%	28%	27%	67%	88%	80%	74%
16. LOCATION								
Street	4%	1%	5%	3%	1%	3%	0%	1%
Station House	5%	23%	5%	8%	8%	22%	9%	9%
Family Court	3%	1%	3%	2%	6%	3%	5%	5%
Probation Office	1%	5%	8%	4%	4%	9%	10%	7%
Telephone	39%	17%	29%	33%	48%	28%	41%	44%
Multiple	6%	9%	14%	9%	17%	6%	31%	21%
17. SITUATION								
Probation Task	26%	9%	22%	22%	38%	9%	7%	24%
Police Task	3%	1%	9%	6%	2%	3%	8%	4%
Solve Crime	1%	0%	4%	2%	4%	0%	1%	3%
Information	21%	24%	19%	21%	27%	45%	37%	32%
Multiple	3%	19%	11%	7%	5%	43%	46%	23%

NOTES: Categories do not add up to 100% for all items. On some items there were considerable numbers of multiple and no responses.

The specific grouping of responses classified in the above categories is presented in Appendix C.

The pattern of interaction displayed in the table shows quite consistent differences across the three sites. While personal and job related contacts with probation are low for the police, the inter-agency contacts are substantially higher for probation officers. The focus of the interaction concerns itself with probation tasks and information verification, and it occurs predominately over the telephone.

A comparison of demographic descriptions of police and probation departments in the regions indicate some differences. Namely, in Albuquerque there are more Hispanics among police officers, probation officers and offenders. Certain religious differences also exist: in Nassau County, a majority of police officers are Catholic and there are more Jewish probation officers. In San Jose, probation officers, unlike those in Nassau or Albuquerque, tend to be older than the police and they hold more senior rank compared to the other probation departments. It may also be noted that in San Jose, the police are considerably higher educated and experience somewhat more personal contact with probation officers than their counterparts under study in other parts of the county.

However, despite these differences, there is a remarkable similarity among the demographic patterns for the three regional areas. In all areas, except San Jose, police officers tend to be older than probation officers. In each area, probation officers are better educated and less experienced than police officers. Probation officers consistently have more contact with the police than vice versa; and the most contact in each regional area takes place over the telephone. When contact does occur, it is related to probation matters and most often involves information verification.

CHAPTER 3

DESCRIPTION OF SURVEY INSTRUMENT

The following instrument was a structured questionnaire covering the following areas:

1. Demographic and job characteristics of respondents;
2. Inter-agency contact:
3. Operational conflict:
4. Dissensus regarding political-legal issues and status and esteem attitudes;
5. Organizational-perceptual conflict vignettes.

The demographic information collected from police and probation officers was described in the last chapter. They are summarized below according to their item number on the final survey instrument.

TABLE III-1

TOPICS INCLUDED IN DEMOGRAPHIC AND JOB CHARACTERISTICS

ITEM NUMBER	ITEM NUMBER
1. Age	8. Years of experience
2. Ethnic group	9. Specialized assignment
3. Religion	10. Category of assignment
4. Education	11. Rank
5. Job-related course enrollment	12. Nature of work
6. Ethnic identity of offender population	13. Type of offender with whome contact occurs
7. Role concept or job image	

The questions tapping inter-agency contact are presented in Table III-2 along with their item numbers on the final survey instrument as follows. Both the demographic and contact variables were developed from the laboratory data, information from conference participants, and through follow-up interviews with other police and probation officers.

TABLE III-2

POLICE-PROBATION CONTACT ITEMS IN FINAL INSTRUMENT

Instructions: (for Police) Many of the questions in the following section refer to probation officers. When the word "probation" officer is used, it refers to an individual who is responsible for supervising offenders who have been brought in on an offense, but placed on probation instead of being sent to prison. A "probation" officer is not a parole officer. A parole officer supervises offenders after they have been released from prison.

When we mention the average police or probation officer, we mean the police or probation officer in the community where you work.

ITEM
NUMBER

13. (Police) In your work during the past year, how often did you have contact with probation officers?

(Probation) In your work during the past year, how often did you have contact with police officers?

None at all	_____
Less than once a month	_____
Once or twice a month	_____
Three or four times a month	_____
More than once a week	_____

14. (Police) In your current police work, how many probation officers do you have contact with?

(Probation) In your current probation work, how many police officers do you have contact with?

None at all	_____
One	_____
Two or three	_____
Four or more	_____

16. (Police) At what location (s) have most of your contacts with probation officers taken place?

(Probation) At what location (s) have most of your contacts with police officers taken place?

None at all ____
On the street ____
In the police station house ____
In the Family Court ____
In a probation office ____
Over the telephone ____
Other (s), please specify ____

17. (Police) In what kinds of situation (s) have most of your contacts with probation officers occurred?

None at all ____
When you were helping the probation officer in a probation-related task ____
When the probation officer was helping you in a police-related task ____
When you and the probation officer were working together to solve a crime ____
Information verification ____
Other (s), please specify ____

(Probation) In what kinds of situation (s) have most of your contacts with police officers occurred?

None at all ____
When the police officer was helping you in a probation-related task ____
When you were helping the police officer in a police-related task ____
When you and the police officer were working together to solve a crime ____
Information verification ____
Other (s), please specify ____

18. (Police) Outside of your job as a police officer, how many probation officers do you ever have personal contact with?

(Probation) Outside of your job as a probation officer, how many police officers do you ever have personal contact with?

None ______
One or two ______
Three to five ______
Six or more ______

The political-legal liberalism scale as well as the status and esteem items on the final instrument were developed from the original laboratory tests at the Albany Conference. The original vignettes provided data which served as the basis for a conflict adaptation formulation. In addition, the organizational conflict vignettes from the Albany Conference were condensed to form two scales: the police perogative and probation autonomy scales. These scales provided data for the analysis of organizational and perceptual conflict.

Of the fifteen hundred questionnaires administered for final analysis, 1,437 yielded usable data. Of the responses included in the final analysis, 1,064 were obtained from police officers, while 393 questionnaires represent responses from probation officers. Approximately 60% of all completed questionnaires were taken from Nassau County, New York. The numbers are as follows:

	Nassau County	San Jose	Albuquerque	Total
Police	598	286	180	1064
Probation	216	145	32	393
	814	431	212	1457

Since a standardized instrument was not readily available to tap many of the attitudinal and perceptual dimensions dealing with agency conflict and dissensus, one of the major tasks was devising a set of instruments which would yield reliable results. The procedures used in selecting items and the methods employed in combining individual items into various scales are briefly described in the following sections.

Operational Conflict

As one of the first steps, it was necessary to define the kind of conflict towards

As one of the first steps, it was necessary to define the kind of conflict towards which police and probation officers would be responding. In order to accomplish this, twelve statements concerning conflict areas that were identified at the Albany Conference were prepared. These statements were evaluated by a small sample of New York State police and probation officers in Syracuse, New York. Based on these responses, seven questions were chosen as providing an adequate representation of possible areas of police-probation operational conflict.

These items were scattered throughout a longer attitude questionnaire. The seven operational conflict questions, which were organized in a Likert scale format, using a agree-disagree continuum, are listed in Table III-3. The scale items were found to be a relatively homogeneous set; based on the entire group of 1,457 respondents, the Spearman-Brown reliability estimate was found to be .89.

TABLE III-3

OPERATIONAL CONFLICT SCALE FOR FINAL INSTRUMENT

Instructions: The following statements are matters of opinion. Some of them you may agree with and others you may not agree with. Please indicate the extent to which you agree or disagree with each of the following statements. Use the following numerical scale and after each item circle the appropriate number.

-3	- 2	-1	+1	+2	+3
Disagree Very Much	Disagree Pretty Much	Disagree A Little	Agree A Little	Agree Pretty Much	Agree Very Much

ITEM NUMBER							
32.	There is a need to reduce conflict between police and probation officers in our area (where you work).	-3	-2	-1	+1	+2	+3
36.	There are very few conflicts existing between the police and probation department in our area.	-3	-2	-1	+1	+2	+3

40.	There is a need to improve cooperation between police and - probation officers in our area.	-3	-2	-1	+1	+2	+3
44.	A situation of serious conflict exists between the police and pro- bation department in our area.	-3	-2	-1	+1	+2	+3
47.	On a personal level, police and probation officers generally get along quite well together in our area.	-3	-2	-1	+1	+2	+3
53.	In the course of carrying out their jobs in our area, probation and police officers seem to have lots of conflict.	-3	-2	-1	+1	+2	+3
57.	Drawing on my own work experience, I think that in our area, there is a great amount of conflict between police and probation officers.	-3	-2	-1	+1	+2	+3

Spearman-Brown reliability estimate .89 (N=1,457)

Dissensus

In order to obtain a clearer picture of the liberal-conservative dimension, a factor analysis was performed on a set of data collected in a pre-test from Nassau County police and probation officers (see Appendix B for pre-test instrument). All the factor analyses reported in this study are based on a normal varimax rotation of a principal axis extraction. The factor analysis produced a seven item liberal-conservative scale from the original four-teen items identified by asterisks in Table III-4.

TABLE III-4

CONSERVATIVE-LIBERAL QUESTIONS FROM PILOT STUDY

Instructions: The following statements are matters of opinion. Some of them you may agree with and others you may not agree with. Please indicate the extent to which you agree or disagree with each of the following statements. Use the following numerical scale and after each item circle the appropriate number.

- -3	- 2	-1	+1	+2	+3
Disagree Very Much	Disagree Pretty Much	Disagree A Little	Agree A Little	Agree Pretty Much	Agree Very Much

ITEM NUMBER	Conservative Statements						
*23.	The majority of judges have gone too far in protecting rights of criminal offenders.	-3	-2	-1	+1	+2	+3
*24.	Most of what passes for rehabilitation is a farce and should be replaced with tougher measures.	-3	-2	-1	+1	+2	+3
*27.	The law has been far too lenient in its treatment of conscientious objectors.	-3	-2	-1	+1	+2	+3
29.	Street demonstrations by homosexual groups such as "gay lib" should be banned as an offense against public morality.	-3	-2	-1	+1	+2	+3
*34.	Penalties for smoking marijuana should be increased.	-3	-2	-1	+1	+2	+3
*38.	Young people should be taught more discipline and respect for authority in the school.	-3	-2	-1	+1	+2	+3

41.	Certain religious groups whose beliefs do not permit them to salute the flag should either be forced to conform or lese be abolished.	-3	-2	-1	+1	+2	+3
*44.	Any country which tolerates as much dissent as the U.S. has recently experienced is headed for disaster.	-3	-2	-1	+1	+2	+3
	Liberal Statements						
28.	The death penalty is barbaric, and should be abolished.	-3	-2	-1	+1	+2	+3
32.	The right of a citizen to protest against any policy of the U.S. government (be it foreign or domestic) must be vigilantly protected.	-3	-2	-1	+1	+2	+3
35.	Marriages between persons of different races should be socially acceptable.	-3	-2	-1	+1	+2	+3
*45.	The action of the National Guard in shooting four Kent State students was a shameful and a completely unnecessary response	-3	-2	-1	+1	+2	+3
48.	Those individuals who openly acknowledge their homosexuality should have the same opportunities for employment and housing as guaranteed by law to other citizens.	-3	-2	-1	+1	+2	+3

*Final item used in scales

NOTE: The asterisks identify items included in the final scale.

In an attempt to further clarify the structure of the conservative-liberal dimension, 26 additional conservative-liberal items were administered to a sample of 120 Suffolk County, New York police and probation officers to form a 40 item Conservative-Liberal Pilot Questionnaire. The entire set of questions dealt with legal policies, social control, and events of a politically controversial nature and are listed in Table III-5.

TABLE III-5

PILOT CONSERVATIVE – LIBERAL QUESTIONNAIRE
Administered to 120 Suffolk County Police and Probation Officers

Instructions: The following statements are matters of opinion. Some of them you may agree with and others you may not agree with. Please indicate the extent to which you agree or disagree with each of the following statements. Use the following numerical scale and after each item circle the appropriate number.

- -3	- 2	-1	+1	+2	+3
Disagree Very Much	Disagree Pretty Much	Disagree A Little	Agree A Little	Agree Pretty Much	Agree Very Much

ITEM NUMBER							
1.	The majority of judges have gone too far in protecting rights of criminal offenders.	-3	-2	-1	+1	+2	+3
2.	Racial imbalances should be corrected wherever they publicly occur —housing, employment, schools.	-3	-2	-1	+1	+2	+3
3.	It should not be necessary to prove that a confession is voluntary in order to have it admitted into evidence.	-3	-2	-1	+1	+2	+3
4.	The individual rights or protest against government policies must be more vigilantly protected.	-3	-2	-1	+1	+2	+3
5.	Street demonstrations by homosexual groups such as "gay lib" should be banned as an offense against public morality.	-3	-2	-1	+1	+2	+3
6.	Most criminals need treatment programs – not punishment.	-3	-2	-1	+1	+2	+3
7.	Most of what passes for rehabilitation is too soft and should be replaced with tougher measures.	-3	-2	-1	+1	+2	+3
8.	Community control of schools	-3	-2	-1	+1	+2	+3

	and other public institutions is a good idea.						
9.	The police should not have to be bothered with going through the process of getting search warrants.	-3	-2	-1	+1	+2	+3
10.	It's a good idea for prisoners to have their own union.	-3	-2	-1	+1	+2	+3
11.	A college president should have their right to fire any teacher whose private life is sexually promiscuous.	-3	-2	-1	+1	+2	+3
12.	The death penalty constitutes cruel and unusual punishment.	-3	-2	-1	+1	+2	+3
13.	The law has been far too lenient in its treatment of conscientious objectors.	-3	-2	-1	+1	+2	+3
14.	The approach taken by the authorities in the Attica disturbances indicated a gross disregard for human life.	-3	-2	-1	+1	+2	+3
15.	Most police should be allowed to detain any person who they have reasonable cause to believe may commit a crime.	-3	-2	-1	+1	+2	+3
16.	Dissenters should have the right to use public monuments, such as the Statue of Liberty in New York, as a means of making their protests.	-3	-2	-1	+1	+2	+3
17.	The Minister who married two homosexuals ought to be barred from the ministry.	-3	-2	-1	+1	+2	+3
18.	Penalties for violating the law are far too harsh.	-3	-2	-1	+1	+2	+3
19.	In school, young people should be taught more discipline and respect for authority.	-3	-2	-1	+1	+2	+3
20.	The action of the National Guard	-3	-2	-1	+1	+2	+3

in shooting four Kent State students was a shameful and completely unnecessary response.

21.	Wire tapping and other forms of government surveillance must be more strictly limited.	-3	-2	-1	+1	+2	+3
22.	Any country which tolerates as much dissent as the U.S. has recently experienced is headed for disaster.	-3	-2	-1	+1	+2	+3
23.	Pornography should be readily available to any adult who wants it.	-3	-2	-1	+1	+2	+3
24.	Penalties for hard drug possession should be increased.	-3	-2	-1	+1	+2	+3
25.	In our society, prisoners are not given enough basic human rights.	-3	-2	-1	+1	+2	+3
26.	Parents should be made financially responsible for the vandalism of their children.	-3	-2	-1	+1	+2	+3
27.	The rights of Black Muslims must be as vigilantly protected as the rights of any other religious group.	-3	-2	-1	+1	+2	+3
28.	If a person doesn't love this Country as it is, he ought to get out.	-3	-2	-1	+1	+2	+3
29.	Trial marriages are a good idea.	-3	-2	-1	+1	+2	+3
30.	Any demonstrator who makes obscene gestures and remarks at a law enforcement officer deserves to be clubbed.	-3	-2	-1	+1	+2	+3
31.	Too much permissiveness is helping to destroy this Country.	-3	-2	-1	+1	+2	+3
32.	Marijuana users should be treated no differently from alcohol and cigarette users.	-3	-2	-1	+1	+2	+3

33.	People who are on welfare should not be allowed to publicly demonstrate and protest about the amount of money they received.	-3	-2	-1	+1	+2	+3
34.	Those individuals who openly acknowledge their homosexuality should have the same opportunities for employment and housing as guaranteed by law to other citizens.	-3	-2	-1	+1	+2	+3
35.	A person (who is mentally ill) who commits a major crime should receive major punishment.	-3	-2	-1	+1	+2	+3
36.	Interracial dating should be socially acceptable.	-3	-2	-1	+1	+2	+3
37.	In order to deal more effectively with the crime problem, we should use more chain gang techniques in our correctional approaches.	-3	-2	-1	+1	+2	+3
38.	Community groups who teach their children not to recite the pledge of allegiance or salute the flag in school ought not receive government funds.	-3	-2	-1	+1	+2	+3
39.	We need to have stricter penalties in order to enforce our laws.	-3	-2	-1	+1	+2	+3
40.	Middle class community groups should have the right to object to the government building low-cost housing projects in their area.	-3	-2	-1	+1	+2	+3

The factor analysis performed on this more comprehensive set of items yielded a ten item political-legal conservatism scale and is presented in Table III-6. Six of the items present a conservative statement; four present a liberal statement. Thus, high scores on the scale do not merely reflect a tendency to either agree or disagree with all statements. The Spearman-Brown reliability estimate based on the entire set of 1,457 respondents is .85.

TABLE III-6

POLITICAL-LEGAL CONSERVATISM SCALE
FOR FINAL INSTRUMENT

Instructions: The following statements are matters of opinion. Some of them you may agree with and others you may not agree with. Please indicate the extent to which you agree or disagree with each of the following statements. Use the following numerical scale and after each item circle the appropriate number.

-3	- 2	-1	+1	+2	+3
Disagree Very Much	Disagree Pretty Much	Disagree A Little	Agree A Little	Agree Pretty Much	Agree Very Much

ITEM NUMBER						
x 30. We need to have stricter penalties in order to enforce our laws.	-3	-2	-1	+1	+2	+3
xx 31. Most criminals need treatment-programs – not punishment.	-3	-2	-1	+1	+2	+3
xx 35. It should be necessary to prove that a confession is voluntary in order to have it admitted into evidence.	-3	-2	-1	+1	+2	+3
x 37. Too much permissiveness is helping to destroy this Country.	-3	-2	-1	+1	+2	+3
xx 42. The rights of Black Muslims must be as vigilantly protected as the rights of any other religious group.	-3	-2	-1	+1	+2	+3
x 43. Any demonstrator who makes oscene gestures and remarks at a law enforcement officer deserves to be clubbed.	-3	-2	-1	+1	+2	+3
x 49. Most of what passes for rehabili-	-3	-2	-1	+1	+2	+3

	tation is too soft and should be replaced with tougher measures.						
xx 50.	The action of the National Guard in shooting four Kent State students was a shameful and completely unnecessary response.	-3	-2	-1	+1	+2	+3
x 55.	In order to deal more effectively with the crime problem, we should use more chain gang techniques in our correctional approaches.	-3	-2	-1	+1	+2	+3
x 56.	The police should not have to be bothered with going through the process of getting search warrants.	-3	-2	-1	+1	+2	+3

Spearman-Brown reliability estimate .85 (N=1,457)

x designates a conservative statement.
xx designates a liberal statement.

Status and Esteem

The four status and esteem items that were first used in the Albany Conference were also employed in the pilot testing and in the final survey instrument without change as presented below. The status dimension reflects an individual's perception of the importance and respect with which he is regarded by others; while esteem is a person's direct estimate of his own self-worth.

TABLE III-7

POLICE AND PROBATION STATUS AND ESTEEM ITEMS FOR FINAL INSTRUMENT

Instructions: The following statements are matters of opinion. Some of them you may agree with and others you may not agree with. Please indicate the extent to which you agree or disagree with each of the following statements. Use the following numerical scale and after each item circle the appropriate number.

-3 Disagree Very Much	-2 Disagree Pretty Much	-1 Disagree A Little	+1 Agree A Little	+2 Agree Pretty Much	+3 Agree Very Much

ITEM NUMBER								
Police 33. Status	Most people think that policemen work at the job they do because they would have a hard time getting another job which pays as much.	-3	-2	-1	+1	+2	+3
Police 46. Esteem	It doesn't take more than the average intelligence of the man in the street to make a good policeman.	-3	-2	-1	+1	+2	+3
Proba- 52. tion Status	Most people think that probation officers work at the job they do because they would have a hard time getting another job which pays as much.	-3	-2	-1	+1	+2	+3
Proba- 39. tion Status	It doesn't take anything more than the average intelligence of the man in the street to make a good probation officer.	-3	-2	-1	+1	+2	+3

Organizational – Perceptual Conflict Vignettes

As described in Chapter One, a number of indirect measures were utilized which appeared quite promising. These measures involved the obtaining of an indication of a person's opinion about an incident involving police and probation officials and a prediction about how police and probation officials might respond to the same incident. The ten organizational vignettes utilized at the Albany Conference served to elicit these responses. Subsequent analysis produced two sub-scales: a police prerogative and a probation autonomy scale. In addition, these vignettes provided data which served as the basis for a conflict adaptation formulation.

A sample vignette is presented in Table III-8 and the entire set are contained in Appendix C. Respondents were asked to evaluate a police or probation incident from three different perspectives: their own, their estimate of the average police response, and their estimate of the average probation response. (This procedure is further detailed in the Instructions section contained in Table III-8.)

TABLE III-8
SAMPLE VIGNETTE
(From Conflict Adaptation Questions)

Instructions: You will find ten situations involving a conflict between a probation and police department. You are asked to do "three" Things:

1. Indicate your opinion about the conflict be checking the appropriate space on the first line entitled "My Opinion."

2. You are then asked to check a space on the next line entitled "Police Opinion" to show how you think the average policeman would respond to the conflict situation.

3. On the next line, by checking a space after the words "Probation Opinion" you will show how you think the average probation officer would see the conflict.

Remember, there are no "correct" answers. Your opinions are what is desired. Take as much time as you need to answer carefully the survey.

ITEM
NUMBER

19. John Jones received a three-year probation term after conviction on a charge of possessing narcotics. Later in a police raid, he is found in the home of Brown, who has a record for narcotics selling. As the police enter the house, Jones apparently emptied the contents of a plastic bag down a toilet and flushed it. The police have information from an undercover informant that Jones had gotten rid of heroin.

    Jones admits drinking excessively for several days, but denies possessing or using drugs. He states that he did not know of the prior arrest of Brown. The police admit they cannot prove the narcotics charge and ask the probation office to recommend revocation of probation for Jones on the basis of violation of a probation rule for association and drinking.

My opinion about the police request is:

	1 Strongly Agree	2 Somewhat Agree	3 Slightly Agree	4 Slightly Disagree	5 Somewhat Disagree	6 Strongly Disagree
My Opinion						
Police Opinion						
Probation Opinion						

Factor analyses were conducted separately for a respondent's own, his perceived police response, and his perceived probation response within each agency. (The results are presented in Appendix C). Consistent results were obtained which identified one factor consisting of four vignettes that was labeled a Police Prerogative Scale and four vignettes labeled a Probation Autonomy Scale (see Table III-9). Based on the 1,457 respondents, the Police Prerogative Scale had a Spearman-Brown reliability estimate of .79 and the Probation Autonomy Scale had a reliability estimate of .78. Only two vignettes were not incorporated; one referred to a probation refusal of a police request to detain a probationer arrested on a minor charge (item 25), and the other concerned a probation refusal to sanction police use of a probationer as a narcotics informer (item 27). Table III-9 describes the vignettes which were employed in each scale. Each respondent received a score on these two scales based on his own response.

TABLE III-9

POLICE PREROGATIVE SCALE AND PROBATION AUTONOMY SCALE FOR FINAL INSTRUMENT

ITEM NUMBER	POLICE PREROGATIVE SCALE
19.	Police request revocation of probationer for rule violation.
20.	Police department requests right to make recommendations to judge.
21.	Police request that information gathered by probation youth workers should be shared with them.
26.	Police contend that they should not have to take probation violators into custody if no crime has been committed.
	Spearman-Brown reliability estimate .79 (N=1,457)

ITEM NUMBER	PROBATION AUTONOMY SCALE
22	Probation department refuses police request for full access to a probationer's case file.
23.	Probation department refuses police department request for a list of names of persons on probation.
24.	Probation department refuses police request to hold probationers in custody pending investigation.
28.	Probation department refuses police request for probation to issue a warrant for investigation of probation violation so that a search desired by the police can take place.
	Spearman-Brown reliability estimate .78 (N=1,457)

As indicated in Chapter One, a major purpose of the research was to determine if there were identifiable conflict adaptation styles that affect the nature of agency and agent-client interaction. Responses to the vignettes were employed to produce a classification of conflict style adaptations necessary to address this question. The basic procedures involved a determination, on an item by item basis, of the discrepancy between a person's own response and his estimated police, and estimated probation responses.

In scoring, the discrepancy in absolute terms between the respondent's opinion and his estimate of the average police officer's response was designated as A. Let us take a simple example for one item.

My opinion about the police request is:

	1 Strongly Agree	2 Somewhat Agree	3 Slightly Agree	4 Slightly Disagree	5 Somewhat Disagree	6 Strongly Disagree
My Opinion		X				
Police Opinion	X					
Probation Opinion					X	

In this case, the A score is 1. These scores were summed over all ten items to yield a total A score. In a similar fashion, the discrepancy between one's own response and the estimated probation response was labeled B. In this illustration the B score was 3. Again, a summation of item B scores was made to obtain a total B score. Perhaps this respondent obtained a total A score of 10 and a total B score of 30. The smaller the score, the closer one's own response is to the estimated response. Thus, in this case, the respondent is closer to the estimated police opinion. A third score, C, was obtained based on the difference between the total A score and the total B score, which in this situation would be 20.

A classifying system employing the three scores was developed so that respondents were categorized as either having a police orientation, a probation orientation, or a moderator (neutral) orientation. The procedure for classification is described in Table III-10.

TABLE III-10

FORMULATION OF CONFLICT ADAPTATION STYLE

1.	MODERATOR when C <15 (1 ½ per item across 10 items)
2.	POLICE ORIENTATION when C > 15 and A < B
3.	PROBATION ORIENTATION when C > 15 and B < A

If the respondent showed relatively little difference between A and B scores (C score less than 15), he was designated as a moderator. If the respondent had a C score of greater than 15, then the determination of orientation was based on whether A or B was greater: if B were greater – he had a police orientation, if A were greater – he displayed a probation orientation.

In addition to the use of this structured questionnaire, a series of interviews were conducted by two mature interviewers six months after the administration of the final instrument. The interviewing was conducted with police and probation officers in Nassau County, New York. Interviewers were instructed to elicit information concerning the amount of contact and the nature of the relationship existing between police and probation officers at interface. They were also instructed to determine the styles of client interaction in practice and the respondents' functional role concept as well as his attitude towards judicial practices. One of the major uses made of this material is to determine distinguishing work-related attitudes and actions among officers with varying conflict adaptation styles.

In summary, the following measures were developed for this research effort: operational conflict scale, political-legal conservatism scale, status and esteem items, police prerogative scale, probation autonomy scale, and interview material based on conflict adaptation illustrating styles of inter-agency and officer-client interaction among police and probation officers.

The measures will be utilized in the succeeding chapters as follows:

1. Chapter 4 contains the data on operational conflict and contact.

2. The dissensus dimension, composed of status and esteem items and a political-legal conservatism scale, is presented and analyzed in relationship to operational conflict in Chapter 5.

3. The police prerogative and probation autonomy scales are presented and studied according to perceptual and operational conflict analyses in Chapter 6.

4. Analysis of the interviews based on conflict adaptation style is presented in Chapter 7.

CHAPTER 4

CONTACT AND CONFLICT

In attempting to examine conflict between two sets of persons, analysis is inevitably directed toward the relationship between the level of contact existing between them and the degree of conflict they express towards each other. For example, it is a widely held assumption that conflict can or should be reduced by greater contact.[1] Thus, scholars on the subject of police-community relations and change agents in the criminal justice system almost invariably urge increased interaction, coordination and cooperation.[2] Only rarely is one cautioned concerning the assumption that contact reduces conflict.[3]

One of the first issues addressed in this study was that assumption. The amount of contact between police and probation officers was assessed by the following question (Table IV-1) in the final survey instrument. For purposes of analysis, the five response possibilities were combined into three categories of contact frequencies: low, medium and high.

TABLE IV-1

AMOUNT OF CONTACT

ITEM NUMBER		
13.	In your work during the past year, how often did you have contact with police (probation) officers?	
	None at all Less than once a month	LOW
	Once or twice a month Three or four times a month	MEDIUM
	More than once a week	HIGH

The frequency of work contacts made by the police and probation officers is reported in Table IV-2 for all respondents and for each of the three communities.

TABLE IV-2

AMOUNT OF POLICE-PROBATION CONTACT BY LOCALITY

		Police		Probation	
AREA SITES	CONTACT	N	%	N	%
All Three Sites	High	66	6%	144	37%
	Medium	166	15%	167	42%
	Low	837	79%	82	21%
	Total	1064	100%	393	100%
Nassau	High	24	4%	74	34%
	Medium	94	16%	85	40%
	Low	480	80%	57	26%
	Total	598	100%	216	100%
San Jose	High	25	9%	56	39%
	Medium	38	13%	66	45%
	Low	223	78%	23	16%
	Total	286	100%	145	100%
Albuquerque	High	11	6%	14	44%
	Medium	40	22%	16	50%
	Low	129	72%	2	6%
	Total	180	100%	32	100%

It is evident from Table IV-2 that probation officers are much more likely than police to have frequent work-related contact. While among the total and in each locality, the modal or typical response for probation is at a medium frequency level, the modal response for police is at a low frequency level.

For example, it can be seen from the table that while 79% of the police experience low contact, 79% of probation officers experience medium or high contact. For all three sites, only 6% of police experience high contact whereas 37% of probation officers experience high contact. It might be recalled that earlier discussion indicated that the contact involving probation officers included interaction with a relatively high percentage of detectives (33% for all three area sites as reported in Item 15, Table 7, Chapter 2); no similar area of concentrated contact for the police was identified.

In comparing the area sites, it may be noted that in Nassau County, a somewhat greater percentage of both police and probation officers experience low contact as compared to San Jose and Albuquerque respondents. For example, 26% of Nassau probation officers experience low contact, as compared to 16% of San Jose and 6% of Albuquerque probation officers. Among the police, 80% of Nassau respondents experience low contact as compared to 78% of San Jose and 72% of Albuquerque police officers.

Having developed a measure of contact, it was then necessary to devise as well a means of scaling the degree of conflict existing between police and probation agents in the three communities under study. Such a measure was needed not only to examine relationships with degrees of contact but several subsequent analyses required a similar scale as well.

Obviously, there are a variety of ways of operationalizing the term conflict, from the number of aggressive remarks exchanged to overt refusals of cooperation such as denials of requests by probation officers for warrants or arrests by police. Because of the scope of this study and the number of respondents involved, the most practical measure available was the level of conflict between police and probation agents perceived by those completing the basic questionnaire employed in this study. Thus, an "operational conflict" scale was developed (Table IV-3) consisting of seven items from the study questionnaire. Five of the statements employed referred to inter-role conflict, while two of the items were related to inter-agency conflict. For each statement, respondents were asked to indicate their extent of agreement or disagreement on a seven point scale.

TABLE IV-3

OPERATIONAL CONFLICT SCALE

ITEM NUMBER

32. There is a need to reduce conflict between police and probation officers in our area (where you work).

36. * There are very few conflicts existing between the police and probation departments in our area.

40. There is a need to improve cooperation between police and probation officers in our area.

44. A situation of serious conflict exists between the police and probation of department in our area.

47. * On a personal level, police and probation officers generally get along quite well together in our area.

53. In the course of carrying out their jobs in our area, probation and police officers seem to have lots of conflicts.

57. Drawing on my own work experience, I think that in our area there is a great amount of conflict between police and probation officers.

*For these two items, agreement indicates "harmony". For all other items, disagreement indicates "harmony".

The mean values of the conflict scores for police and probation officers are presented in Table IV-4 both by specific site and for the total group. For each site and for the total group, probation officers perceive more harmony (less operational conflict) than police officers. The general extent of operational conflict does not appear to be extremely high, at least as indexed by the present scale. All of the subgroup means are above the scale midpoint of 4.0, or towards the harmony pole of the scale.

TABLE IV-4

OPERATIONAL CONFLICT OF POLICE AND PROBATION OFFICERS IN THREE LOCALITIES

LOCATION	Nassau		San Jose		Albuquerque		Total	
ROLE OF RESPONDENT	Police	Proba-tion	Police	Proba-tion	Police	Proba-tion	Police	Proba-tion
MEAN HARMONY	5.1	5.4	4.7	5.1	4.6	5.3	4.9	5.3
N	598	216	286	145	180	32	1064	393

\NOTES: The possible range of scores is from 1.0 to 7.0 with scale midpoint of 4.0. The higher means indicate more harmony (lower conflict). The lower means indicate less harmony (higher conflict).

An application of the t test to evaluate the difference between police and probation means revealed that for each site the differences were significant below the .05 level.

THE RELATIONSHIP OF CONFLICT AND CONTACT

Having developed measures for the two dimensions, it is possible to examine the extent to which there is a relationship between contact and conflict. For this purpose, scores on the conflict scale are reduced to high and low categories. The high category represents any degree of agreement that conflict exists (any scale score of 4.0 or more) whereas the low category represents any degree of disagreement that conflict exists (any scale score of 3.9 or less). A cross tabulation was made between these two measures of conflict and degree of contact experienced according to the three contact categories described above in Table IV-1 (see also Section 2, Appendix C for conflict and contact categorization). These findings are examined separately for police and probation respondents.

TABLE IV-5

DEGREE OF CONFLICT AND AMOUNT OF CONTACT FOR POLICE OFFICERS.

	CONTACT							
	Low		Medium		High		Total	
CONFLICT	N	%	N	%	N	%	N	%
High	432	52%	63	38%	13	22%	508	48%
Low	397	48%	102	62%	47	78%	546	52%
Total	829	100%	165	100%	60	100%	1054	100%

$X^2 = 28.63, P < .01$
$V = .16, G = - .36$

As may been seen in Table IV-5, among police officers, higher contact is clearly associated with lower conflict. In fact, the contrast between extremes of police officer contact is particularly striking: 78% of officers with high contact express low conflict, while only 48% of low contact officers express low conflict. Thus, it is apparent that among the police, contact is negatively associated with conflict: the higher the degree of contact with probation staff the lower the degree of perceived conflict with that staff.

Turning, now, to the relationship between the variables of contact and operational conflict for probation officers, the data are presented in Table IV-6.

TABLE IV-6

DEGREE OF CONFLICT AND AMOUNT OF CONTACT FOR PROBATION OFFICERS.

	CONTACT							
	Low		Medium		High		Total	
CONFLICT	N	%	N	%	N	%	N	%
High	38	49%	75	47%	61	45%	174	47%
Low	40	51%	84	53%	76	55%	200	53%
Total	78	100%	159	100%	137	100%	374	100%

$X^2 = .40, P < .82$
$V = .03, G = -.05$

In contrast to the contact-conflict relationship for the police, there is no significant difference between the amount of contact and the level of conflict expressed by probation officers. Forty-five percent of probation officers with high contact express high conflict as compared to 49% of those with low contact who express high conflict. Thus, there is only a 4% difference for probation between contact level and the amount of conflict.

At the simplest level, it is clear that contact does not automatically lead to low conflict. In order to understand more fully the situation where contact does reduce conflict, we turn to a different set of analyses. First, the question presents itself as to whether any particular types of police-probation interaction are more associated with conflict than other types?

In order to arrive at an answer to this question, the following item was included in the final instrument: the precise wording varied depending whether the police or probation staff were the respondents.

TABLE IV-7

SITUATIONS OF CONTACT

ITEM NUMBER	
17.	In what kinds of situation(s) have most of your contacts with probation officers occurred?
	None at all ______
	When you were helping the probation officer in a probation-related task ______
	When the probation officer was helping you in a police-related task ______
	When you and the probation officer were working together to solve a crime ______
	Information verification ______
	Other(s), please specify ______

The most frequent types of situational contacts reported by both police and probation officers are "police helping probation" and "information verification". Probation officers not only report more frequent contacts, but also are more likely to be involved in multiple types of situational contact. Relatively fewer respondents report contacts when both are "working together" or when "the probation officer is helping the police".

Responses of the police are classified and reported in Table IV-8. The data shown and subsequent analysis in this section is confined to those police respondents who indicate at least some contact with probation officers.

TABLE IV-8

DEGREE OF CONFLICT AND THE NATURE OF CONTACT SITUATION FOR POLICE OFFICERS

Conflict	Situation of Contact											
	Police helping Probation		Probation Helping		Working Together		Information Verification		Multiple		Total	
	N	%	N	%	N	%	N	%	N	%	N	%
High	77	33%	30	48%	7	37%	105	48%	28	35%	247	40%
Low	155	67%	33	52%	12	63%	115	52%	51	65%	366	60%
Total	232	100%	63	100%	19	100%	220	100%	79	100%	613	100%

NOTE: 42% of police officers express no situation of contact.

$$X^2 = 12.19, p < .05$$
$$V = .14$$

Significant associations appear between the situation of contact and the amount of conflict. Specifically, there are two situations of contact in which the likelihood of conflict is higher: these are when the officer on a police-related task (48%), and in the situation of information verification (48%). In contrast, among police officers whose contact situation entails helping a probation officer on a probation-related task, only 33% express high conflict. Officers who have multiple contacts and work together on crime solving with probation officers also tend to be relatively low on conflict (i.e., 35% and 37% respectively). It is clear that in situations where the police are seeking to achieve a goal related to their agency function with the assistance of probation officers, information verification being one specific type, they perceive the highest level of conflict.

Since the amount of contact and at least two specific situations of contact appear to be significantly related to the level of perceived conflict, it was decided to examine the joint impact of the two variables. Table IV-9 describes the results of this examination. As was the case earlier, the analysis is confined to those officers with some contact.

In order to facilitate the comparisons, contact situations were collapsed into two categories: those which had a higher probability of conflict, namely information verification and the situation of probation helping police on police-related tasks (Situation A); and those which had a lower probability of conflict, specifically police helping probation on a probation task, working together to solve a crime and multiple situations (Situation B). (The more detailed table is presented as Table IV-9 in Section 7 of Appendix C).

TABLE IV-9

PERCENTAGE OF POLICE OFFICERS WITH HIGH CONFLICT BY NATURE OF CONTACT SITUATION AND AMOUNT OF CONTACT, OFFICERS WITH CONTACT ONLY

Amount of Overall Contact	Percent of Police with High Conflict	
	Situations A	Situations B
High	33% (18)	15% (40)
Medium	51% (67)	28% (94)
Low	47% (196)	41% (194)
Total	47% (281)	34% (228)

NOTES: Situations A include information verification and probation helping police; Situations B include all other categories.

N appearing in parenthesis refers to the denominator on which the percentages are based.

% refers to percentage of that denominator with high conflict.

The findings in Table IV-9 suggest that there may be situationally specific features generating conflict independent of the amount of contact. Particularly at high and medium contact levels, officers with Situation A type contacts are much more likely to report conflict than officers with Situation B type contacts. The difference is smaller but in the same direction among officers with low contact.

For officers with Situation B type contacts, the greater the amount of contact the lower the conflict. For Situation A type contacts, this relationship is not particularly clear.

Turning now to a parallel analysis for probation officers, Table IV-10 includes those probation officers who report some contact with police and examines the association between the nature of the contact situation and the amount of conflict.

TABLE IV-10

DEGREE OF CONFLICT AND THE NATURE OF THE SITUATION OF CONTACT FOR PROBATION OFFICERS

Conflict	Situation of Contact											
	Police Helping Probation		Probation Helping Police		Working Together		Information Verification		Multiple		Row Total	
	N	%	N	%	N	%	N	%	N	%	N	%
High	43	45%	8	50%	6	60%	56	44%	42	55%	155	46%
Low	52	55%	8	50%	4	40%	70	56%	51	55%	185	54%
Total	95	100%	16	100%	10	100%	126	100%	93	100%	340	100%

NOTE: 13% of probation officers express no situation of contact.

X^2 = 1.05, $P < .9$
V = .06

As can be seen from the table, except for those categories where there are relatively few cases, the type of situation in which contact occurs for probation officers appears to have relatively little impact on the amount of conflict reported by probation officers.

In summary, the findings with respect to the police suggest that not only is low contact linked to high conflict, but two types of contacts, information verification and probation helping police, increase the risks of conflict. No such pattern emerged with respect to probation officers. Apparently the points of high conflict for police function; for probation officers conflict situations appear to be more generalized.

In addition to examining the types of situations of contact, an analysis was made of the location of contact obtained from the following question (Table IV-11).

TABLE IV-11

LOCATIONS OF CONTACT

ITEM NUMBER	
16.	At what location(s) have most of your contacts with probation officers taken place? None at all ______ On the Street ______ In the police station house ______ In the family court ______ In a probation office ______ Over the telephone ______ Other(s), please specify ______

While conflict was not found to be related to this variable for either police (Appendix Table IV-12, Section 7, Appendix C) or for probation officers (Appendix Table IV-13, Section 7, Appendix C), some information about the context of contact is provided by Table IV-12.

TABLE IV-12
LOCATION OF INTER-ROLE CONTACT FOR POLICE AND PROBATION OFFICERS

LOCATION	POLICE	PROBATION
Telephone	56%	50%
Multiple	15%	24%
Station House	14%	11%
Family Court	4%	6%
Probation Office	6%	8%
Street	5%	1%
	100	100
	(635)	(344)

Over half of both police and probation officers report that the locus of most contacts is the telephone conversation. The station house is the next most frequently reported location. Considering the fact that a substantial number of the multiple contact respondents would include the telephone location of contact, the telephone location of contact is the overwhelming important concern for the analysis of the police-probation locus of interaction.

OCCUPATIONAL VARIABLES AND CONFLICT

Another level of analysis was directed towards discovering the extent to which conflict was associated with a number of occupational variables. Among those analyzed were category of assignment, rank, length of work experience, nature of work (i.e. supervisory, field or administrative), specialized assignment (i.e. narcotics, morals, intake, research and staff), job focus (i.e. community service, law enforcement or other occupational orientations), whether job related courses were being taken, and the type officer that contact occurred with (i.e. for the police this involved contact with Adult, Family or Juvenile Division probation officers; and for probation it entailed contact with either juvenile specialists, detectives, patrolmen, lieutents or a combination multiple category).

It was discovered that among these occupational variables, only the length of work experience, rank, and the category of assignment were related to conflict. It is to these three variables then, we shall turn our attention. In each case, the amount of contact was established first and held constant when the relationship with conflict was examined. The data with respect to length of work experience are presented first. The categories employed are presented in Table IV-13 while Tables IV-14 and IV-15 describe how work experience relates to the amount of contact with the opposite agency personnel.

TABLE IV-13

EXPERIENCE

ITEM NUMBER	
8.	Total years of police (probation) experience (only municipal, county, state, federal, or other public agency): Less than 6 years — LITTLE 7-15 years — MIDDLE 16 or more years — MUCH

TABLE IV-14

AMOUNT OF CONTACT BY THE AMOUNT OF EXPERIENCE OF POLICE OFFICERS (N=1,048)

CONTACT	EXPERIENCE		
	LITTLE %	MIDDLE %	MUCH %
HIGH	2%	8%	8%
MEDIUM	10%	17%	21%
LOW	88%	75%	71%
TOTAL	100%	100%	100%
N	(395)	(400)	(253)

TABLE IV-15

AMOUNT OF CONTACT BY THE AMOUNT OF EXPERIENCE OF POLICE OFFICERS (N=1,048)

CONTACT	EXPERIENCE		
	LITTLE %	MIDDLE %	MUCH %
HIGH	38%	34%	30%
MEDIUM	44%	39%	50%
LOW	18%	27%	20%
TOTAL	100%	100%	100%
N	(235)	(117)	(20)

Basically both tables reveal that the amount of contact has little relationship with the amount of experience. It may be noted in Table IV-14 that the majority of the police at all levels of experience have low contact. For example, while only 2% of police officers with little experience have high contact, 88% of them indicate low contact. Regardless of the experience of probation officers, the level of contact with police tends to be at medium or high levels (Table IV-15).

Having established the relationships between experience and contact, it is now appropriate to examine the existence of conflict present when the amount of contact is accounted for. The relationships between conflict and experience are presented in the following tables (Tables IV-16 and IV-17).

TABLE IV-16
PERCENTAGE OF POLICE OFFICERS WITH HIGH CONFLICT
BY AMOUNT OF EXPERIENCE AND AMOUNT OF CONTACT (N=1,048)

CONTACT	EXPERIENCE					
	LITTLE		MIDDLE		MUCH	
	%	N	%	N	%	N
HIGH	22%	(9)	32%	(31)	5%	(20)
MEDIUM	51%	(41)	40%	(70)	26%	(54)
LOW	63%	(345)	51%	(299)	35%	(179)
TOTAL	61%	(395)	48%	(400)	31%	(253)

NOTE: N in parenthesis refers to denominator population.
% refers to percentage of that denominator with high conflict.

TABLE IV-17
PERCENTAGE OF PROBATION OFFICERS WITH HIGH CONFLICT
BY AMOUNT OF EXPERIENCE AND AMOUNT OF CONTACT (N=372)

CONTACT	EXPERIENCE		
	LITTLE % N	MIDDLE % N	MUCH % N
HIGH	50% (90)	40% (40)	0% (6)
MEDIUM	50% (103)	47% (45)	30% (10)
LOW	55% (42)	47% (32)	0% (4)
TOTAL	51% (395)	44% (117)	15% (20)

NOTE: N in parenthesis refers to denominator population.
% refers to percentage of that denominator with high conflict.

What is the joint impact of experience and contact on the level of conflict? Regardless of contact levels, police officers with much experience report lower levels of conflict. Also, regardless of experience, the level of contact influences conflict. The cumulative impact is considerable. Only 5% of police officers with high contact and much experience report conflict. This contrasts with the 63% of police with low contact and little experience.

These relationships are the same for probation officers. As may be seen in Table IV-17, conflict is least present among those with much experience. As occurred with the police, the most striking difference occurs between little experienced probation officers with low contact, 55% of whom report conflict, as compared to much experienced probation with high contact among whom 0% report conflict. For both police and probation, experience is a significant predictor of conflict with those with sixteen or more years experience expressing the least conflict. The next occupational variable explored is organizational rank. Procedures similar to those used in examining the effect of experience are used here. The categories of rank classification are presented in Table IV-18 and their relationship to degree of contact is shown in Table IV-19.

TABLE IV-18

RANK

ITEM NUMBER 11.	RANK POLICE	CATEGORY	GRADE PROBATION
	Patrolman Detective (investigator) Corporal	LOW	Probation officer trainee Permanent probation officer
	Sergeant Detective Sergeant	MIDDLE	Senior Probation Officer Supervisor
	Lieutenant Detective Lieutenant Administrator (Captain or above)	HIGH	Principal Probation Officer (senior supervisor) Probation administrator (or above)

TABLE IV-19

AMOUNT OF CONTACT BY RANK OF POLICE OFFICER (N=1,047)

CONTACT	RANK		
	LOW %	MIDDLE %	HIGH %
HIGH	4%	14%	6%
MEDIUM	15%	16%	18%
LOW	81%	70%	76%
TOTAL	100%	100%	100%
N	(777)	(190)	(80)

TABLE IV-20

AMOUNT OF CONTACT BY RANK OF PROBATION OFFICER (N=369)

CONTACT	RANK		
	LOW %	MIDDLE %	HIGH %
HIGH	38%	36%	33%
MEDIUM	44%	42%	38%
LOW	18%	22%	29%
TOTAL	100%	100%	100%
N	(194)	(151)	(24)

As may be observed in the two preceding tables, regardless of rank, contact is predominately low for the police and at a middle to high level for probation. However, among probation officers, those with high rank are somewhat more likely to indicate low contact.

In examining the issue as to whether rank is associated with conflict, the relationships are presented in Tables IV-21 and IV-22.

TABLE IV-21

PERCENTAGE OF POLICE OFFICERS WITH HIGH CONFLICT BY RANK AND AMOUNT OF CONTACT (N=1,047)

CONTACT	RANK					
	LOW		MIDDLE		HIGH	
	%	N	%	N	%	N
HIGH	19%	(26)	30%	(27)	0%	(5)
MEDIUM	38%	(120)	36%	(31)	43%	(14)
LOW	56%	(631)	45%	(132)	28%	(61)
TOTAL	52%	(777)	41%	(190)	29%	(80)

NOTE: N in parenthesis refers to denominator population.
% refers to percentage of that denominator with high conflict.

TABLE IV-22

PERCENTAGE OF POLICE OFFICERS WITH HIGH CONFLICT BY RANK AND AMOUNT OF CONTACT (N=1,047)

CONTACT	RANK					
	LOW		MIDDLE		HIGH	
	%	N	%	N	%	N
HIGH	48%	(73)	46%	(55)	13%	(8)
MEDIUM	49%	(85)	48%	(63)	22%	(9)
LOW	56%	(36)	42%	(33)	29%	(7)
TOTAL	50%	(194)	46%	(151)	21%	(24)

NOTE: N in parenthesis refers to denominator population.
% refers to percentage of that denominator with high conflict.

In comparing the findings in the preceding two tables, it can been seen among probation that at all contact levels, low rank is associated with high conflict and high rank is associated with low conflict. Whereas 56% of low ranking probation officers at low contact express conflict, among high ranking officers at high contact only 13% express conflict.

Among the police, the relationship of low rank and high conflict exists only at the low contact level, at which 56% of those with low rank express conflict as compared to only 28% of high ranking officers who express conflict. Rank is a predictor of conflict for probation at all contact levels, but for police it is a predictor at low contact only.

In examining the final occupational variable, category of assignment, the categorizations employed are shown in Table IV-23 and the relationship to contact to Tales IV-24 and IV-25.

TABLE IV-23

CATEGORY OF ASSIGNMENT

ITEM NUMBER	
10.	POLICE Category of assignment (if you are a patrolman or a detective assigned to juvenile (youth division) work, or a headquarters assignment, check only that assignment box and not the patrol or detective boxes). Patrol Headquarters Detective Other Juvenile
10.	PROBATION Category of assignment: Juvenile Division of Family Court Another Division of Family Court Adult Division

TABLE IV-24

AMOUNT OF CONTACT BY CATEGORY OF POLICE ASSIGNMENT (N=960)

CONTACT	CATEGORY OF ASSIGNMENT			
	PATROL %	DETECTIVE %	JUVENILE %	HEADQUARTERS %
HIGH	0%	3%	40%	12%
MEDIUM	5%	31%	46%	20%
LOW	95%	66%	14%	68%
TOTAL	100%	100%	100%	100%
N	(541)	(201)	(80)	(138)

TABLE IV-25

AMOUNT OF CONTACT BY CATEGORY OF PROBATION ASSIGNMENT (N=348)

CONTACT	CATEGORY OF ASSIGNMENT		
	JUVENILE DIVISION %	FAMILY COURT %	ADULT DIVISION %
HIGH	36%	24%	44%
MEDIUM	53%	26%	39%
LOW	11%	50%	17%
TOTAL	100%	100%	100%
N	(128)	(34)	(186)

Table IV-24 indicates that police officers in juvenile assignments have the most contact and patrolmen the least. For example, whereas 95% of patrolmen have low contact with probation, only 14% of police in juvenile assignments have low contact. On the other hand, probation officers in the Adult Division have the most contact with police and those assigned to non-juvenile work in the Family Court (involving family related matters excluding delinquency such as non-support, abuse, adoption, etc.) have the least. The relationship between the amount of conflict and the category of assignment are presented in Tables IV-26 and IV-27.

TABLE IV-26

PERCENTAGE OF POLICE OFFICERS WITH HIGH CONFLICT BY CATEGORY OF ASSIGNMENT AND AMOUNT OF CONTACT (N=96)

CONTACT	CATEGORY OF ASSIGNMENT							
	PATROLMAN		DETECTIVE		JUVENILE		HEADQUARTERS	
	%	N	%	N	%	N	%	N
HIGH	0%	(1)	14%	(7)	22%	(32)	29%	(17)
MEDIUM	39%	(28)	40%	(62)	41%	(37)	30%	(27)
LOW	59%	(512)	37%	(132)	64%	(11)	40%	(94)
TOTAL	58%	(541)	37%	(201)	36%	(80)	37%	(138)

NOTE: N in parenthesis refers to denominator population.
% refers to percentage of that denominator with high conflict.

TABLE IV-27

PERCENTAGE OF PROBATION OFFICERS WITH HIGH CONFLICT
BY CATEGORY OF ASSIGNMENT AND AMOUNT OF CONTACT (N=348)

CONTACT	CATEGORY OF ASSIGNMENT					
	JUVENILE DIVISION		FAMILY COURT		ADULT DIVISION	
	%	N	%	N	%	N
HIGH	50%	(46)	25%	(8)	44%	(81)
MEDIUM	57%	(68)	33%	(9)	38%	(73)
LOW	29%	(14)	47%	(17)	41%	(32)
TOTAL	52%	(128)	38%	(34)	41%	(186)

NOTE: N in parenthesis refers to denominator population.
% refers to percentage of that denominator with high conflict.

Table IV-26 indicates that among police officers with low contact, those classified as detectives and headquarters personnel tend to perceive substantially lower conflict than either patrolmen or juvenile officers.

As evidenced by Table IV-27, Juvenile Division probation officers express the most conflict at mid and high contact levels (50% and 57) respectively) and the least conflict at low contact (29%).

It is interesting to observe from the data that while increased interaction is associated with low conflict for police juvenile specialists, increased contact is associated with high conflict for juvenile probation officers. There appears to be something involved in the nature of high interaction with police on the part of probation officers specializing in juvenile cases that is conflict prone. One might surmise that since only 8% of police work is in juvenile assignments as compared to 28% of probation work, probation officers in juvenile assignments who experience high police contact would find themselves dealing with police who do not share their juvenile oriented interests.

In summary, it has been shown that when the amount of contact is held constant, conflict is least evident among police and probation officers with the most experience (i.e. 16 or more years of work experience). While high rank is associated with low conflict for probation officers, it is not among the police. Lastly, it was demonstrated that while increased interaction is associated with low conflict for police juvenile specialists, increased contact is associated with high conflict for probation officers in juvenile assignments.

DEMOGRAPHIC VARIABLES AND CONFLICT

The relationship of demographic characteristics to conflict was also examined. Such an analysis was important in itself in attempting to identify groups with high risks of conflict. In addition, it appeared important to determine whether such characteristics qualified the previous findings in regard to the connection between contact and conflict.

It was discovered that while religion and educational attainment were not related to conflict, age and off-duty (personal) contact were. Thus, we will begin by exploring the relationship of age to conflict. Before doing so it will be useful to describe the relationships between the amount of contact and age. These are presented in Tables IV-29 and IV-30. The categories of age classification are contained in Table IV-28.

TABLE IV-28

AGE

ITEM NUMBER	AGE	
	Under 30	YOUNGER
	30-44	MIDDLE
	Over 45	OLDER

TABLE IV-29

AMOUNT OF CONTACT BY AGE OF POLICE OFFICER (N=1,052)

CONTACT	AGE		
	YOUNGER %	MIDDLE %	OLDER %
HIGH	3%	6%	12%
MEDIUM	11%	17%	21%
LOW	86%	77%	67%
TOTAL	100%	100%	100%
N	(377)	(531)	(144)

TABLE IV-30

AMOUNT OF CONTACT BY AGE OF PROBATION OFFICER (N-370)

CONTACT	AGE		
	YOUNGER %	MIDDLE %	OLDER %
HIGH	42%	34%	30%
MEDIUM	41%	46%	37%
LOW	17%	20%	33%
TOTAL	100%	100%	100%
N	(157)	(140)	(73)

As evidenced in Table IV-29, the police at all age levels experience predominately low contact. However, there is some tendency for contact to increase with age. For example, whereas only 14% of younger police officers experience medium to high contact, 33% of older police officers fall into these categories.

The relationship between age and contact for probation officers is somewhat different. As presented in Table IV-30, older probation officers experience the least contact. For example, whereas 83% of younger probation officers experience medium to high contact,

67% of older probation officers experience medium to high contact. The relationships between conflict and age are presented in Tables IV-31 for the police and Table IV-32 for probation officers.

TABLE IV-31

PERCENTAGE OF POLICE OFFICERS WITH HIGH CONFLICT BY AGE AND AMOUNT OF CONTACT (N=1,052)

CONTACT	AGE					
	YOUNGER		MIDDLE		OLDER	
	%	N	%	N	%	N
HIGH	46%	(11)	16%	(31)	17%	(18)
MEDIUM	44%	(43)	38%	(92)	30%	(30)
LOW	65%	(323)	46%	(408)	35%	(96)
TOTAL	62%	(377)	43%	(531)	32%	(144)

NOTE: N in parenthesis refers to denominator population
% refers to percentage of that denominator with high conflict.

TABLE IV-32

PERCENTAGE OF PROBATION OFFICERS WITH HIGH CONFLICT BY AGE AND AMOUNT OF CONTACT (N=370)

CONTACT	AGE					
	YOUNGER		MIDDLE		OLDER	
	%	N	%	N	%	N
HIGH	55%	(66)	47%	(47)	14%	(22)
MEDIUM	57%	(65)	48%	(65)	26%	(27)
LOW	77%	(26)	39%	(28)	29%	(24)
TOTAL	59%	(157)	46%	(140)	23%	(73)

NOTE: N in parenthesis refers to denominator population
% refers to percentage of that denominator with high conflict.

As can be seen from Table IV-31, at all levels of contact conflict is most evident among younger police officers. For example, at low contact 65% of younger police officers express conflict as compared to the 35% of older police officers who express conflict. The two variables of age and contact produce a cumulative impact on conflict. The most striking difference occurs between younger police at low contact, 65% of whom report conflict, as compared to older police at high contact among whom only 17% report conflict. It is also apparent that regardless of age, conflict tends to be lower among those with greater contact.

These relationships are the same for probation officers. As evidenced in Table IV-32, high conflict is more likely to be found among younger probation officers. For example, at low contact, 77% of younger probation officers express conflict as compared to 29% of older police officers. As occurred with the police, the most striking difference occurs between young probation officers with low contact, 77% of whom report conflict, as compared to older probation officers at high contact among whom only 14% report conflict.

Thus, for both police and probation, age is a significant predictor of conflict with officers under thirty expressing the most conflict. Contact seems to have a modulating effect in that young police officers with very low contact and young probation officers with very low contact express the most conflict; but a higher degree of conflict exists among the younger officers at all levels of contact.

Why youth should be associated with higher conflict among both police and probation officers is a matter of interest since it seems to contradict the conventional wisdom that places hope for cooperation in youth. Younger officers in general do not have the same degree of autonomy and flexibility in decision making as do older officers. Perhaps, this might contribute to a posture of greater conflict. Furthermore, younger officers tend to lack the self-confidence garnered from work experience and are thereby more likely to assume a defensive conflict-prone position. David Rafky, for example, reports that younger police officers (under 30 years of age) are more likely to get into trouble due to the fact that they are more inclined than older police officers to attach and express denigrating labels in expressing their attitudes.[4] Thus, whether the cause be a lack of autonomy, self-confidence, self-control, and/or immaturity, the findings in this study clearly indicate that for the purposes of conflict management, younger officers are of primary concern in future study and conflict management programs.

In comparing contact frequency according to age as well as experience and rank, it has been shown that for the police—contact tends to increase with age; and among probation officers–contact tends to decrease with age and rank. Thus, a very clear pattern is evident. Conflict is least likely to be present in situations wherein older, more experienced policc officers (who tend to have more contact with probation than do younger policemen) interact with probation; and it is least likely to occur when older, more experienced, high ranking probation officers interact with the police. On the other hand, conflict is most likely to be present among younger, less experienced police and probation officers.

The next variable examined is that of off-duty (personal) contact. As was done with the other variables, the amount of contact was established first and, held constant when the relationship with conflict was examined. The relationships between the amount of contact (official) and off-duty (personal) contact are presented in Tables IV-34 and IV-35. The categories used for off-duty (personal) contact are presented in Table IV-33.

TABLE IV-33

OFF-DUTY (PERSONAL) CONTACT

ITEM NUMBER	For Police and Probation	
18.	Outside of your job as a probation (police officer, how many police (proba tion) officers do you ever have personal contact with?	
	None	LOW
	1 or 2	MEDIUM
	3-5 6 or more	HIGH

TABLE IV-34

AMOUNT OF OFFICIAL CONTACT BY OFF-DUTY (PERSONAL) CONTACT OF POLICE OFFICERS (N=1,047)

OFFICIAL CONTACT	OFF-DUTY CONTACT		
	LOW %	MEDIUM %	HIGH %
HIGH	5%	4%	16%
MEDIUM	13%	21%	28%
LOW	82%	75%	56%
TOTAL	100%	100%	100%
N	(749)	(226)	(72)

TABLE IV-35

AMOUNT OF CONTACT BY OFF-DUTY (PERSONAL) CONTACT
OF PROBATION OFFICER (N=370)

OFFICIAL CONTACT	OFF-DUTY CONTACT		
	LOW %	MEDIUM %	HIGH %
HIGH	22%	27%	57%
MEDIUM	46%	52%	31%
LOW	32%	21%	12%
TOTAL	100%	100%	100%
N	(115)	(118)	(137)

Both tables IV-34 and IV-35 indicate an association between a high degree of official contact with a higher degree of personal contact.

Taking a look at the total amount of interaction, consisting of both official and off-duty contact, of police with probation, as indicated in Table IV-36, 59% of police officers have low official and low personal contact.

TABLE IV-36

PERCENTAGE OF POLICE WITH VARYING DEGREES OF OFF-DUTY (PERSONAL) AND OFFICIAL CONTACT WITH PROBATION (N=1,047)

OFFICIAL CONTACT	OFF-DUTY CONTACT				
	LOW %	MEDIUM %	HIGH %	TOTAL %	N
HIGH	4%	1%	1%	6%	63
MEDIUM	9%	5%	2%	16%	167
LOW	59%	15%	4%	78%	817
TOTAL	72%	21%	7%	100%	
N	754	220	73		1047

NOTE: The denominator for all percentages is the total number of police, N=1,047.

Among probation, there is a tendency towards higher official and personal contact. As indicated in Table IV-37, 21% of probation officers experience high official and high personal contact.

TABLE IV-37

PERCENTAGE OF PROBATION WITH VARYING DEGREES OF OFF-DUTY (PERSONAL) AND OFFICIAL CONTACT WITH POLICE (N=370)

OFFICIAL CONTACT	OFF-DUTY CONTACT				
	LOW %	MEDIUM %	HIGH %	TOTAL %	N
HIGH	7%	9%	21%	37%	137
MEDIUM	13%	17%	12%	42%	155
LOW	10%	7%	4%	21%	78
TOTAL	30%	33%	37%		
N	111	122	137		370

NOTE: The denominator for all percentages is the total number of probation, N=370.

Thus, data indicate that while probation officers have far more official and personal interaction with police than do police with probation, both police and probation officers with high official contact are also likely to experience high off-duty interaction.

The relationship between the amount of conflict and personal contact is presented in the following tables.

TABLE IV-38

PERCENTAGE OF POLICE OFFICERS WITH HIGH CONFLICT BY PERSONAL CONTACT AND AMOUNT OF CONTACT (N=1,047)

OFFICIAL CONTACT	OFF-DUTY CONTACT					
	LOW		MIDDLE		HIGH	
	%	N	%	N	%	N
HIGH	29%	(38)	10%	(10)	8%	(12)
MEDIUM	36%	(97)	46%	(48)	30%	(20)
LOW	54%	(614)	52%	(169)	35%	(40)
TOTAL	50%	(749)	49%	(226)	29%	(72)

NOTE: N in parenthesis refers to denominator population.
% refers to percentage of that denominator with high conflict.

TABLE IV-39

PERCENTAGE OF PROBATION OFFICERS WITH HIGH CONFLICT BY PERSONAL CONTACT AND AMOUNT OF CONTACT (N=370)

OFFICIAL CONTACT	OFF-DUTY CONTACT					
	LOW		MIDDLE		HIGH	
	%	N	%	N	%	N
HIGH	28%	(25)	50%	(32)	49%	(78)
MEDIUM	36%	(53)	56%	(61)	48%	(43)
LOW	51%	(37)	48%	(25)	44%	(16)
TOTAL	39%	(115)	53%	(118)	48%	(137)

NOTE: N in parenthesis refers to denominator population.
% refers to percentage of that denominator with high conflict.

It can be seen from Table IV-38 that at all contact levels, police officers with low personal contact tend to have higher conflict. Also, regardless of the amount of personal contact, those with lower amounts of official contact have higher conflict. A most striking difference occurs between those with low official and low personal conflict, 54% of whom express conflict, in contrast to those with high official and high personal contact among whom only 8% express conflict.

Inspection of Table IV-39 reveals that among probation officers, the amount of conflict is not clearly related to either variable. Personal contact does not produce lower conflict; indeed among those with high work contact. Thus, while the police display a consistent pattern of low contact (both official and off-duty) being associated with high conflict; for probation, work related contacts remain high, but when personal contacts also are high then conflict is likely to be high. This finding might indicate the presence of an interactional subcultural transmission process wherein police subcultural values are transposed upon probation officers with high personal (off-duty) contact (in addition to high official, work-related contact) such that a resultant inter-role conflict occurs for these probation officers between the demands of probation professionalism and the implicit expectations stemming from the subcultural values of the police.

A final series of contact and conflict analyses were undertaken which employed the important demographic variable of ethnicity. For these purposes, the major ethnic categories of White, Black and Spanish-American were utilized in classifying the ethnic background of both police and probation officers as well as their clients.

In examining the ethnicity variables, the amount of contact was established first, and, then, held constant as the relationships with conflict were examined. The first of these was the ethnicity of the officer variable. The relationships between the amount of contact and ethnicity of the officer are presented in Tables IV-40 and IV-41.

TABLE IV-40

AMOUNT OF CONTACT BY ETHNICITY OF POLICE OFFICER (N=1,040)

CONTACT	ETHNICITY OF OFFICER		
	WHITE %	BLACK %	SPANISH-AMERICAN %
HIGH	6%	12%	2%
MEDIUM	15%	29%	17%
LOW	79%	59%	81%
TOTAL	100%	100%	100%
N	(975)	(17)	(48)

TABLE IV-41

AMOUNT OF CONTACT BY ETHNICITY OF PROBATION OFFICER (N=367)

CONTACT	ETHNICITY OF OFFICER		
	WHITE %	BLACK %	SPANISH-AMERICAN %
HIGH	35%	28%	53%
MEDIUM	43%	36%	47%
LOW	22%	36%	0%
TOTAL	100%	100%	100%
N	(336)	(14)	(17)

Table IV-40 indicates that among the police, all ethnic subgroups experience mostly low contact with probation officers. However, while the number of minority officers are small, the data suggest that Black police are more likely to experience contact than either White or Hispanic police officers. For example, 41% of Blacks have medium to high contact as compared to 19% of Hispanics and 21% of Whites.

Table IV-41 indicates that Hispanic probation officers are the most likely to have contact with the police. Whereas 58% of Hispanic officers experience high contact, only 35% of White and 28% of Black probation officers experience high contact.

In relation to the ethnicity of the officer and conflict, Tables IV-42 and IV-43 present the data.

TABLE IV-42

PERCENTAGE OF POLICE OFFICERS WITH HIGH CONFLICT BY ETHNICITY OF OFFICER AND AMOUNT OF CONTACT (N=1,040)

CONTACT	ETHNICITY OF OFFICER					
	WHITE		BLACK		SPANISH-AMERICAN	
	%	N	%	N	%	N
HIGH	22%	(55)	55%	(2)	0%	(1)
MEDIUM	34%	(150)	60%	(5)	88%	(8)
LOW	52%	(770)	70%	(10)	56%	(39)
TOTAL	48%	(975)	65%	(17)	60%	(48)

NOTE: N in parenthesis refers to denominator population.
% refers to percentage of that denominator with high conflict.

TABLE IV-43

PERCENTAGE OF PROBATION OFFICERS WITH HIGH CONFLICT BY ETHNICITY OF OFFICER AND AMOUNT OF CONTACT (N=367)

CONTACT	ETHNICITY OF OFFICER					
	WHITE		BLACK		SPANISH-AMERICAN	
	%	N	%	N	%	N
HIGH	44%	(119)	50%	(4)	33%	(9)
MEDIUM	40%	(144)	40%	(5)	13%	(8)
LOW	48%	(73)	60%	(5)	0%	(0)
TOTAL	43%	(336)	50%	(14)	24%	(17)

NOTE: N in parenthesis refers to denominator population.
% refers to percentage of that denominator with high conflict.

Table IV-42 shows that at all contact levels, White police officers have the least conflict. For example, at mid contact, 34% of Whites indicate conflict as compared to 88% of Spanish and 60% of Black officers. Table IV-43, on the other hand, indicates that at all contact levels, Spanish probation officers have the least conflict.

We can state with caution that the ethnicity of the officer appears to be a predictor of conflict; White police and Hispanic probation officers express the least conflict. However, it is interesting to observe that despite the fact their number is small, Hispanic police officers experience the most conflict with probation officers. Thus, it may be noted that while a Hispanic police officer is most likely to experience conflict with probation officers, a Hispanic probation officer is least likely to experience conflict with the police.

The second ethnicity variable, the ethnicity of the offender whom the officer primarily deals with, is contained in Table IV-44. The relationships between the amount of contact and the ethnicity of the offender are presented in Tables IV-45 and IV-46.

TABLE IV-44

ETHNICITY OF OFFENDER WITH WHOM OFFICER GENERALLY DEALS

ITEM NUMBER	For Police and Probation	
6.	What type offender do you most often come in contact with?	
	White	_____
	Negro or Black	_____
	Spanish-American	_____
	Other	_____

TABLE IV-45

POLICE REPORT OF AMOUNT OF PROBATION CONTACT BY ETHNICITY OF OFFENDER WITH WHOM POLICE OFFICER OFFICER GENERALLY DEALS (N=1,040)

CONTACT	ETHNICITY OF OFFENDER			
	WHITE %	BLACK %	SPANISH %	OTHER %
HIGH	5%	4%	7%	6%
MEDIUM	15%	24%	13%	15%
LOW	80%	72%	80%	79%
TOTAL	100%	100%	100%	100%
N	(317)	(142)	(159)	(422)

TABLE IV-46

PROBATION REPORT OF AMOUNT OF POLICE CONTACT BY ETHNICITY OF OFFENDER WITH WHOM PROBATION OFFICER GENERALLY DEALS (N=366)

CONTACT	ETHNICITY OF OFFENDER			
	WHITE %	BLACK %	SPANISH %	OTHER %
HIGH	35%	33%	46%	35%
MEDIUM	49%	46%	44%	31%
LOW	16%	21%	10%	34%
TOTAL	100%	100%	100%	100%
N	(171)	(24)	(61)	(110)

Table IV-45 indicates that irrespective of ethnicity of the modal offender, as has been found repeatedly, most police interaction involves low contact with probation. Table IV-46 indicates that probation officers who report working predominately with Hispanic offenders are more likely to indicate that they have high contact with the police.

The relationships between the amount of conflict and the ethnicity of the offender are presented in the following tables.

TABLE IV-47

PERCENTAGE OF POLICE OFFICERS WITH HIGH CONFLICT BY ETHNICITY OF OFFENDER AND AMOUNT OF CONTACT (N=1,040)

CONTACT	ETHNICITY OF MODAL OFFENDER							
	WHITE		BLACK		SPANISH		OTHER	
	%	N	%	N	%	N	%	N
HIGH	13%	(16)	40%	(5)	37%	(11)	19%	(27)
MEDIUM	32%	(47)	38%	(34)	75%	(20)	32%	(62)
LOW	47%	(254)	49%	(103)	67%	(128)	52%	(333)
TOTAL	43%	(317)	46%	(142)	66%	(159)	47%	(422)

NOTE: N in parenthesis refers to denominator population.
% refers to percentage of that denominator with high conflict.

TABLE IV-48

PERCENTAGE OF PROBATION OFFICERS WITH HIGH CONFLICT BY ETHNICITY OF OFFENDER AND AMOUNT OF CONTACT (N=366)

CONTACT	ETHNICITY OF MODAL OFFENDER							
	WHITE		BLACK		SPANISH		OTHER	
	%	N	%	N	%	N	%	N
HIGH	42%	(60)	50%	(8)	57%	(28)	41%	(39)
MEDIUM	52%	(83)	36%	(11)	52%	(27)	32%	(32)
LOW	39%	(28)	40%	(5)	67%	(6)	54%	(37)
TOTAL	46%	(171)	42%	(24)	56%	(61)	43%	(110)

NOTE: N in parenthesis refers to denominator population.
% refers to percentage of that denominator with high conflict.

Table IV-47 indicates that police officers whose primary offender contact occurs with Spanish offenders tend to report more inter-role conflict. Police officers at high contact levels tend to have more conflict if they interact primarily with Black and Hispanic offenders. Except for officers dealing with Blacks, the general contact-conflict relationship of high contact and low conflict persists.

Table IV-48 indicates that among probation officers there is a suggestion that the Hispanic ethnicity of an offender is associated with higher conflict. For example, among high contact probation officers, 57% of those whose primary offender interaction is Hispanic express conflict as compared to 42% of those with primarily White offender interaction.

In summary, it may be concluded that while the preliminary analysis consists of small numbers in some of the ethnic categories so that it is difficult to generalize, the data present findings to suggest more intensive follow up study.

For example, it has been shown that there is a relationship for both police and probation officers expressing high conflict among whom there appears to be a primary offender interaction with Hispanics. Also, it has been demonstrated that police officers of Hispanic ethnicity tend to express high conflict with probation.

In attempting to understand the role of Hispanic ethnicity in contributing to police-probation conflict, a knowledge of Hispanic culture is indispensable: particularly an understanding of the values placed upon feeling-oriented relationships, the role of vocabulary in bilingual communications, and the central theme of machismo. The studies of probation counseling of offenders of Hispanic heritage by Felix Chaves and Jose Arcaya are most informative in bringing crucial distinctions to the fore.[5]

Chaves and Arcaya present a description of behavior pattern needs that might be particularly difficult to obtain in our society: feeling-oriented relationships, formal communication of personal respect, recognition of the importance of machismo, understanding of dependency needs as contrasted to self-determination, personal concern as compared to objective fact finding, and caring as contrasted to ethical advice.[6]

There is much evidence to support the notion that a police officer, especially, would be most likely to experience something less than respect and deference.[7] A Hispanic police officer might be more sensitive in his interaction with probation when these cultural expectations are not met; and, perhaps, this could contribute to police-probation conflict. Nevertheless, the question of Hispanic ethnicity among police in conflict with probation and the function of Hispanic ethnicity among offenders contributing to police-probation conflict is one that calls for further field study.

SUMMARY OF CONTACT AND CONFLICT

In conclusion, therefore, it has been shown that the typical probation officer has far more contact (most of which were actually telephone contacts) with the police than does the typical police officer with probation. Situations wherein the police attempt to obtain help or information from probation to perform their duties are associated with the most conflict. While increased interaction is associated with low conflict for police juvenile specialists, increased contact is associated with high conflict for probation juvenile specialists. It was surmised that since juvenile specialists comprise a far higher percentage of probation officers (28%) than police (8%), the fact that juvenile specialists among probation would most likely be interacting with police who do not share a similar orientation might account for more conflict with increased contact.

After discovering the general patterning of the amount, situations, loci, and context of contact, it was possible to distinguish additional demographic and occupational variables associated with conflict.

In studying these variables, predictors of conflict were indicated. It was illustrated that for both police and probation, youth is related to high conflict and that much experience is related to low conflict. It was surmised that perhaps younger and less experienced officers might have less autonomy and flexibility in decision making such that they might be more conflict prone. In addition, it was suggested that younger officers might lack the self confidence and control garnered from work experience; and, thereby, they would more likely assume a defensive conflict prone posture.

Although the number of minority officers in the survey are small, it can be stated with caution that while Hispanic probation officers experience low conflict, Hispanic police officers experience high conflict. An attempt at a partial explanation of these ethnic differences was made by relating literature from those with experience in counseling Hispanics. It was concluded that a conflict of Anglo-Hispanic mores would more likely be experienced by lower status police officers than by probation officers. Nevertheless, any further speculation as to the reasons for the association of Hispanic ethnicity and police-probation, inter-role conflict necessitates more detailed field study.

Lastly, it was discovered that for the police, an increase in both work related and off-duty contact with probation officers is associated with lower conflict. Among probation officers, it was shown that while work related contacts remained high, when personal contacts also are high then conflict is likely to be high.

It was suggested that these high work-related and off-duty contact and high conflict results for probation officers can be explained by the existence of an informal attitude structure prevalent in the world of the police. Namely, these attitudes may be referred to as the police social code wherein the individual officer is expected to get around the letter of the law (including professional rules) in order to enforce law and order. Quite often, as documented by the Knapp Commission and other students of the police,[8] there is an expectation that the proper stance of being someone who can be trusted is synonymous with being someone who understands that shortcuts have to be taken and that personal loyalty is the highest virtue.

This informal police code (similar in some respects to the inmate social code in its emphasis on solidarity and loyalty) is often antithetical to the professionalism espoused by most probation officers in their education, training and work performance.

It can be argued that once a probation officer has high off-duty (personal) contact with the police, he is exposed to the implicit expectation that he, too, is someone who can be trusted to function according to the code. As a result, when a probation officer has high work related and off-duty contact, the conflicts are intensified because of the police code which contradicts probation professionalism.

NOTES

1. See Robert R. Blake, and Jane S. Mouton, "The Intergroup Dynamics of Win-Lose Conflict and Problem-Solving Collaboration in Union Management Realtions," in Intergroup Relations and Leadership, ed. by Muzafer Sherif (New York: John Wiley and Sons, 1962); Robert R, Blake, Jane Mouton, and Herbert Shepard, "An Intergroup Problem-Solving Approach to Mergers," in Managing Intergroup Conflict in Industry, eds. Robert Blake, Herbert Shepard, and Jane Mouton (Houston, Texas: Gulf Pub. Co., 1964), pp. 146-152; John M. Dutton, and Richard E. Walton, "Interdepartmental Conflict and Cooperation: Two Contrasting Studies," Human Organization 25 (1966): 207-220; Jerry G. Ells and Vello Sermat, "Motivational Determinants of Choice in Chicken and Prisoner's Dilemma," Journal of Conflict Resolution 12 (Sept. 1968): 374-380; Rensis Likert, New Patterns in Management (New York: McGraw Hill, 1961); Richard E. Walton and John M. Dutton, "Interdepartmental Conflict and It's Management: A General Model and Review," Krannert Graduate School of Industrial Administration, Purdue University, March 1968; Richard E. Walton, Interpersonal Peacemaking: Confrontations and ThirdParty Consultation (Reading, Mass.: Addison-Wesley Pub. Co., 1969).

2. See Louis Radelet, The Police and the Community: Studies (Beverly Hills: Glencoe Press, 1973); Hans Toch, et al., Agents of Change: A Study in Police Reform (New York: John Wiley and Sons, 1975).

3. Morton Deutsch, The Resolution of Conflict (New Haven: Yale University Press, 1973), pp. 382-388; Neeley Gardner, Group Leadership (Wash., D.C.: National Training and Development Service, 1974); John Thibaut, "The Development of Contractural Norms in Bargaining: Replication and Variation," Journal of Conflict Resolution 12, No. 1 (March1969): 102-112.

4. David M. Rafky, "Police Attitudes and Labeling," Journal of Police Science and Administration, 1, No. 1 (March 1973): 78.

5. Jose Arcaya, "The Multiple Realities Inherent in Probation Counseling," Federal Probation 37, No. 4 (Dec. 1973): 60-62; Felix J. Chaves, "Counseling Offenders of Spanish Heritage," Federal Probation 40, No. 1 (March 1976): 29-32.

6. Ibid.

7. David Bouma, Kids and Cops (Grand Rapids, Michigan: Eerdmans, 1969); Paul Chevigny, Police Power (New York: Pantheon Books, 1969); George L. Kirkham, "A Professor's Street Lessons," FBI Law Enforcement Bulletin 43 (March 1974): 14-22; Irving Piliavin, "Police-Community Alienation," Andover, Mass.: Warner Modular Publications, 1973); Jerome Skolnick, Justice Without Trial (New York: John Wiley and

Sons, 1966); E. A. Thibault and N. L. Weiner, "The Anomic Cop," Humboldt Journal of Social Relations 1 (Fall 1973): 36-41.

[8]. M. G. Aultman, "A Social Psychological Approach to the Study of Police Corruption," Journal of Criminal Justice 4, No. 4 (Winter 1976): 323-332; Thomas Barker, "Peer Group Support For Police Occupational Deviance," Criminology 15, No. 3 (Nov. 1977): 353-366; Herbert Beigel, "The Investigation and Prosecution of Police Corruption," The Journal of Criminal Law and Criminology 65, No. 2 (June 1974): 156; Paul Chevigny, Police Abuses in New York City (New York: Holt, Rinehart and Winston, 1969); The Knapp Commission Report on Police Corruption (New York: George Braziller, 1973); Patrick Murphy, "Police Corruption," Police Chief (December 1973): 36-37, 72; Mark Pogrebin and Burton Atkins, "Probable Causes For Police Corruption: Some Theories," Journal of Criminal Justice 4, No. 1 (Spring 1976): 9-16: 9-16; L. Savitz, "The Dimensions of Police Loyalty," in Police in Urban Society, ed. Harlan Hahn (Beverly Hills, California: Sage, 1971), pp. 213-225; L.W. Sherman, Police Corruption: A Sociological Perspective (Garden City, New York: Doubleday, 1974); J. H. Skolnick, Justice Without Trial (New York: John Wiley, 1966); M. Symonds, "Emotional Hazartds of Police Work," in The Ambivalent Force, eds. A. Niederhoffer and A. Blumberg, (Waltham, Mass.: Ginnand Co., 1970), pp. 58-64; J. Van Maanen, "Working the Street: A Developmental View of Police Behavior," in The Potential For Reform of Criminal Justice, ed. Herbert Jacob (Beverly Hills, California: Sage, 1974), pp. 83-130; I. Younger, "The Perjury Routine," National (May 1967): 596-597.

CHAPTER 5

DISSENSUS, STATUS AND ESTEEM

This chapter is devoted to an analysis of the role of dissensus in attitudes as a factor influencing conflict between police and probation officers. The term dissensus refers to a "difference in attitudes or values". In addition to describing what individuals consider to be important, attitudes and values represent broad guidelines to action.[1] Findings from the early Albany Conference suggested that police and probation officials held strong differences in attitude regarding legal processes, approaches toward offenders, tolerance of deviance, faith-in-people, and in the status and esteem of the two positions. (Appendix A contains the data presenting the differences in attitudes between police and probation officials.) What was not possible at the Albany conference was to relate these differences in value to independent measures of conflict, nor was it possible to chart the extent to which such differences existed in "the real world". This study attempts to address both questions.

In order to develop a satisfactorily comprehensive and functional measure of relevant attitudes, various dimensions of conservatism and liberalism were examined: political-economic,[2] tradition and change,[3] toleration of non-conformity,[4] attitudes toward democratic principles,[5] and radicalism-conservatism. The resultant Political-Legal Liberalism Scale was developed following the extensive pre-testing described in the survey instrument section of Chapter 3. This scale directly relates to issues associated with police and probation concerns.

The ten items, listed in Table V-1, using a Likert scale format and an agree-disagree continuum, comprise the Political-Legal Liberalism Scale.

TABLE V-1

POLITICAL-LEGAL LIBERALISM

Political-Legal Liberalism Scale

1. We need to have stricter penalties in order to enforce our laws.
2. It should be necessary to prove that a confession is voluntary in order to have it admitted into evidence.
3. The rights of Black Muslims must be as vigilantly protected as the rights of any other religious group.
4. Most of what passes for rehabilitation is too soft and should be replaced with tougher measures.
5. The police should not have to be bothered with going through the process of getting search warrants.
6. Most criminals need treatment programs—not punishment.
7. Too much permissiveness is helping to destroy this country.
8. Any demonstrator who makes obscene gestures and remarks at a law enforcement officer deserves to be clubbed.
9. The action of the National Guard in shooting four Kent State students was a shameful and completely unnecessary response.
10. In order to deal more effectively with the crime problem, we should use more chain gang techniques in our correctional approaches.

The mean responses to the political-legal ideological attitudinal scale are presented in Table V-2.

TABLE V-2

POLITICAL-LEGAL LIBERALISM

Means and N	Nassau		San Jose		Albuquerque		Total	
	Police	Probation	Police	Probation	Police	Probation	Police	Probation
x	4.1	5.4	4.2	5.6	4.2	5.5	4.1	5.5
N	598	216	286	145	180	32	1064	393

NOTES: The possible range of scores is from 1.0 to 7.0 with scale midpoint of 4.0
The higher means indicate more liberalism.
The lower means indicate less liberalism.
An application of the t test to evaluate the difference between police and

probation means revealed that for each site the differences were significant below the 0.1 level.

The findings on political-legal liberalism indicate the same results as at Albany, namely, that in each of the three communities the police are less liberal than probation officers. It should be noted, however, that the police responses have a mean (4.1) which places them in a neutral position on the items while the probation officers' mean score (5.5) is toward the more liberal end. Until normative data on such items are obtained from other respondent groups, it is not possible to determine how typical or extreme these particular means should be considered. Nevertheless, the difference along this continuum suggests that dissensus on this dimension may provide one basis for intergroup conflict.

The subject of police attitudes and the so-called police personality has provided much material for popular accounts and broad generalizations.[7] The assumption that the attitudes of police officers must be changed is a most pervasive one.[8] Emphasis on education for the police officer so that his attitudes, often equated with nasty prejudices, can be turned around have been steadily increasing during the last two decades. However, since no significant effect on the attitudes of the working police officer by conventional education programs has been demonstrated,[10] one is forced to reexamine the original question as to what does or does not constitute a police attitude.

A number of studies have reported that some salient components of what has been described in sundry fashion as a conventional or conservative value system may be discovered among police officers.[11] However, these findings do not form the basis for a generalized personality construct. Nevertheless, there are many generalizations and stereotypes of the police based upon unscientific accounts or at best half-truths.

The first shibboleth is that of authoritarianism. The following statement is archetypical, "In fact, the typical policeman, as he is portrayed in the literature, is almost a classic example of the authoritarian personality."[12] Others suggest that rigid childrearing practices might be related in that "those who remain in police jobs are those who ‘can take it’ and for whom ‘conformity to the system’ does not pose a difficult problem”[13] Commissions and study groups continue to publish statements about authoritarian police officers[14]such as the following:

> “Police are notorious for being poorly educated, for being insecure individuals. Since they know they are poorly trained and poorly educated and largely incompetent, they expect to be challenged by anybody the approach.”[15]

In addition, the police have been described in graphic terms by Arther Niederhoffer, among others, as immensely cynical.[16]

Yet, when these broad generalizations about policemen are subjected to closer examination, it is often discovered that these conclusions regarding the police personality are, at best, facile. As an example, a recent empirical assessment of the Neiderhoffer Police Cynicism Scale shows that, to date, no adequate measure of police cynicism exists.[17] Further, this critical assessment indicates that police cynicism (depending upon particular types of cynicism associated with particular individual or organizational attributes) is multidimensional.[18]

Although the denigrating stereotypes might function as convenient rhetoric in the service of upper middle class elitism, they do not fare well when subject to careful assessment. As another illustration, a study reported by Trojanowicz shows that police officers are less likely to counteract with aggression against a belligerent than are social workers.[19] In addition, there is empirical evidence to suggest that the police are no more authoritarian or prejudiced than comparison groups of comparable education[20] and social situation.[21]

In reference to police attitudes, one is able to assert that while some salient components of what might be described as conventionalism, dogmatism and general conservatism have been found to exist among the police,[22] these facts cannot form the basis for a generalized personality construct (whether it be the authoritarian, cynical or suspicious personality).

What can be stated is that the police display conservative attitudes of a political-legal nature (that are multi-dimensioned and cognitively derived) in relation to their work. Also, police attitudes occur in a context that is specific enough (according to the particulars of the institutional setting) and broad enough (according to societal influences) to belie generalizations about and stereotypes of the police personality.

DISSENSUS (POLITICAL-LEGAL LIBERALISM) AND CONFLICT

The question as to whether the strains caused by dissensus of a political-legal nature would be associated with conflict is examined in Table V-3. The following table presents data enabling us to ascertain whether individuals differing in political-legal attitudes are likely to express higher degrees of inter-role conflict.

TABLE V-3

DISSENSUS (POLITICAL-LEGAL LIBERALISM) AND CONFLICT

ATTITUDES	PERCENTAGE WITH HIGH CONFLICT			
	POLICE		PROBATION	
	%	(N)	%	(N)
LIBERAL	40.9%	(569)	49.3%	(209)
CONSERVATIVE	57.5%	(485)	43.0%	(165)
TOTAL	48.6%	(1054)	46.5%	(374)

NOTE: Respondents with scores of 4.0 or higher were considered liberal. All others were classified as conservative.

N N in parenthesis refers to denominator population.
% refers to percentage of that denominator with high conflict.

X^2 = 29.83, $P < .01$ X^2 =, 1.21, $P<.70$

(G = -0.15, V = 0.17) (G = +0.13, V = 0.06)

The findings in Table V-3 show that there is an association between political-legal attitudes and inter-role conflict. Among the police, conservative officers are significantly more likely to express high conflict; while among probation officers, liberal respondents are somewhat more likely to express high inter-role conflict. Thus, it appears that the value system of the respondents in regard to these political-legal issues does constitute one source of inter-role conflict

In reference to the previous findings about contact, it was found that among police, high conflict was less among officers with high contact (Table IV-5). The question arises as to whether high contact police officers are more likely to be those with liberal views? The answer to this question is contained in the following table.

TABLE V-4

POLITICAL-LEGAL ATTITUDES OF POLICE OFFICERS BY AMOUNT OF INTER-ROLE CONTACT (N=1,054)

CONTACT	PERCENTAGE WITH LIBERAL ATTITUDES	
HIGH	66.7%	(60)
MEDIUM	57.1%	(169)
LOW	52.4%	(825)

NOTE: N in parenthesis refers to denominator population.

$X^2 = 5.63$, $P < .10$, $G = +0.15$

The analysis reveals that police officers with high amounts of contact are more likely to express liberal attitudes.

The question that is now before us is to what extent to attitudes and contact have a joint effect on the amount of inter-role conflict expressed by police officers. For information bearing on this question, we turn to Table V-5. Those who scored 4.0 or below have been classified as low in liberalism, those scoring 4.1 or above have been classified as high.

TABLE V-5

PERCENTAGE OF POLICE OFFICERS WITH HIGH CONFLICT BY LIBERALISM AND AMOUNT OF CONTACT (N=1,054)

CONTACT	LIBERALISM			
	LOW (Conservative)		High (Liberal)	
	%	N	%	N
HIGH	25%	(20)	20%	(40)
MEDIUM	47%	(70)	32%	(95)
LOW	61%	(395)	45%	(435)
TOTAL	58%	(485)	41%	(569)

NOTE: N in parenthesis refers to denominator population.
% refers to percentage of that denominator with high conflict.

The results from the table suggest that the variables of political-legal attitude and contact each have an independent effect on the amount of conflict. For each level of contact, whether high, medium or low, liberal police officers express less conflict. Also, for both liberal and conservative officers, the greater amount of conflict is expressed by those with low contact, and the least amount of conflict is expressed by those with high contact. The joint effect of the two variables has a substantial impact on conflict: only 20% of liberal police officers with high contact express high conflict, whereas 61% of conservative police officers with low contact express high conflict.

While the relationship between attitude and conflict was not as strong among probation officers (Table V-3), and the relationship between contact and conflict was virtually nonexistent for this group (Table IV-6), the same analysis was conducted for probation as was reported for police.

In Table V-6, the relationship between political-legal attitudes and contact is examined.

TABLE V-6

POLITICAL-LEGAL ATTITUDES OF PROBATION OFFICERS
BY AMOUNT OF INTER-ROLE CONTACT (N=374)

CONTACT	PERCENTAGE WITH LIBERAL ATTITUDES	
HIGH	52.6%	(137)
MEDIUM	53.4%	(159)
LOW	66.7%	(78)

NOTE: N in parenthesis refers to denominator population.

X^2 = 4.91, P <.10
F = -0.15

The analysis reveals that probation officers with low levels of contact with police tend to be the most liberal. Relatively little difference on liberalism is found between those with high and medium contact. Thus, while police with increased interaction with probation are more liberal (Table V-4), probation officers with increased contact are less liberal (Table V-6).

In answer to the question as to the joint impact of contact levels and political-legal attitudes on the conflict expressed by probation officers, the findings are presented in Table V-7.

TABLE V-7

PERCENTAGE OF PROBATION OFFICERS WITH HIGH CONFLICT BY LIBERALISM AND AMOUNT OF CONTACT (N=374)

CONTACT	LIBERALISM			
	LOW (Conservative)		High (Liberal)	
	%	N	%	N
HIGH	46%	(65)	43%	(72)
MEDIUM	41%	(74)	53%	(85)
LOW	42%	(26)	52%	(52)
TOTAL	43%	(165)	49%	(209)

NOTE: N in parenthesis refers to denominator population.
% refers to percentage of that denominator with high conflict

The analysis indicates that the results are not particularly strong or consistent. At both medium and low contact levels, there is a suggestion that liberals express more conflict. The trend is not apparent for those with high contact levels. Also, it may be recalled that for police, the impact of attitude on conflict was stronger for those with low and medium contact.

In general, with reference to the question as to whether dissensus is associated with conflict, there has been much support for the concept that people tend to display a favorable disposition towards those with a perceived similarity of values.[23] Conversely, it has been maintained that individual and groups have difficulty in understanding and interacting with others who are very dissimilar in basic values.[24] These findings tend to support these views at least in part.

The field data findings in this study have demonstrated that, as at the Albany Conference, the police are significantly more conservative on political-legal issues than are probation officers. In addition, the association between conservatism on these issues and conflict (which had not been tested at the Albany Conference) was found to be quite evident among the police. Furthermore, the results demonstrate that for the police, both high conservatism on political-legal issues and a situation of low contact each have an independent effect in contributing to conflict. Among probation officers, however, neither variable of political-legal attitude nor contact was significantly related to conflict.

STATUS AND ESTEEM

A second important source of conflict identified by researchers and of particular interest here is that which rests on differences in personal esteem and perceived status among members of a system.[25] For our purpose we use the definition suggested by Vincent O'Leary and Donald Newman who described status as the relative social ranking of an individual by others (probation officers are accorded one level of social importance and acceptance by the community; police officers another) and esteem as the individual's own ranking of his position.[26] The assumption is made that the strains caused by differences in the assessment of one's worth by others as opposed to one's own assessment is the root of much conflict between those occupying different but complementary roles.

At the Albany Conference, police and probation delegates were asked to compare their jobs in terms of the esteem with which they viewed them and their estimate of the status others accorded them.[27] Both police and probation officials attributed higher status to the probation task as compared to the police task. With respect to esteem, however, the police saw themselves as fully professional and worthy of self-respect as probation officers.

The following questions comprise the status and esteem items from the final instrument. They were responded to on a Likert scale format, using an agree-disagree continuum.

TABLE V-8

POLICE AND PROBATION STATUS AND ESTEEM

ITEM 33.	Police Status. Most people think that policemen work at the job they do because they would have a hard time getting another job which pays as much.
ITEM 46.	Police Esteem. It doesn't take more than the average intelligence of the man in the street to make a good policeman.
ITEM 52.	Probation Status. Most people think that probation officers work at the job they do because they would have a hard time getting another job which pays as much
ITEM 39.	Probation Esteem. It doesn't take anything more than the average intelligence of the man in the street to make a good probation officer.

Table V-9 presents the mean responses to the status and esteem items and measures of statistical significance.

TABLE V-9

STATUS AND ESTEEM SCORES OF POLICE AND PROBATION OFFICERS
SOCIETAL VIEWS (STATUS)

SOCIETAL VIEWS	TOTAL	Nassau	San Jose	Albuqu.
I. Police estimate police status	5.5	5.5	5.5	5.4
Probation estimate probation status	6.0xx	6.0xx	5.9Xxx	6.3xx
II. Police estimate probation status	5.7	5.7	5.8	5.7
Probation estimate police status	5.6	5.5x	5.8	5.8
PERSONAL VIEW (ESTEEM)				
III. Police perceive police esteem	5.6	5.6	5.7	5.8
Probation perceive probation esteem	5.9xx	5.8x	5.8	6.3xx
IV. Police perceive probation esteem	5.4	5.3	5.5	5.6
Probation perceive police esteem	5.6x	5.5x	5.6	6.3xx
Police (N)	(1064)	(598)	(286)	(180)
Probation (N)	(393)	(216)	(145)	(32)

NOTE: The possible range of scores is from 1.0 to 7.0 with scale mid-point of 4.0. Respondents with scores of 4.0 or higher were assigned high status and high esteem, whereas those with scores below 4.0 were assigned low status and esteem.

The higher means indicate greater status or esteem.
The lower means indicate less status or esteem.

xx t value significant at .01 level
x t value significant at .05 level

Summarizing the findings in regard to status, it may be noted that:

1. Probation officers perception of their status is higher than police officers perception of their own status.
2. Probation officers perception of police status differs from police officer perception of police status.
3. Probation officers perception of their own status is higher than police perception of probation status.

Thus, the major conflict lies in the differential perceptions of probation status held by police and probation. These general findings tend to persist within each of the three sites.

Following the same analysis for the esteem measure, it may be noted that:

1. The probation report of their esteem is higher than police report of their own esteem. (The difference is somewhat less than for status.)
2. The probation officers accordance of esteem to police does not differ from the level of esteem accorded to police by police.
3. The probation report of their esteem is substantially higher than esteem accorded to probation by police.

Thus, the major conflict stems from the discrepancies in esteem attributed to probation officers by the two occupational groups.

These data differ somewhat from the Albany Conference preliminary findings in that while the direction of differences is the same, the degree of difference is greater. At Albany, the police saw themselves (esteem) as equally professional as probation. In the field survey, however, the issue of esteem differences is magnified such that the police see themselves as worthy of more professional respect than probation.

The status and the cross-position esteem differentials that were observed here could be considered as the accordance of professional respect, and inevitably lead to the question raised by O'Leary and Newman: do the kinds of difference in status and esteem which were noted have an impact on conflict? More specifically we shall examine such questions as: Do probation officers who accord low status to police differ in their expressions of conflict from those who accord high status to police officers? Do such expressions vary among police who differ in the status they accord probation officers? Are the patterns similar for the dimension of esteem? Finally, what is the impact on conflict of the interaction of contact with the status and esteem variables?

An analysis of the impact on conflict of differential status attributions to the other occupational function is presented in the following table where the findings on status are presented for both police and probation respondents.

TABLE V-10

PERCENTAGE OF RESPONDENTS WITH HIGH CONFLICT BY STATUS ACCORDED THE OTHER OCCUPATIONAL ROLE

STATUS ACCORDED OTHER ROLE	POLICE RESPONDENTS % WITH HIGH CONFLICT	(N)	PROBATION RESPONDENTS % WITH HIGH CONFLICT	(N)
HIGH	40.8%	(727)	42.3%	(269)
LOW	65.1%	(327)	57.1%	(105)
TOTAL	48.4%	(1054)	46.5%	(374)

NOTE: N in parenthesis refers to denominator population.

% refers to percentage of that denominator with high conflict.

X^2 = 54.89, P<.01 X^2 = 8.01, P < .01

V = .23, G = +0.47 V = .14, G = +0.32

In Table V-11, similar findings may be discovered utilizing the esteem measure.

TABLE V-11

PERCENTAGE OF RESPONDENTS WITH HIGH CONFLICT BY ESTEEM ACCORDED THE OTHER OCCUPATIONAL ROLE

STATUS ACCORDED OTHER ROLE	POLICE RESPONDENTS % WITH HIGH CONFLICT	(N)	PROBATION RESPONDENTS % WITH HIGH CONFLICT	(N)
HIGH	44.3%	(697)	40.3%	(270)
LOW	55.5%	(357)	65.5%	(104)
TOTAL	48.1%	(1054)	46.8%	(374)

NOTE: N in parenthesis refers to denominator population.

% refers to percentage of that denominator with high conflict.

X^2 = 12.17, P <.01 X^2 = 18.31, P < .01

V = 11, G = +0.23 V = .26, G = +0.46

A comparison of the results from Tables V-10 and V-11 indicate clearly that differences in perceived status and esteem are associated with conflict. Among the police, the relationship is stronger for the status measure; and among probation officers, the relationship is stronger for the esteem measure.

An inspection of the contact patterns between probation and police officers indicated that high contact groups are somewhat more likely to accord high status and esteem to the other occupational group. For this reason, the previous analyses were repeated with the inclusion of the amount of contact. In Table V-12, an analysis is made of the relationship between status accorded probation by police and conflict for each of the three categories of contact.

TABLE V-12
PERCENTAGE OF POLICE OFFICERS WITH HIGH CONFLICT
BY STATUS ACCORDED AND AMOUNT OF CONTACT
WITH PROBATION OFFICERS (N=1,054)

AMOUNT OF CONTACT	STATUS ACCORDED PROBATION BY POLICE: LOW — % WITH HIGH CONFLICT	(N)	HIGH — % WITH HIGH CONFLICT	(N)
HIGH	28%	(18)	19%	(42)
MEDIUM	49%	(37)	35%	(128)
LOW	70%	(272)	44%	(557)
TOTAL	65%	(327)	41%	(727)

NOTE: N in parenthesis refers to denominator population.
% refers to percentage of that denominator with high conflict.

The findings from Table V-12 indicate that the factors of status levels and contact levels each contribute independently to conflict. For each of the three contact levels, police officers report less conflict if they accord high status to probation. Also, the police with high levels of contact report lower conflict whether they accord probation high status or not. The two variables of status and contact have a cumulative impact on conflict: while 70% of low contact police who accord low status to probation report high conflict, high conflict is reported by only 19% of high contact police who accord high status to probation.

A similar analysis was conducted for probation officers (Table V-13).

TABLE V-13

PERCENTAGE OF PROBATION OFFICERS WITH HIGH CONFLICT BY STATUS ACCORDED AND AMOUNT OF CONTACT WITH POLICE OFFICERS (N=374)

	STATUS ACCORDED POLICE BY PROBATION			
AMOUNT OF CONTACT	LOW		HIGH	
	% WITH HIGH CONFLICT	(N)	% WITH HIGH CONFLICT	(N)
HIGH	60%	(37)	39%	(100)
MEDIUM	61%	(43)	42%	(116)
LOW	48%	(25)	49%	(53)
TOTAL	57%	(105)	42%	(269)

NOTE: N in parenthesis refers to denominator population.
% refers to percentage of that denominator with high conflict.

The results are more complex than those obtained for the police. For probation officers with low contact with the police, conflict is not related to status accorded to police. It is related, however, among probation officers who have high or medium amounts of contact. Again, the impact of contact on conflict is not very direct for probation officers. There is some suggestion that among the probation officers according high status to police, higher contact is associated with lower conflict. This does not appear to be the case for probation officers who assign low status to police; indeed, for this group, the greatest conflict is reported by those with higher contact.

The relationship of conflict and contact with esteem, in addition to status, was also examined for both groups. The findings for the police are presented in Table V-14.

TABLE V-14

PERCENTAGE OF PROLICE OFFICERS WITH HIGH CONFLICT
BY ESTEEM ACCORDED AND AMOUNT OF CONTACT
WITH PROBATION OFFICERS (N=1,054)

AMOUNT OF CONTACT	ESTEEM ACCORDED PROBATION BY POLICE			
	LOW		HIGH	
	% WITH HIGH CONFLICT	(N)	% WITH CONFLICT	(N)
HIGH	35%	(17)	16%	(43)
MEDIUM	42%	(50)	37%	(115)
LOW	59%	(290)	48%	(539)
TOTAL	56%	(357)	44%	(697)

NOTE: N in parenthesis refers to denominator population.
% refers to percentage of that denominator with high conflict.

The analysis in Table V-14 reveals much the same pattern as previously commented upon for status. Both factors of amount of contact and esteem attributed to probation officers demonstrate an independent and cumulative relationship with conflict.

The findings for probation officers are presented in Table V-15.

TABLE V-15

PERCENTAGE OF PROBATION OFFICERS WITH HIGH CONFLICT
BY ESTEEM ACCORDED AND AMOUNT OF CONTACT
WITH POLICE OFFICERS (N=374)

AMOUNT OF CONTACT	ESTEEM ACCORDED PROLICE BY PROBATION			
	LOW		HIGH	
	% WITH HIGH CONFLICT	(N)	% WITH CONFLICT	(N)
HIGH	63%	(35)	38%	(102)
MEDIUM	63%	(48)	41%	(111)
LOW	67%	(21)	42%	(57)
TOTAL	63%	(104)	40%	(270)

NOTE: N in parenthesis refers to denominator population.
% refers to percentage of that denominator with high conflict.

It may be seen in Table V-15 that while esteem accorded to police is linked to low conflict, for each of the three contact groups, again, the amount of contact shows no relationship with conflict.

SUMMARY

The findings in this chapter revealed that in terms of dissensus involving a political-legal value system, police and probation officers significantly differ in their attitudes. Probation officers tend to be more liberal than police officers (as they did at the Albany Conference); they are more strongly committed to civil libertarian views and a rehabilitative philosophy. In addition, it was demonstrated that those police officers who are most conservative tend to express more inter-role conflict. Among the probation officers, political-legal dissensus is not significantly related to inter-role conflict.

In reference to differences along status and esteem (professional respect) dimensions, it was shown that both police and probation officers believe (as occurred at the Albany Conference) that society attributes more status to probation officers; and probation officers esteem their role more highly than police officers esteem policing. However, in the field study, police officers accord higher esteem, or professional respect, to policing than they do to probation. At the Albany Conference, the police saw themselves (esteem) as approximately equally worthy of professional respect in comparison to probation officers.

While there has been much literature to the effect that policemen feel themselves stigmatized by indices of low status,[28] there have been occasional indicators[29] that confirm this study's findings, namely, that the police evaluate themselves (esteem) highly in according high professional respect to their occupational function.

There is substantial evidence from this study that the differential status and esteem accorded the other occupational role is linked to the amount of reported inter-role conflict. High conflict tends to be found when low status and esteem are accorded the other occupation. Furthermore, this is not merely a function of different amounts of contact. The relationship persists within high, medium and low contact subgroups. For police, the factors of status and esteem accorded probation and amount of contact show strong independent and cumulative impact on conflict. Among the police, the factor of accorded status was somewhat stronger than accorded esteem in its relationship to conflict; and, among probation officers, the factor of accorded esteem was somewhat stronger than accorded status in its relationship to conflict.

In conclusion, therefore, in any future study or management projects regarding conflict between police and probation officers, it may be asserted that significant areas of concern in reference to the police are strong conservative attitudes of a political-legal nature and the accordance of low status (and secondarily the accordance of low esteem or professional respect) to probation. Among probation officers, the accordance of low esteem (professional respect) to the police (and secondarily the accordance of low status) constitutes a significant area of potential inter-role conflict.

NOTES

[1] Andrew F. Sikula, "The Values and Value Systems of Municipal Policemen," Police (May 1972): 59.

[2] T. W. Adorno et. Al., The Authoritarian Personality (New York: Harper & Row, 1950), p. 169; W.A. Kerr, Manual of Instruction for Tulane Factors of Liberalism-Conservatism (Chicago: Psychometric Hicks, "Construction and Validation of a Thurstone Scale of Liberalism-Conservatism" Journal of Applied Psychology 50 (1966): 9-12.

[3] W. J. Boldt and J. B. Stroud, "Changes in the Attitudes of College Students," Journal of Educational Psychology 25 (1934): 611-619; H. Hysenck, "Primary Social Attitudes," International Journal of Opinion and Attitude Research 1, No. 3 (1947); Theodore F. Lentz and colleagues of The Attitude Research Laboratory, C & R Opinionaire Test Manual (St. Louis: Character Research Association, Dept. of Education, Washington University, 5th printing, 1950); Herbert McClosky, "Conservatism and Personality," American Political Science Review 58 (1958): 27-45; J. Morgan, I. Sirageldin, and N. Baerwaldt, Productive Americans (Ann Arbor, Michigan: Survey Research Center. 1966).

[4] Vincent O'Leary and Donald J. Newman, "Conflict Resolution in Criminal Justice," Journal of Research in Crime and Delinquency (July 1970): 106-107; Samuel A. Stouffer, Communism, Conformity, and Civil Liberties (Garden City, New York: Doubleday & Company, Inc. 1955), pp. 262-266.

[5] Herbert McClosky, "Consensus and Ideology in American Politics," American Political Science Review 58 (1964): 361-382; Louis A. Noble and Ransom E. Noble, "A. Study of the Attitudes of College Students Toward Civil Rights," Journal of Social Psychology 42 (1954): 289-297: James W. Prothro and Charles M. Grigg, "Fundamental Principles of Democracy: Bases of Agreement and Disagreement," Journal of Politics 22 (1960): 276-294.

[7] See David Bouma, Kids and Cops (Grand Rapids, Michigan: Eerdmans, 1969); Paul Chevigny, Police Power (New York: Pantheon Books, 1969); Arther Niederhoffer, Behind The Shield (New York: Doubleday, 1967); Jerome Skolnick, Justice Without Trial (New York: John Wiley and Sons, 1966); E. A. Thibault and N. L. Weiner, "The Anomic Cop," Humboldt Journal of Social Relations 1 (Fall 1973): 36-41.

[8] See American Bar Association, Standards Relating to the Urban Police Function (New York: Institute of Judicial Administration, 1973), p. 15; Arthur F. Brandstatter, "A Career Concept for Police," The Journal of Criminal Law, Criminology and Police Science 61, No. 3 (Sept. 1970): 440.

[10] Dennis C. Smith and Elinor Ostrom, "The Effects of Training and Education on Police Attitudes and Performance: A Preliminary Analysis," in The Potential for Reform of Criminal Justice, ed. Herbert Jacob (Beverly Hills, California: Sage Publications, 1974), pp. 45-81; Normal L. Weiner, "The Effect of Education on Police Attitudes," Journal of Criminal Justice 2, No. 4 (1974): 317-328.

[11] Robert D. Finney, "A Police View of Social Workers," Police (February 1972): 59-63; Jonathan S. Raymond et. Al., "A Source of Potential Social Conflict: Police versus Addict Value Structures," International Journal of Criminology and Penology 3, No. 3 (August 1975): 275; Andrew F. Sikula, The Values and Value Systems of Municipal Policemen, Police (May 1972): 59-63; James J. Teevan, Jr., and Bernard Dolnick, "The Values of the Police: A Reconsideration and Interpretation," Journal of Police Science and Administration 1, No. 3 (Sept. 1973): 366-369.

[12] Robert W. Balch, "The Police Personality: Fact or Fiction?" The Journal of Criminal Law, Criminology, and Police Science, 63, No. 1 (March 1972): 107.
[13] Ruth Levy, "Predicting Police Failures," Journal of Criminal Law, Criminology, and Police Science 58, No. 2 (1967): 275.

[14] American Civil Liberties Union, "Police Power and Citizens' Rights," p. 16.

[15] City of New York Commission on Human Rights, "Community Values and Conflict 1967: A Conference Report," p. 74.

[16] See Michael Banton, The Policeman in the Community (New York: Basic Books, 1964); David J. Bordua, The Police: Six Sociological Essays (New York: John Wiley and Sons, 1967); Arthur Niederhoffer, Behind the Shield (New York: Doubleday, 1967), pp. 199-248.

[17] Robert M. Regoli, "An Empirical Assessment of Niederhoffer's Police Cynicism Scale," Journal of Criminal Justice 4, No. 3 (1976): 231-241.

[18] Ibid., p. 237.

[19] Robert Trojanowicz, "The Policeman's Occupational Personality," The Journal of Criminal Law, Criminology, and Police Science, 62, No. 4 (Dec. 1971): 558.

[20] D. H. Bayley and H. Mendelsohn, Minorities and the Police: Confrontation in America (New York: The Free Press, 1969); Alexander Smith et. Al., "Authoritarianism in Police College Students and Non-Police College Students," Journal of Criminal Law, Criminology and Police Science 59, No. 3 (1968): 440-443.

[21] David M. Rafky, "Police Attitudes and Labeling," Journal of Police Science and Administration 1, No. 1 (March 1973): 65-86; C. E. Teasley and Leonard Wright "The Effects of Training on Police Recruity Attitudes," Journal of Police Science and Administration 1, No. 2 (June 1973): 241-248.

[22] T. W. Adorno et. Al., The Authoritarian Personality (New York: Harper U Row, 1950), p. 973; Else Brunswik-Frenkel,, "Further Explorations by A Contributor to 'The Authoritarian Personality', in Studies in the Scope and Method of The Authoritarian Personality, eds. Richard Christie and Marie Jahoda (Glencoe, Illinois: The Free Press, 1954), p. 227; Frederick I. Klyman and Joanna Kruckenberg, "Methodology for Assessing Citizen Perceptions of Police," Journal of Criminal Justice 2, No. 3 (Fall 1974): 222; Grame R. Newman et. Al., "Authoritarianism, Religiosity, and Reactions to Deviance," Journal of Criminal Justice 2, No. 3 (Fall 1974): 258; Jonathan S. Raymond et. Al, "A Source of Potential Social Conflict: Police versus Addict Value Structures," International Journal of Criminology and Penology 3, No. 3 (August 1975): 275; Milton Rokeach. "The Nature and Meaning of Dogmatism," Psychological Review 61, No. 3 (1954): 195.

[23] Louis Festinger, "Informal Social Communication," Psychological Review 57 (1950): 271-282; E. E. Jones and H. B. Gerard, Foundations of Social Psychology (New York: John Wiley and Sons, 1967); T. M. Newcomb, Personality and Social Change (New York: Dryden, 1943); M. Rokeach, The Open and Closed Mind (New York: Basic Books, 1969); M. Rokeach and L. Mezel, "Race and Shared Belief as Factors in Social Choice," Science 151 (1966): 167-172; D. D. Stein, "The Influence of Belief Systems on Interpersonal Preference: A Validation Study of Rokeach's Theory of Prejudice," Psychological Monographs 80, 1966.

[24] Jonathan S. Raymond et. Al., "A Source of Potential Social Conflict: Police versus Addict Value Structures," International Journal of Criminology and Penology 3, No. 3 (August 1975): 267-278; Stephen Schacter, "Deviation, Rejection and Communication," Journal of Abnormal and Social Psychology 46 (1951): 190-207; David Summers, "Conflict, Compromise and Belief Change in a Decision-Making Task," Journal of Conflict Resolution 12, No. 2 (June 1968): 215-221.

[25] Dae H. Chang and Charles H. Zastrow, "Police Evaluative Perceptions of Themselves, The General Public and Selected Occupational Groups," Journal of Criminal Justice 4, No. 1 (Spring 1976): 17-27; Robert D. Finney, "A Police View of Social Workers," Police (February 1972): 59-63; R. Kahn and D. Wolfe, "Role Conflicts in Organizations," in Power and Conflict in Organizations, eds R. Kahn and E. Boulding (New York: Basic Books, Inc., 1964)., pp. 115-126; Jon Miller and Lincoln Fry, "Measuring Professionalism in Law Enforcement," Criminology 14, No. 3 (Nov. 1976): 401-413.

[26] Vincent O'Leary and Donald J. Newman, "Conflict Resolution in Criminal Justice," Journal of Research in Crime and Delinquency (July 1970): 108.

[27] These questions were adapted from Michael Banton, The Policeman in the Community (New York: Basic Books, Inc., 1964).

[28] Paul Jacobs, Prelude to Riot (New York: Random House, 1966), p. 48; Elmer J. Johnson, Crime, Correction and Society (Homewood, Illinois: Dorsey Press, 1964), p. 443; Gunnar Myrdal, An American Dilemma (New York: Harper and Bros., 1944), p. 540; James R. Thompson, "Supreme Court and the Police: 1968," Journal of Criminal Law, Criminology and Police Science 57, No. 4 (Dec. 1966): 425; Hans Toch, "Cops and Blacks: Warring Minorities," The Nation (April 21, 1969): 491; Nelson Watson and James Sterling, Police and Their Opinions (Wash., D.C.: International Association of Chiefs of Police, 1969), p. 7.

[29] Dae H. Chang and Charles H. Zastrow, "Police Evaluative Perceptions of Themselves, The General Public and Selected Occupational Groups," Journal of Criminal Justice 4, No. 1 (Spring 1976): 26; Jon Miller and Lincoln Fry, "Measuring Professionalism in Law Enforcement," Criminology 14, No. 3 (Nov. 1976): 409.

CHAPTER 6

ORGANIZATIONAL CONFLICT AND PERCEPTUAL DISTORTION

It is well documented that conflicts may arise as two organizations interact with each other and require similar resources.[1] Due to the fact that police and probation officials have responsibility for executing tasks which at certain points intersect, questions arise as to the nature of discrepancies between the two groups as they share responsibility for handling offenders and seek to serve their own organizational requirements in the process.[2]

At the Albany Conference, it was found that there were marked discrepancies between the two groups on a number of organizational issues.[3] One procedure useful in identifying these discrepancies was a scale consisting of a number of vignettes presenting police-probation interactions. From the original vignettes employed at the conference, ten were selected for inclusion in the final field instrument. As was indicated in Chapter 3, factor analyses performed on the responses from the field data identified two scales composed of four items each. The items in the final scale, Police Prerogatives, are presented in Table VI-1; the items in the second scale, Probation Autonomy, are presented in Table VI-2. Based on the 1,457 respondents, the Police Prerogative Scale had a Spearman-Brown reliability estimate of .79 and the Probation Autonomy Scale had a reliability estimate of .78. (The development of the scales is further detailed in Chapter 3).

TABLE VI-1

POLICE PREROGATIVE SCALE

You will find ten situations involving a conflict between a probation and police department. You are asked to do "three" things:

1. Indicate your opinion about the conflict by checking the appropriate space on the first line entitled "My Opinion".
2. You are then asked to check a space on the next line entitled "Police Opinion" to show how you think the average policeman would respond to the conflict situation.
3. On the next line, by checking a space after the words "Probation Opinion" you will show how you think the average probation officer would see the conflict.

Remember, there are no "correct" answers. Your opinions are what is desired. Take as much time as you need to answer carefully the survey.

ITEM 19. John Jones received a three-year probation term after conviction of a charge of possessing narcotics. Later, in a police raid, he is found in the home of Brown, who has a record for narcotics selling. As the police enter the house, Jones apparently emptied the contents of a plastic bag down a toilet and flushed it. The police have information from an undercover informant, that Jones had gotten rid of heroin.

Jones admits drinking excessively for several days, but denies possessing or using drugs. He states he did not know of the prior arrest of Brown. The police admit they cannot prove the narcotics charge and ask the probation office to recommend revocation of probation for Jones on the basis of violation of probation rule for association and drinking.

ITEM 20. The legislature is considering new penal and criminal law revisions. One proposal is for the police department to be given the right to make recommendations directly to the court on whether individuals should be granted probation or not. The probation department opposes this proposal, contending that recommendations should be made only on the basis of a balanced weighing of all the facts by professionally trained probation staff. The police department argues that the probation department should continue to submit their reports, but that it should be able also to make its views known directly to the sentencing judge.

ITEM 21. The Probation Department is starting a new program of working with offenders in groups and gangs. In order for the program to be effective, the probation department argues that youths will have to learn to trust the probation officers. Gang members will be told that anything that the probation officer learns will be held in strictest confidence. The police contend information about illegal acts not be withheld by the probation department.

The probation department argues that it is important for them to be able to work with the youthful gangs and to withhold such information. The police contend it must be shared.

ITEM 26. When a probationer violates any of the conditions of his probation, the polilce department is asked by the probation department to put him in custody for a review of his case by the court. This review may result in continuance of probation or commitment to an institution. The Police Department argues that if the probationer has committed new violations of the law they will arrest him. Otherwise, the probation department should have the responsibility for taking persons into custody who are simply charged with violation of probation rules. The probation department argues that arrest is a police function, and they should not be required to arrest probationers. The Police Department refuses.

TABLE VI-2

PROBATION AUTONOMY SCALE

ITEM 22. Police Officer Phelps is working on a forgery case. He has some leads which indicate that Harry Kelp, a probationer may be involved. Phelps asked Probation Officer Garrison if he could read the file of Kelp to see if there is any information in his background which may help him settle the case. The probation officer says he is willing to tell Phelps anything if he will let him know what kind of information he wants. Phelps contends that he is not sure of the kind of information he needs and it would be helpful if he could read the file without having it screened first by Probation Officer Garrison. Garrison refuses to turn the file over for Officer Phelps' inspection, stating that certain information is not relevant and should not be made available.

ITEM 23. The Police Department asked the Adult Probation Department to provide them with an up-to-date list including an address, some background information and a photograph of everyone placed on probation. The purpose is to let selective policemen, especially detectives, know who is on probation in various areas or the city in the event of the commission of a crime. The Probation Department says it will be glad to give information to police on specific individuals but are opposed to giving the Police Department such a blanket list. It contends that it is unfair to the offender and could lead to unnecessary harassment.

ITEM 24. The Police Department has arrested John Jones at the scene of an assault on an elderly man who was struck from behind. Jones has a prior record of assault and is on probation for manslaughter. No one had a direct view of the assailant. Jones was picked up within a few minutes of the assault in the next block running away. The police contend that they need time to find persons who might have witnessed the assault. They ask the probation department to place a "hold" on the defendant so he will be held in custody until the investigation is completed. The probation department contends that there are no know violations of probation against this man and refuse to place a hold against him.

ITEM 28. The Police Department tells the Probation Officer that Frank O'Neill, a probationer, is suspected of possessing stolen goods obtained from a burglary. The police do not have enough information presently to secure a search warrant, but urge the Probation Department to issue a warrant for investigation of probation violation so that a search might take place. The Probation Department argues that their policy does not permit them to arrest probationers under those circumstances. The Police Department argues that the probationer has violated his probation on several occasions by drinking and this could be used as a basis for arresting a probationer. Material from the burgarly could be found during a valid search. The Probation Department refuses.

These organizational conflict vignettes were designed to answer the following questions:

1. Are there significant differences between police and probation on organizational decisions involving inter-agency interaction?

2. Does perceptual distortion exist, and, if so, is it more evident among one group than the other?

3. What is the relationship between operational conflict and views held about police prerogative or probation autonomy issues?

The mean responses to the eight items incorporated in the two scales are presented in Table VI-3. Data are presented separately for police and probation respondents; comparable findings from the Albany Conference are also included in Table VI-3.

TABLE VI-3

RESPONSES OF POLICE AND PROBATION OFFICERS TO OPERATIONAL SITUATIONS, ALBANY AND FIELD RESPONDENTS

VIGNETTE SUMMARY WITH FIELD ITEM NUMBER	LOCATION	POLICE	PROBATION	DIFFERENCE
19. Police request revocation of probation for rule violation when new crime can't be proved	ALBANY FIELD	2.7 1.9	4.1 3.4	1.4 1.5
20. Police department believes it should be given right to make recommendations go judge	ALBANY FIELD	2.7 1.8	4.5 4.2	1.8 2.4
26. Police contend probation department should be required to arrest probation violators.	ALBANY FIELD	2.2 2.5	4.3 4.0	2.1 1.5
22. Probation department refuses police request for access to a probationer's case file.	ALBANY FIELD	4.5 3.9	2.6 2.4	1.9 1.5
23. Probation department refuses police department request for a list of names of persons on probation	ALBANY FIELD	3.5 3.6	1.4 2.0	2.1 1.6
24. Police department argues that a man with serious prior record should not recieve probation	ALBANY FIELD	3.2 3.8	5.0 4.3	1.8 .5
28. Probation department refuses police request to hold probationer in custody pending investigation	ALBANY FIELD	2.6 3.5	2.0 2.4	.6 1.1

NOTES: The higher the score the greater the disagreement with the question.

An application of the t test to evaluate the difference between police and probation means revealed that for each item, the difference among field respondents were significant below the .01 level.

**There were 15 police respondents at the Albany Conference, 1064 in the field. The number of probation respondents were 16 and 393 respectively.

On all four items concerning police prerogatives, probation are more likely to disagree than are the police respondents. This finding is obtained at both the Albany Conference and in the field testing. For example, in reference to item 20, while the police at Albany and those in the field agree that a police department should be given the right to make recommendations directly to a judge; probation officers oppose such a prerogative being accorded to the police.

On the four items presenting probation autonomy conerns, the police are more likely to disagree than are probation respondents. In reference to item 23, for instance, probation respondents at Albany and those in the field agree with the refusal of the probation department to supply the police with a list of names of persons on probation. The police do not agree with the probation department's exercise of their autonomy in refusing such a request.

Scores on the four items scales: Police Prerogatives and Probation Autonomy were obtained by summing item scores. Mean items scores were calculated (scale score/4); these scores are presented in Table VI-4 for police and probation respondents. The findings for the scales confirm the findings obtained on individual items. Police respondents are substantially higher on according police prerogatives; while probation respondents are substantially higher on probation autonomy. These findings appear not only for the total group but for each of the three sites.

The differences between police and probation respondents on these two organizational vignette scales are presented in Table VI-4.

TABLE VI-4

MEAN SCORES ON POLICE PREROGATIVE AND PROBATION AUTONOMY SCALES BY POLICE AND PROBATION RESPONDENTS, TOTAL GROUP AND THREE STUDY SITES

TOTAL GROUP	N	POLICE PREROGATIVES	PROBATION AUTONOMY
Police	(1064)	4.6	3.5
Probation	(393)	3.1	4.7
NASSAU			
Police	(598)	4.9	3.3
Probation	(216)	2.9	5.2
ALBUQUERQUE			
Police	(180)	4.1	3.5
Probation	(32)	2.9	5.2
SAN JOSE			
Police	(286)	4.4	3.5
Probation	(145)	3.0	4.5

NOTE: The possible range of scores is from 1.0 to 6.0 with scale midpoin of 3.5. Respondents with means of 3.5 or higher were considered high scorers and those with means below 3.5 were considered low scorers.

An application of the t test to evaluate the difference between police and probation means revealed that for each site the differences were significant below the .01 level.

There are some differences among the three study sites in the amount or prerogative and autonomy accorded to the two agencies. The police prerogative scores tend to be highest for Nassau County respondents (both police and probation officers), and lowest for Albuquerque respondents (both police and probation officers).

In contrast, Albuquerque respondents accord the most autonomy to probation officers. The scales appear sufficiently sensitive to reveal not only inter-organizational but inter-site differences as well.

PERCEPTUAL DISTORTIONS

A final question that arises at this point is whether different normative positions on police and probation organizational issues lead to different degrees of operational conflict. In other words, what is the relationship between the operational conflict scale and respondent scores on the autonomy and prerogative scales.

The answer to this question is contained in Table VI-5 wherein the relationships for both police and probation officers between probation autonomy and police prerogatives and operational conflict are presented.

TABLE VI-5
RELATIONSHIPS BETWEEN PROBATION AUTONOMY AND POLICE PREROGATIVE SCORES AND OPERATIONAL CONFLICT

RESPONDENTS	PERCENTAGE WITH HIGH CONFLICT			
	PROBATION AUTONOMY		POLICE PREROGATIVES	
	LOW	HIGH	LOW	HIGH
POLICE	52.7% (269)	43.7% (238)	48.5% (312)	47.7% (196)
PROBATION	45.9% (68)	46.9% (106)	45.8% (82)	47.2% (92)

It may been seen from Table VI-5 that the only significant relationship is that which exists for the police; among whom less conflict is found among those with higher commitment to probation autonomy. (This relationship is significant according to X^2 analysis at the .01 level.)

In attempting to explain why police officers with high conflict assign low priority to probation organizational requests, some reference to the police role requirements and organizational structure would be germane.

It has been well documented that the police function is wide ranging, related in some respects to social work, and ambiguous.[4] Furthrmore, Albert J. Reiss, Jr., maintains:

> "Whenever participants in a number of roles in different organizations have authori ty to make these decisions is hierarchically determined so that the deci sion at each level is open to review at the next, the stage is set for conflict among the participants."[5]

It would appear that in addition to the ambiguity in role requirements and the hierarchial police organization structure, police frustration is exacerbated by the fact, corroborated by the data in this study, that the police experience much conflict in receiving information from probation officers in general. Some critics assert that while we insist that the police do our dirty work, we do not take responsibility for this decision in providing the necessary support.[6]

Whatever one's conception of proper police functioning, a comparison of how our police are utilized with the English police constable is revealing. Wayne Jackson, Assistant Chief of Probation in the Administrative Office of the United States Court, reports:

> "Police are used routinely to perform some of the duties generally accomplished by U.S. probation officers in the presentence process. Ancillary police reports are prepared that complement the social enquiry (presentence report) at the dispositional hearing. Police reports delineate the defendant's prior arrest record, employment history, and general reputation in the community."

While it is true that the problems in the United Kingdom are not the same as those in the United States, the fact that police with high conflict relate negatively to probation autonomy decisions may reflect more upon the lack of organizational planning on a systems basis than deficiencies on the part of the police. In other words, the police may be quite reluctant, resulting in the expression of operational conflict, to accord autonomy to probation when they feel that their own professional discretion is not duly recognized and provided for.

Anther approach to the study of organizations in conflict is centered in perceptual distortions which prevent a clear image of the duties, functions, and purposes of one organization from reaching another in conflict with it.[8] As was indicated in Table VI-1, for each vignette, respondents were asked to indicate their opinion about the appropriateness of the organizational request along a six point scale anchored form Strongly Agree (1) to Strongly Disagree (6). In addition to obtaining one's own response or Actual Score, respondents were asked to predict both the typical response of one's own occupational group and of the other occupational group (see Instructions section of Table VI-2). Discrepancy measures could then be calculated between various pairs of responses.

At Albany, it was possible to observe that both groups overestimated the amount of conflict which actually existed between them.[9] In general, data at the Albany Conference showed that probation officials were more inaccurate in predicting police responses than were the police in predicting probation responses. We were interested in discovering whether these differences would hold up in the field.

The findings from the field study showing the actual and predicted responses on the police prerogative scale for each group of police and probation officers in the three localities are presented in Table VI-6.

TABLE VI-6

POLICE PREROGATIVE SCALE: COMPARISONS OF ACTUAL AND PREDICATED RESPONSES FOR ORGANIZATIONAL MEMBERS BY POLICE AND PROBATION RESPONDENTS, TOTAL GROUP AND THREE STUDY SITES

	ACTUAL RESPONSE	ATTRIBUTED TO	POLICE PREDICTIONS	PROBATION PREDICTIONS	INACCURACY OF POLICE	PROB.
TOTAL						
	4.6	Police	4.8	4.7	+ .2	+.1
	3.1	Probation	2.4	2.9	- .7	- .2
	+1.5	DISCREPANCY	+2.4	+1.8	+ .9	+.3
NASSAU						
	4.9	Police	4.9	4.8	.0	- .1
	3.2	Probation	2.4	3.0	-.8	- .2
	+1.7	DISCREPANCY	+2.5	+1.8	+.8	+.1
ALBUQUERQUE						
	4.1	Police	4.5	4.3	+.4	+.2
	2.9	Probation	2.3	2.6	-.7	-.3
	+1.2	DISCREPANCY	+2.3	+1.7	+1.1	+.5
SAN JOSE						
	4.4	Police	4.7	4.7	+.3	+.3
	3.0	Probation	2.4	2.7	-.6	- .3
	+1.4	DISCREPANCY	+2.3	2.0	+.9	+.6

NOTES: Inaccuracy was obtained by subtracting the actual response from the perceived response.

Discrepancy was obtained by subtracting the probation score from the police score.

Numbers of respondents as well as the significance level of the mean differences are presented in Table VI-4.

It may be seen in Table VI-6 that both groups of respondents believe that the police will grant more prerogatives to police than will be granted to police by probation officers. They are both accurate in the general direction of this prediction, for the police do accord more perogatives to police than does probation accord to police. However, both groups overexaggerate the amount of the actual difference between them. In examining the total group, for example, it may be seen that the actual discrepancy is +1.5 while the police predict a discrepancy of +2.4 and probation officers predict a discrepancy of +1.8. This general pattern is repeated in each site. Thus, one may conclude that in reference to police prerogatives:

1) Police score higher than probation respondents.
2) Both police and probation are aware that the police will accord higher preroga tives to the police than will be accorded to them by probation officers.
3) Both police and probation exaggerate the actual differences between the groups in their predictions.
4) The police exaggerate the differences more than do probation officers.
5) The greatest perceptual conflict (the most inaccurate predictions) is demon strated by the police in their attribution of probation opposition to the accor dance of police prerogatives.

Findings on probation autonomy in relation to perceptual distortion are presented in Table VI-7.

TABLE VI-7

PROBATION AUTONOMY SCALE: COMPARISONS OF ACTUAL AND PREDICTED RESPONSES FOR ORGANIZATIONAL MEMBERS BY POLICE AND THREE STUDY SITES

TOTAL	ACTUAL RESPONSE	ATTRIBUTED TO	POLICE PREDICTIONS	PROBATION PREDICTIONS	INACCURACY OF POLICE	PROB.
	4.7	Probation	5.0	4.8	+.3	+ .1
	3.5	Police	3.1	2.4	-.4	-1.1
	+1.2	DISCREPANCY	+1.9	+2.4	+.7	+1.2
NASSAU	4.7	Probation	4.9	4.8	+.2	+.1
	3.3	Police	3.1	2.4	-.2	- .9
	+1.4	DISCREPANCY	+1.8	+2.4	+.4	+1.0
ALBU-QUERQU	5.2	Probation	5.0	5.4	-.2	+ .2
	4.0	Police	3.3	2.8	-.7	-1.2
	+1.2	DISCREPANCY	+1.7	+2.6	+.5	+1.4
SAN JOSE	4.5	Probation	5.0	4.7	+.5	+.2
	3.5	Police	2.9	2.5	-.6	-1.0
	+1.0	DISCREPANCY	+2.1	+2.2	+1.1	+1.2

NOTES: Inaccuracy was obtained by subtracting the actual response from the perceived responses.

Discrepancy was obtained by subtracting the probation score from the police score.

Numbers of respondents as well as the significance level of the mean differences are presented in Table VI-4.

Table VI-7 indicates that there is considerable parallelism with the findings reported for the police prerogative scale (Table VI-6). In regard to probation autonomy, the following may be stated:

1) Probation officers score higher than police officers.
2) Both groups are accurate in recognizing that probation officers score higher than police on the accordance of probation autonomy.

3) Both police and probation overexaggerate the extent of the differences between them.
4) Probation officers exaggerate the differences more than the police.
5) The greatest perceptual conflict is demonstrated by probation officers in their attribution of police opposition to the accordance of probation autonomy.

These findings are obtained not only for the total group, but in each of the three sutdy sites. Thus, it has been demonstrated that while actual differences on organizational issues do exist between police and probation, there exists a perception of even greater differences than are actually present. Furthermore, as a result of the field study, we are able to qualify the indications of perceptual conflict uncovered at the Albany Conference. It has been shown in the field data that in reference to organizational interaction involving issues of police prerogatives, police officers display the greatest perceptual conflict in their attribution of the extent of probation opposition to the accordance of police prerogatives. In regard to organizational issues of probation autonomy, probation officers express the greatest perceptual conflict in their estimate of the amount of police opposition to the accordance of autonomy to probation.

In comparing the preliminary findings at Albany to the survey data, it was discovered that (as occurred at Albany) probation officers were more inaccurate in overestimating police opposition to probation autonomy issues than were the police in their estimations or probation opposition to police prerogative issues. Further, it was found that the respondents in the field perceived less distance between themselves and their own group than did the Albany participants (who were high ranking officials). Lastly, the field respondents showed more distance between police and probation organizations on issues reflecting their own group's interests. Thus, with the exception of the greater perceived distance between respondents and their own group, the field data shows the same direction (with greater magnitude) of organizational conflict and perceptual distortion that was discovered at the Albany Conference.

SUMMARY

In conclusion, therefore, in answer to the three questions posed at the beginning of this chapter, the following have been demonstrated.

1) Significant differences do exist between police and probation officers on the orga nizational conflict vignettes illustrating police prerogative and probation autonomy issues.
2) A significant relationship between probation autonomy and conflict exists for the police among whom those who accord low probation autonomy also express higher conflict.
3) Perceptual distortion is present for both police and probation; and, as occurred at the Albany Converence, perceptual distortion is more pronounced among proba tion than police officers.

In addition to the presence of organizational conflict, a particular pattern of perceptual distortion is evident such that each group over estimates the other group's opposition to issues affecting one's own group. In other words, the police express perceptual conflict by over estimating probation opposition to police prerogative decisions; and probation officers express perceptual conflict (to a greater extent) by over estimating police opposition to probation autonomy decisions.

The data in this study should bring to the attention of both police and probation agencies the fact that perceptual conflicts do exist between their respective agencies. For the police, these findings would seem to specify the organizational-interaction decision area or probation autonomy as the most crucial for further research on conflict management. Likewise, for probation, the results of the study indicate a need for more concerted attention to their own perceptual distortions regarding the degree of police opposition to probation autonomy concerns.

NOTES

[1] John D. Adams, Organizational Development and Change (Wash., D.C.: National Training and Development Service, 1974); Chris Argyris, Integrating the Individual and the Organization (New York: Wiley, 1964); Chris Argyris, Interpersonal Competence and Organizational Effectiveness (Homewood, Ill.: The Dorsey Press, 1962); Chris Argyris, Management and Organizational Development (New York: McGraw-Hill, 1971); Dean C. Barnlund and Franklyn S. Haiman, "A Philosophy and Method of Change." In Small Group Communication, edited by Robert S. Cathcart and Larry A. Samovar (Dubuque, Iowa: William C. Brown Co., 1970), pp. 206-215; Robert R. Blake, Jane S. Mouton and Richard L. Sloma, "An Actual Case History of Resolving Intergroup Conflict in Union-Management Relations," in Managing Intergroup Conflict in Industry, edited by Robert Blake, Herbert Shepard and Jane Mouton (Houston, Texas: Gulf Pub. Co., 1964), pp. 155-195; Robert R. Blake, Jane Mouton and Herbert Shepard, "An Intergroup Problem-Solving Approach to Mergers," in Managing Intergroup Conflict in Industry, edited by Robert Blake, Herbert Shepard and Jane Mouton (Houston, Texas: Gulf Publishing Co., 1964), pp. 146-152; Robert R. Blake, Jane S. Mouton and Herbert Shepard, "Strategies for Improving Headquarters-Field Relations," in Managing Intergroup Conflict in Industry, edited by Robert Blake, Herbert Shepard and Jane Mouton (Houston, Texas: Gulf Publishing Co., 1964), pp. 114-121; Elise Boulding, "Further Reflections on Conflict Management," in Power and Conflict in Organizations, edited by Robert Kahn and Elise Boulding (New York: Basic Books, 1964), pp. 146-150; Douglas Brown, The Human Nature of Organizations (New York: American Management Associations, 1973); Lester Coch and John French, Jr., "Overcoming Resistance to Change," In Group Dynamics, edited by Dorwin Cartwright and Alvin Zander (New York: Harper & Row, 1968), pp. 336-350; George Cvetkovich, "Small Group Dynamics in Extended Judgment Situations," in Human Judgment and Social Interaction, edited by Leon Rappoport and David Summers (New York: Holt, Rinehart and Winston, 1973), pp. 315-335; Morton Deutsch, "The Effects of Cooperation and Competition upon Group Process," in Group Dynamics, edited by Dorwin Cartwright and Alvin Zander (New York: Harper & Row, 1968), pp. 461-482; Leonard Doob, Resolving Conflict in Africa (New Haven: Yale University Press, 1970); John M. Dutton and Richard E. Walton, "Interdepartmental Conflict and Cooperation: Two Contrasting Studies," Human Organization 25 (1966); 207-220; William M. Evans, Organization Theory (New York: John Wiley and Sons, 1976): Edward Gross, "Symbiosis and Consensus As Integrative Factors in Small Groups," in Small Group Communication, edited by Robert S. Cathcart and Larry A. Samovar (Dubuque, Iowa: William C. Brown Co., 1970), pp. 63-71; Harvey A. Hornstein and David Johnson, "The Effects of Process Analysis and Ties to His Group Upon the Negotiator's Attitudes Toward the Outcomes of Negotiations," Journal of Applied Behavioral Science 2 (1966): 449-463; James W. Julian and Franklyn A. Perry, "Cooperation Contrasted with Intra-Group and Inter-Group Competition," in Small Group Communication, edited by Robert S. Cathcart and Larry A. Samovar (Dubuque, Iowa: William C. Brown Co., 1970), pp. 89-91; Daniel Katz, "Approaches to Managing Conflict," in Power and Conflict in Organizations, edited by Robert Kahn and Elise Boulding (New York: Basic Books, 1964), pp. 104-115; Clerk Kerr, Labor and Management in Industrial Society (New York: Doubleday and Co., 1964), Rensis Likert and Jane G. Likert, New Ways of Managing Conflict (New York: McGraw-Hill, 1976); Jay W. Lorsch and Alan Sheldon, "The Individual in the Organization: A Systems View," in Managing Group and Intergroup Relations, edited by Jay W. Lorsch and Paul R. Lawrence (Homewood, I11.: Richard D.

Irwin, Inc., 1972), pp. 161-182; Norman R. F. Maier, Problem Solving and Creativity: In Individuals and Groups (Belmont, California: Brooks Cole Pub. Co., 1970); Anant R. Negandhi, Organizational Theory in an Open System (New York: Kennikat Press Corp., 1975); Everett M. Rogers and Rekha-Agarwala Rogers, Communication in Organizations (New York: Free Press, 1976); Muzafer Sherif, "Intergroup Relations and Leadership, in Intergroup Relations and Leadership, edited by Muzafer Sherif (New York: Wiley and Sons, 1962), pp. 3-21; James C. Taylor, Technology and Planned Organizational Change (Ann Arbor, Mich.: Institute for Social Research, The University of Michigan, 1971); Kenneth W. Thomas, "Issues in Management of Conflict," in Management of Conflict, edited by Stewart Shapiro (Los Angeles: Institute of Industrial Relations, Univ. of California, March 13, 1973), pp. 5-22; Victor A. Thompson, Bureaucracy and Innovation (University, Alabama: University of Alabama Press, 1976); Richard E. Walton, Interpersonal Peacemaking: Confrontations and Third Party Consultation (Reading, Mass.: Addison-Wesley Pub. Co., 1969); Richard Walton, "Third Party Roles in Interdepartmental Conflict," Industrial Relations 7, No. 1 (October 1967): 29-43; Richard E. Walton and John M. Dutton, "Interdepartmental Conflict and Its Management: A General Model and Review," Krannert Graduate School of Industrial Administration, Purdue University, March 1968); Karl E. Weick, The Social Psychology of Organizing (Reading, Mass.: Addison-Wesley Pub. Co., 1969); Gerald Zaltman, Robert Duncan and Jonny Holleck., Innovations and Organizations (New York: John Wiley and Sons, 1973).

[2] Vincent O'Leary and Donald J. Newman, "Conflict Resolution in Criminal Justice," Journal of Research in Crime and Delinquency 7, No. 2 (July 1970): 99-119.

[3] Vincent O'Leary and Edward Ryan, A Study of Conflict Resolution in Criminal Justice, a publication of the Probation Management Institute, administered by the National Council on Crime and Delinquency, October 1969, pp. 26-30.

[4] See Michael Banton, The Policeman in the Community (New York: Basic Books, 1964); David J. Bordua, The Police: Six Sociological Essays (New York: John Wiley and Sons, 1967); Louis A. Radelet, The Police and the Community: Studies (Beverly Hills: Glencoe Press, 1973), p. 288; Quinn Tamm, "Equal Justice-Under Law," The Police Chief 33, No. 11 (Nov. 1966), p. 6; Richard Ward, "The Police Role: A Case of Diversity," The Journal of Criminal Law, Criminology and Police Science 62, No. 1 (March 1971), p. 586; James Q. Wilson, Varieties of Police Behavior (Cambridge: Harvard University Press, 1968).

[5] Albert J. Reiss, Jr., The Police and the Public (New Haven: Yale University Press, 1971), p. 132.

[6] William Westley, "The Escalation of Violence Through Legitimation," The Annuals 364 (March 1966): 126.

[8] Kenneth Boulding, "The Individual as a Party of Conflict," in Conflict and Defense, edited by K. Boulding (New York: Harper & Bros., 1962), pp. 80-104; Morton Deutsch, The Resolution of Conflict (New Haven: Yale University Press, 1973); Robert Faris, "Interaction Levels and Intergroup Relations," in Intergroup Relations and Leadership, edited by Muzafer Sherif (New York: Wiley and Sons, 1962); Roger Fisher, "Fractionating Conflict," in Conflict Resolution, edited by Clagett Smith (Notre Dam, Indiana: University of Notre Dame Press, 1971), pp. 157-169; Neely Gardner, Group Leadership (Wash., D.C.: National

Training and Development Service, 1974); Kenneth R. Hammond, "The Cognitive Conflict Paradigm," in Human Judgment and Social Interaction, edited by Leon Rappoport and David Summers (New York: Holt, Rinehart and Winston, 1973), pp. 188-205; Kenneth R. Hammond and Berndt Brehmer, "Quasi-Rationality and Distrust: Implications for International Conflict," in Human Judgment and Social Interaction, edited by Leon Rappoport and David Summers (New York: Holt, Rinehart and Winston, 1973), pp. 338-391; Ronald G. Havelock and Mary C. Havelock, Training for Change Agents (Ann Arbor, Michigan: Institute for Social Research, 1973); Colin Kessel, "Effects of Group Pressure and Commitment on Conflict, Adaptability, and Cognitive Change," in Human Judgment and Social Interaction, edited by Leon Rappoport and David Summers (New York: Holt, Rinehart and Winston, 1973), pp. 296-303; William M. Knapp and Jerome E. Podell, "Mental Patients, Prisoners, and Students with Simulated Partners in a Mixed-Motive Game." Journal of Conflict Resolution 2 (June 1967): 235-241; Carl E. Kuhlman, Monroe J. Miller and Erol Gungor, "Interpersonal Conflict Reduction: The Effects of Language and Meaning,: in Human Judgment and Social Interaction, edited by Leon Rappoport and David Summers (New York: Holt, Rinehart and Winston, 1973), pp. 229-237; Eric H. Neilson, "Understanding and Managing Intergroup Conflict," in Managing Group and Intergroup Relations, edited by Jay W. Lorsch and Paul R. Lawrence (Homewood, I11.: Richard B. Irwin, 1972), pp. 329-343; Robert D. Nye, Conflict Among Humans (New York: Springer Pub. Co., 1973); John A. Seiler, "Diagnosing Interdepartmental Conflict," in Managing Group and Intergroup Relations, edited by Jay W. Lorsch and Paul R. Lawrence (Homewood, I11.: Richard D. Irwin, 1972), pp. 310-324; Herbert W. Simons, "The Carrot and Stick as Handmaidens of Persuasion in Conflict Situations," in Perspectives on Communication in Social Control, edited by Gerald W. Miller and Herbert W. Simons (Englewood Cliffs, New Jersey: Prentice-Hall, 1974), pp. 178-184; A. S. Tannenbaum, Control in Organizations (New York: McGraw-Hill, 1968); Frederick J. Todd, Kenneth R. Hammond and Marilyn M. Wilkins, "Differential Effects of Ambiguous and Exact Feedback on Two-Person Conflict and Compromise," Journal of Conflict Resolution 10, No. 1 (March 1966); 88-97; Stanton Wheeler, "Role Conflict in Correctional Communities," in Prison: Studies in Institution Organization and Change (New York: Holt, Rinehart and Winston, 1961), pp. 229-259; Abraham Zaleznik and David Moment, The Dynamics of Interpersonal Behavior (New York: John Wiley and Sons, 1964).

[9] Vincent O'Leary and Edward Ryan, op. cit., pp. 30-36.

CHAPTER 7

CONFLICT ADAPTION STYLES

In addition to providing organizational conflict and perceptual distortion data, the vignettes were also utilized as the instrument for classifying respondents on their conflict adaptation styles. A system was developed so that respondents were categorized as either having a police adaption style, a probation adaptation style, or a moderator orientation style, (i.e. neither strongly police nor probation oriented). Basically, respondents were classified by whether their own responses on the vignettes were closer to those they predicted for police or those they predicted for probation. If there was relatively little difference between two, a respondent was classified as a "moderator". If there was a substantial difference, the respondent was classified as having either a "probation adaption" or "police adaptation" according to which group score the respondent's own score was closer. Thus, the typology incorporated scores from three different scales. The formulations of the typology are presented in more detail in Table VII-1 and were described in further detail in Chapter 3.

The typology was constructed in order to explore how various adaption styles (police, probation or moderator) related to measures of patterns of contact. Additionally, an effort was made to determine how these various styles differed on a series of measures of attitude and job interactions. In order to obtain these data, a series of interviews were conducted by two mature interviewers six months after the administration of the study instrument. Neither interviewer had been involved in the administration of the instrument.

Contact Patterns And Adaptation Styles

Table VII-1 describes the manner in which the vignette scores were classified to produce the adaptation styles that were the basis of the analysis that follows. The distribution of police and probation respondents by their conflict adaptation styles are shown in Table VII-2.

TABLE VII-1

CONFLICT ADAPTION TYPOLOGY

As applied to the three responses to each organizastional conflict vignette:	The formula was computed as follows:
Response 1 My opinion Response 2 My estimation of the average police officer's response Response 3 My estimation of probation officer's response	If the difference between Response 1 and 2 equals A, and If the difference between Response 1 and 3 equals B, and If the difference between A and B equals C

DESIGNATED TYPOLOGY CLASSIFICATIONS

MODERATOR	Then, if C <1 1/2 per item, the respondent displays a Moderator Adaption designed as Group III.
POLICE ADAPTION	If C> 1 1/2 per item and if A<B, the respondent displays a Police Orientation designated as Group I.
PROBATION ADAPTION	If C > 1 1/2 per item and if B<A, the respondent displays a Probation Orientation designated as Group II.

NOTE: Since 10 items were used for classifying conflict adaptation, 15 (10 x 1 1/2 per item) was the assigned difference used to designate the conflict adaption of the respondent.

TABLE VII-2

CONFLICT ADAPTION TYPES OF POLICE AND PROBATION RESPONDENTS, NASSAU COUNTY

CONFLICT ADAPTATION	PROBATION RESPONDENTS N	PROBATION RESPONDENTS %	POLICE RESPONDENTS N	POLICE RESPONDENTS %
Police	14	15%	46	42%
Moderator	33	34%	63	57%
Probation	49	51%	1	1%
TOTAL	96	100%	110	100%

$X_2 = 71.90, P < .01$
$V = 0.69$

It may be seen from Table VII-2 that the probation respondents display a predominantely probation adaptation (51%), whereas the police respondents express a moderator adaption (57%). It should be noted, as well, that while less than 1% of police respondents express a probation adaptation, 15% of the probation officers indicate a police adaptation. Thus, among this pool of respondents, we have two rather interesting groupings: a significant minority of probation officers with a police adaptation and a majority of police with a moderator adaption.

Moving to the next level of analysis, we shall explore how conflict adaptations differ among respondents who have various contact patterns. To this end, Tables VII-3 and VII-4 present the relationship between conflict adaptation and category of assignment for police and probation officers. The data for these tables, as well Tables VII-5 and VII-6, were secured by the interview process to be described in the next setion.

TABLE VII-3
CONFLICT ADAPTATION AND POLICE CATEGORY OF ASSIGNMENT, NASSAU COUNTY

CONFLICT	CATEGORY OF ASSIGNMENT									
	JUVENILE		COMMUNITY RELATIONS		DETECTIVE		NARCOTIC		TOTAL	
	N	%	N	%	N	%	N	%	N	%
Police Adaption	10	29%	0	0%	22	48%	14	64%	46	42%
Moderator Adaption	24	68%	7	100%	24	52%	8	36%	63	57%
Probation Adaption	1	3%	0	0%	0	0%	0	0%	1	1%
Total	35	100%	7	100%	46	100%	22	100%	110	100%

X^2 analysis was computed by collapsing the 1 probation adaptation respondent into the moderator adaptation category.

$$X^2 = 13.65, P < .01$$
$$V = .35$$

TABLE VII-4
CONFLICT ADAPTATION AND PROBATION CATEGORY
OF ASSIGNMENT, NASSAU COUNTY

CONFLICT	CATEGORY OF ASSIGNMENT					
	ADULT DIVISION		FAMILY DIVISION		TOTAL	
	N	%	N	%	N	%
Police Adaption	14	21%	0	0	14	15%
Moderator Adaption	19	29%	14	47%	33	34%
Probation Adaption	33	50%	16	53%	49	51%
Total	66	100%	30	100%	96	100%

$X^2 = 8.32, P < .05$
$V = .29$

Characteristics of the police respondents as documented in Table VII-3 are as follows: 57% of the police indicate a moderator adaption, 42% express a police adaptation, and only 1% display a probation adaption. Further, definite linkages with adaption types may be noted. Police assigned to juvenile or community relations categories are more likely to have a moderator rather than police adaptation. Narcotics officers are more likely to have a police adaptation, while detectives tend to be rather evenly split between police and moderator adaptations.

While the relationship for probation is not as strong as it is for the police, Table VII-4 does indicate that 51% of the probation officers indicate a probation adaptation, 34% express a moderator adaptation, and 15% express a police adaptation. It can be seen from Table VII-4 that all of the officers with a police adaptation (14) are situated in the Adult Division. It is also evident that officers in the Family Division are more likely to display a moderator adaptation oat 47% compared to only 29% of the Adult Division.

Thus, the data indicate that police respondents tend to choose a moderator position (57%), while the probation officers choose a prbation adaptation (51%). It is also shown that police officers in juvenile and community relations assignments along with probation officers in the Family Division are the most oriented toward a moderator position. While the probation adaptation position is practically nonexistent among the police, the police adaptation is strongest among police officers with narcotic assignments and among a small group of Adult Division probation officers.

Shifting to a more general level, Tables VII-5 and VII-6 describe the relationship between conflict adaptation style and the amount of contact between police and probation.

TABLE VII-5

CONFLICT ADAPTION AND AMOUNT OF CONTACT FOR POLICE OFFICERS, NASSAU COUNTY

CONTACT	CONFLICT ADAPTATION							
	POLICE ADAPTATION		MODERATOR ADAPTATION		PROBATION ADAPTATION		TOTAL	
	N	%	N	%	N	%	N	%
HIGH	6	13%	15	24%	1	100%	22	22%
MEDIUM	24	52%	36	57%	0	0%	60	55%
LOW	16	35%	12	19%	0	0%	28	25%
TOTAL	46	100%	63	100%	1	100%	110	100%

NOTES: High contact = more than once a week
Medium contact = one to four times a month
Low contact = less than once a month or more

X^2 analysis was computed for all police conflict adaptation relationships by collapsing the 1 probation adaptation respondent into the moderator adaptation category.

X^2 = 4.69, $P<.10$
V = .21

TABLE VII-6

CONFLICT ADAPTION AND AMOUNT OF CONTACT FOR PROBATION OFFICERS, NASSAU COUNTY

CONTACT	CONFLICT ADAPTATION							
	POLICE ADAPTATION		MODERATOR ADAPTATION		PROBATION ADAPTATION		TOTAL	
	N	%	N	%	N	%	N	%
HIGH	11	79%	21	64%	9	18%	41	43%
MEDIUM	2	14%	7	21%	21	43%	30	31%
LOW	1	7%	5	15%	19	39%	25	26%
TOTAL	14	100%	33	100%	49	100%	96	100%

X^2 = 25.61, $P < .01$
V = .37

As shown in Table VII-5, the police with a moderator adaptation experience more contact with probation than those with a police adaptation: 24% of moderators experience high contact as compared to 13% of respondents with a police adaptation. Among probation, Table VII-6 shows that those with police and moderator adaptations experience more contact with the police than those with a probation adaptation: 79% of police adapters and 64% of moderators experience high contact as compared to only 18% of those with a probation adaptation.

CONFLICT ADAPTATION STYLES

A major purpose of this chapter is to describe the relationship of adaptation styles to various expressed attitudes and types of interaction between probation and police officials and their offender clients. The data for these analyses were drawn from a series of interviews conducted during a two month period in 1972 by two interviewers some six months after the questionnaires used in the study were distributed and collected. The interviewing was confined to police and probation officers in Nassau County and was conducted in the respondent's work settings. The interviewers were instructed to elicit information concerning

a) the category of assignment of the interviewee,

b) the amount of contact (high, medium or low) existing with members of the other agency, i.e. police with probation and vice versa,

c) the nature of the relationship with members of the other agency (positive, neutral or negative),

d) the style of client interaction (law enforcement, personal adjustment or processing),

e) the attitude towards the courts (jail shy, revolving door, or O.K.).

As a result of the way in which the schedules were coded, the interviewers knew the conflict adaptation group to which the interviewee belonged. This development was inadvertent in that the original intention was for the interviewing to occur without knowledge of the interviewee's conflict adaptation. The data presented above concerning job assignments and degree of contact should not be affected by the information known to interviewee, but some caution should be exercised when examining attitudes and interactions. The data in this chapter in these regards should be regarded as illustrative rather than as establishing independently the strength of those relationships.

The potential pool of interview respondents was limited to those who had been willing to affix their name to their questionnaire schedules. From the total of 220 Nassau probation officers, the 96 officers who had signed the questionnaire were interviewed. Since few police officers had much interagency contact (as compared to probation officers) and since it was more difficult tolocate police officers for interview purposes within the allotted time and budget, it was decided to focus interviews with the police on those categories of police who had the greatest interagency contact. Accordinlgy, police officers in juvenile, narcotics, detective and community relations assignments were interviewed. The interviews were conducted with 110 police officers who had been identified by signature and who were situated in one of the formentioned categories of assignment.

From these inverviews it was possible to flesh out the behavioral characteristics of each of the adaptation styles. The following section describes in brief some of the elements of each of the adaptation styles as revealed by interviews in the field:

Probation Adaptation Style

It should be recalled that 51% (Table VII-4) of probation respondents express a probation adaptation whereas only 1 police respondent indicates this adaptation. Thus, our description concerns itself exclusively with probation officers. It should be noted that these probation adapters have minimal police contact (Table VII-6 shows that only 18% experience high contact). The exception to their general negative assessment of the police is contained in the following representative descritpion of the juvenile aid police officer:

> "I personally use the police as a resource. Now, I'm talking about juvenile aid police for they are not looking for arrests, like the others, but rather for assistance. In investigation, I use them as a source of all kinds of information about the kid -- including their feeling about the client. I ask them for their feelings about the client's family and his environment. In supervision, I would use them as another source. I would leave a list of my clients with the police. They would call me and I would go down to the JAB (Juvenile Aid Bureau) and try to work it out with the police."

Many probation officers in this group are highly indignant about police officers who express negative opinions about their clients especially when they may have had only one contact with the offender. Their attitude is that of helping the client, often to the point of mediating between him and the police. This orientation is represented in the following case description:

> "I had a case where a sixteen year old shot somebody. The police couldn't find him so they called me. I then sent out word in the community and contacted his brother who was also on probation. He turned himself in to me rather than the police because he was afraid that the police would shoot him. He was armed and had had resentment against the police. He realized that I was trying to help him."

Police Adaptation Style

Forty-two percent of the police respondents and 15% of probation respondents demonstrated a police adaptation (Table VII-2). According to category of assignment, police in narcotic assignments (Table VII-3) are most likely to express a police adaptation, and all of the 14 probation officers with this adaptation are located in the Adult Division (Table VII-4).

Police Adaptation Probation Officers

Probation officers with a police adaptation display a strong inclination to engage in law enforcement tasks in conjunction with the police as independent peace officers. The following case represents this inclination.

> "The police had a report that an individual was having what they described as orgies and drug sessions in a home. The individual was being supervised by the County Probation Department. The Police Department requested that we get a search warrant. This department proceeded to go to court and we got a warrant based on the information received from the Suffolk police. Surveillance was placed on the house, and one Friday night the police observed several youngsters entering the house. The police contacted the supervisor of the Nassau probation who in turn contacted three of his probation officers.
>
> They met with the police at 3:00 A.M. Saturday morning, and they raided the house making thirteen arrests. There were nine males and four females (two of the females were under age). Everyone was unclothed or almost, and they had been sniffing gasoline or kerosene and had been using body paint. In the eyes of the police and the three probation officers, it was an orgy scene."

These officers have much police contact (Table VII-6 shows that 79% experience high contact). However, what is distinctive to this group is the nature of the contact. Common characteristics of this interaction are as follows:

(1) They visit the police department personally.
(2) They often call the police with helpful information
(3) Many of them call the police on a weekly basis just tocheck on clients.

(4) They will stop to talk to the police on the street when they are visiting clients.

The probation officers in this group comment quite often how the police help them and how they help the police in solving cases. There is a strong feeling that since the police go out of their way to help us, we should go out of our way to help them. The implication is quite strong on the part of these officers that they and the police are collaborative substystems with a superordinate goal of law enforcement. They feel that their information coordination with the police has to be maintained on a personal level.

In respect to client interaction, probation officers with a police adaptation would not hesitate to revoke a probationer "the first time he steps out of line," and to serve warrants personally on the probationer. Most of them feel that they do not have enough time to consider rehabilitation methods.

Although the department does not encourage its officers to carry weapons and has issued a directive that no probation officer can wear a gun in his office, many of these officers indicate that they feel obliged to carry guns. The reasons are as follows:

(1) It is necessary to protect oneself in case the probationer is a hard drug user or becomes violent:
(2) if the client knows they have a gun, he has more respect for the officer;
(3) since they are peace officers; they feel entitled to carry a gun.

Some officers did not say they carried guns but inferred as much. For example, one officer stated that if a client was uncooperative, he would open his jacket to show him that he "meant business." Another officer stated, "To keep a client on the straight and narrow, I open my jacket and let him see what I've got inside."

There is also widespread feeling in this group that cases of repeated recidivism indicate a need for more incarceration. "If a client relapses into his previous mode of behavior and breaks probaton, it is reasoned, "he should be punished." It is often stated that if there were a violation and the court just puts him back on probation, the threat of getting a violation loses its sting. Accordingly, this group doesn't like the fact that one client can tell another not to worry about a violation because "it only means getting back on the same merry-go-round."

The following case description represents the feeling that not enough offenders are incarcerated.

> "One of my probationers is thirty-two years old, he has been on and off probation since 1960. He's mainlined heroin since 1964. He's been in numerous correctional facilities and he is a certified addict. He committed a crime in this county and we investigated him. Due to his prior record of recidivism, we recommended incarceration, but the judge put him on probation. While he was out on bail pending disposition, he committed a crime in another county. He was arraigned there and allowed to go out on bail. When the sentencing date came, he never showed up. A warrant has been issued for his arrest. What good is it? This guy has been around for so many years, I don't think there is anything in the world that probation can ever do for him. I think we have a responsibility to society to keep people like him locked up and off the streets."

Probation officers state that receiving information from probationers who are acting as informers is very common. Also, police officers often give them information and recommendations concerning clients. These recommendations vary from general discussions to specific considerations about how to deal with a "nasty offender" and are not perceived as an inappropriate or unwelcomed invasion of their function.

Police Adaptation Police Officers

Among the police, the police adapters indicate that their interaction with probation is often informal and very close with specific probation officers helpful in solving cases. The willingness of some probation officers to receive the police officer's recommendations on "nasty" offenders is often commented upon in this group as a highly favorable situation. The interaction of this group with police adapters and some moderators among probation officers is characterized by one of mutual admiration for the extra efforts and courtesies afforded by the police to probation and dependence by probation officers on the police. An example of this milieu is afforded in the following case recounted by a probation officer:

> "I received a call one morning from a detective asking about an outstanding warrant we had on a probationer. I checked and found that it was still outstanding. Hours later, the police called to inform me that the arrest had been made. This was a courtesy to us, you realize, by the police department. You see they don't get credit for an arrest that they made for the probation department, as it is counted as a rearrest. The police are very, very cooperative in many of these arrests for us."

The majority of the police adaptation police officers have a positive assessment of their interaction with probation (52%), Table VII-8) as indicated by the following case descriptions:

> "I have contact all the time with POs. Two or three were just here this morning. They were here for some information on a kid. We have the name file and we readily share our information: sale, possessor, user of drugs, etc. The PO was trying to set up a better system of communication. They are welcome. We have an effective working relationship. The can come and call anytime."

Those police who express a negative evaluation of probation interaction (30%, Table VII-9) most often cite the lack of access to probation files and the naivete of probation officers. These are characteristics not likely to be descriptive of police adaptative probation officers but more likely of probation adaptive officers. The following case descriptions indicate common reactions toward this group:

> "The feeling seems to be that we are out to get the kid, the POs to help him. So they hold back information."

> "On their part, at times, they are unwilling to share their information. I can think of one case where the PO betrayed our trust and confidence in order to keep the confidence of the kid."

> "It's strange to me that probation files are closed. It's a one-way street."

> "The probation department's holding back information is hindering us. They never share information. And those who have, have been admonished."

These police adapters feel that there should be more cooperation with probation, even though most probation officers have the wrong attitude, as evidenced in the following accounts:

> "I believe that POs believe too much in rehabilitation. They are peace officers. Probation should have a better sense of law enforcement."
>
> I'don't believe the working relationship between the departments should be closer. We are in immediate contact with the defendant and have more knowledge. We probably in most cases have more information to share that does not get in on the written report because of the lack of contact with POs. We should try to get better contact between the arresting officer and the investigating officer and the probation officer."

Thus, the police-adaptation police officers believe in more interaction with probation (even though many probation officers have wrong attitudes) in order to facilitate law enforcement tasks. This feeling is shared by police adapters among probation officers. Further case accounts of probation and police officers with a police adaptation style are contained in section one of Appendix D.

Moderator Adaptation

The moderator adaptation is represented among 57% of the police respondents and 34% of probation respondents (Table VII-2). Among the police, Table VII-3 showed that those in juvenile (68%) and community relations assignments (100%) are most likely to express moderator adaptations; whereas with probation, Table VII-4 demonstrated that this adaptation is most likely to occur among those assigned to the Family Division (47%).

Moderator Adaptation Police Officers

Police officers with a moderator orientation express a desire for more cooperative interaction with probation. The following statement describes their attitude:

> "I think both departments could benefit from cooperation. Possibility, if we had more information from the probation department, our job would be more effective."

However, they are quite adamant, unlike the police adaptation officers, in their opposition to probation officers engaging in law enforcement tasks as represented in the following case accounts:

> "Some POs would like to be law enforcement officers, in on the enforcement end of it. They violate offenders on probation. They want to go in on arrests, take over our job. Sometimes this happens. We have to tell him 'Let us take care of it. You take care of probation."

> "One time a new PO tried to force one of the probationers to work for us as an informer. This is just not right."

In addition, these moderator police officers express disapproval of allowing close cooperation between police oriented specialists and probation officers and they express fear of law enforcement abuses. The following description is representative of this reaction:

> "The strikeforce and undercover men should not have contact with the probation department. Sometimes, they might act without really knowing the larger problems of departmental coordination. They (the police) have only seen the problems of recidivism and are too narrow."

Furthermore, these moderator police officers express criticism of harsh probation approaches as evidenced in the following case description (further descriptions are contained in section two of Appendix D):

> "Just as the ghetto or living community of a minority group is strange and unsure territory for the POs, the probation department does not seem to recognize that this is the same pro-

blem for those who have to come to Mineola from Roosevelt, or Freeport, etc. All these large buildings seem like a real example of the secure establishment, unfriendly and accusing. And sometimes when a PO unthinkingly tells a client to 'sit and wait your turn!' he should not be surprised then that at the first opportunity the person disappears."

In comparing the moderator police officers to police officers with a police adaptation, it is evident that the moderators share the general client-reintegration attitude of probation officers while the police adapters feel that probation is too soft on clients. While both groups of police want more cooperation with the probation department, the motivations for this desire are quite distinct. The police adapters feel that more cooperation is necessary to facilitate law enforcement tasks, whereas the moderator group feels that more coordination is necessary in order to allow for more effective program and system development. In fact, the moderators are critical of harsh tactics being used by probation officers as well as being critical of increased cooperation involving police officers with a "narrow" law enforcement perspective.

Among moderator police offenders, the following case descriptions best describe their role orientation which is neither strict law enforcement nor social work:

"It's hard to define our role, it's enforcement yet it it isn't. We try to get involved with people."

"I have gotten away from locking people up. I'm more social oriented but I'm not a social worker."

"We are preventative rather than social worker or law enforcement."

"I try to be on good terms with the offender, be a bit understanding."

Moderator Adaptation Probation Officers

The moderator probation officers believe in cooperation with the police, but in structured situations rather than informally. These moderators stress techniques of dealing with clients as opposed to the ideological approaches of law enforcement or social work. Problems are described in terms of dysfunctions rather than as bad acts due to a wrong ideology or to bad people (i.e. frustrated cops, liberal do-gooders, uncaring, soft people, hard-ass individuals). The officers emphasize the system and speak of the effect of process interrelationships rather than in terms of protecting society of remotivating the disturbed client.

These officers indicate a non-judgmental approach as represented in the following case description:

> "I have a case now that I'm investigating where the boy was in a children's shelter. While in the shelter, one of the workers befriended this kid. The man is a Black Muslim and a very devout follower. This kid was in trouble because of drugs. I did my investigation and asked for evaluations from a number of sources. When I received the results, I noted that this boy needed very structured supervision. I also noticed that his family situation was weak and there was no authority figure present. I called a conference with my supervisor and the shelter worker. We all decided that we could let the boy out of the shelter if he would attend the well organized documented drug program the Muslim sect had in the boy's neighborhood. The worker at the shelter and another man who worked with kids on drugs agreed to work with the boy. We then put this client on probation to help coordinate his overall progress with the Muslim program."

Among probation officers, while police adapters speak and act in terms of the ideology of protecting society, and probation adapters stress personality and motivating and relating to the client as well as liberal ideology and probation status concerns, moderators speak in terms of process, coordination and program specifics.

OTHER TYPOLOGIES

In comparing the three conflict adaptations to standard typologies of probation officers, one is struck by the similiarity among them. Daniel Glaser reports three classifications determined by Ohlin, Piven and Pappenfort after interviews with all the probation and parole officers in one state.[1] They were as follows:

1. The punitive officer is the guardian of middle-class community morality; he attempts to coerce the offender into conforming by means of threats and punishment and his emphasis is on control, protecting the community against the offender, and systematic suspicion of those supervision.
2. The protective agent vacillates between protecting the offender and protecting the community. His tools and direct assistance, lecturing, and praise and blame. He is recognized by his ambivalent emotional involvement with the offender and others in the community as he shifts back and forth in taking sides with one against the other.
3. The welfare worker has as his ultimate goal the improved welfare of the client, a condition achieved by helping him in his individual adjustment within limits imposed by the client's capacity. He feels that the only genuine guarantee of community protection lies in the client's personal adjustment since external conformity will be only temporary and adjustment more difficult.[2]

In comparing Glaser's description to the orientations discovered in the conflict adaptation interviews, it would be quite feasible to relate the typologies as follows:

(1) The punitive officer closely resembles the police adapter.

(2) The protective officer displays many of the characteristics of the moderator.

(3) The welfare worker closely parallels the probation adapter.

A second probation typology is presented by Walter L. Barkdull who is the Assistant Director of the California Department of Corrections. The three classifications are as follows:

1. The community control officer

"An officer may specialize the surveillance. Working closely with local law enforcement units, he can determine whether the probationer is living where he says he does, working where he is supposed to (and regularly), how he spends his leisure hours and with whom, whether he's out at odd hours, if he's drinking, and in some circumstances whether he's taking a prescribed alcohol antagonist or other required medicine. This officer can also administer antinarcotic examinations and tests in appropriate cases."[3]

2. The facilitator (A title assigned based upon Barkdull's description).

"Another team officer may specialize in finding employment or other placement, continuing education or job training, helping the client get necessary licenses, credit and other bona Fides, locating housing, and providing any necessary temporary assistance."[4]

3. The caseworker (Again, this title was assigned based upon the description).

> "Still a third officer may provide help with material or family problems, counseling to help the client deal with everyday adversities, and other highly professional casework services."[5]

A third probation typology is offered by Ted Palmer of the Youth Studies Center at the University of Southern California. The data for Palmer's project was collected at the Santa Monica Area Office of the Los Angelos Probation Department. Interviews were held with one hundred and seventy-eight juvenile probationers and twenty-six probation officers. Palmer's three classifications are as follows:

1. The surveillance/self-control oriented officers. The following six core characteristics define this group of individuals: These officers are likely to

"(a) think and/or act in terms of controls and limits
(b) be relatively tough-minded and exacting
(c) have a moralistic orientation
(d) manifest relatively much covert or overt aggression-hostility
(e) manifest certain social undesirable characteristics
(f) manifest current personal problems, in the form of certain anxieties or defensive attitudes."[6]

In connection with probationers, Palmer describes the concerns of these officers as follows:

> "In addition to looking upon the 'control of behavior' as the primary objective with probationers, they are likely to indicate that the typical probationer has (1) gotten into trouble because 'he's simply doesn't care what the rules are, but just goes ahead and does what he wants'; also, they are likely to believe that (2) delinquency more often results from there being too little rather than too much control over youths. It would appear that to these officers, the strength of the recalcitrant or unpredictable impulses which are seen to be implicated in the youths' delinquency, must be countered by equally powerful or unrelenting controls, both external and, where possible, internal in nature."[7]

2. The relationships/self-expression oriented officers. These officers are likely to:

"(a) indicate considerable concern with establishing/maintaining an atmosphere for a working relationship, and for mutual communication with youths.
(b) interact with the youths more on a familiar than on a formal basis: are less socially distant.
(c) be relatively involved -- personally or emotionally -- with the youths.
(d) express concern -- in connection with treatments foci -- with impulses and needs associated with feelings of guilt, hostility, aggression, or rejection.
(e) focus their techniques and goals around the youth's internal, psychological processes."[8]

This group's approach to probationers is described as follows:

"They appear to view their personal relationship with the probationers (or with their parents) as the vehicle through which the youths may be brought to recognize and cultivate certain personality or socially desired attributes, and to modify their self-image. This process may be seen as paving the way for the above mentioned satsifying experience and feelings. Thus, for example, the officers may try to counteract the youths' feelings of hostility, by: accepting their feelings, expressing confidence in them; recognizing their efforts, and -- in a counseling, friendly, brotherly (or sisterly) manner -- encouraging further efforts; 'doing extra things' for them; and, conveying sincerity."[9]

3. The surveillance/self-expression oriented officers.

Some of the core characteristics of these officers are as follows:

"(a) be oriented toward change and activity
(b) think/and/or act in terms of controls and limits."[10]

Palmer states that although control of the youngsters' behavior is not the central-treatment goal of these officers, they are ready to use their authority, but in a manner (unlike the surveillance/self-control group) that is not impersonal or formalized.[11] Their approach to probationers is described as follows:

"However, unlike (relationship/self-expression) they are not apt to prefer thinking about things to doing things.

Nor is there evidence to suggest that they usually concentrate upon an improvement of the youths' self-concept, or upon the youths' comfort in or ability to cope with an unyielding or non-understanding environment. There are, on the contrary, various indications that they believe it is possible for individuals to energetically, and directly, modify unsatisfactory external conditions."[12]

A cross section of these probation typologies along with the three conflict adaptation styles is presented in the following table.

TABLE VII-7

CROSS CLASSIFICATION OF PROBATION TYPOLOGIES

Conflict Adaptation	Probation and Parole Typology (reported by Glaser)	Probation Tasks (described by Barkdull)	Palmer's Probation Typology
I. Police Adapter	I. Punitive	I. Community Control	I. Surveillance/self-control
II. Probation Adapter	II. Welfare Worker	II. Caseworker	II. Relationship/self-expression
III. Moderator	III. Protective	III. Facilitator	III. Surveillance/self-expression

Although conceptualizations of police typologies and classifications are legion, [13] the major dichotomy, with innumberable variations thereof, is that of control and service. A recent comprehensive yet succinct operational classification is that of the three dimensional task analysis of local policing developed by Dr. William Brown.[14] The matrix model of Brown provides a typology of police activities based upon official response to community and individual needs of both a control and service nature. It would appear, also, that this central police classification dichotomy of control and service closely parallels the police (control) and moderator (service) adaptations of the police. Since police and probation officers are involved in both control and service functions, the matrix model [15] provides a structured mechanism for defining the parameters of further field research in conflict resolution.

In any attempt to arrive at a common conflict adaptation taxonomy, perhaps, the positive aspects in the innovate use of labels need to be reaffirmed. While conflict resolution often connotes resolution away from something undesirable, it should be remembered that what has been perceived as negative often becomes a crucial catalyst in efforts for change. In the words of Hans Toch:

> "Each man becomes an expert on the problem exemplified by him; each evolves systematic ways of solving the problem, and each is able to monitor his progress and that of others. The man becomes not only 'rehabilitated' but evolves into a resource to his department - a professional who can help other men reduce the chances of future violent encounters."[16]

The possibility exists that with further research and planning, change programs proceeding from information concerning conflict adaptations may be established as a prelude to effective coordination and responsive as well as responsible system development.

ADAPTATION STYLES, ATTITUDES AND INTERACTIONS

Having described in some detail the characteristics of the various adaptation styles, we now turn to the relationship between them and certain specific attitudes and interaction patterns. The interviewers were instructed to classify respondents, on the basis of interview material, into three interaction styles (positive, neutral or negative) reflecting their inter-agency contrasts. The distribution of police and probation respondents by interaction styles is shown in Table VII-8.

TABLE VII-8
INTERACTION STYLES OF POLICE AND PROBATION RESPONDENTS, NASSAU COUNTY

INTERACTION STYLE	PROBATION RESPONDENTS N	PROBATION RESPONDENTS %	POLICE RESPONDENTS N	POLICE RESPONDENTS %
POSITIVE	26	27%	38	35%
NEUTRAL	29	30%	53	48%
NEGATIVE	41	43%	19	17%
TOTAL	96	100%	110	100%

$X^2 = 16.47$, $P < .01$
$V = .28$

The table indicates that the police have a predominately neutral or positive estimation of police-probation interaction (83%) as compared to probation (57%). Table VII-8 also demonstrates that while 43% of the probation respondents are negative in their estimation of police-probation interaction, only 17% of the police are negative. Thus, as was noted earlier with questionnaire data, probation officers display a significantly greater degree of negativism regarding police-probation interaction than do the police.

The next question to be addressed is that of the relationship between the type of adaptation and the style of interaction. In Table VII-9, the findings are presented for police respondents.

TABLE VII-9

CONFLICT ADAPTATION AND POLICE-PROBATION INTERACTION STYLES, POLICE RESPONDENTS, NASSAU COUNTY

INTERACTION STYLE	CONFLICT ADAPTATION							
	POLICE ADAPTATION		MODERATOR ADAPTATION		PROBATION ADAPTATION		TOTAL	
	N	%	N	%	N	%	N	%
POSITIVE	24	52%	13	21%	1	100%	38	35%
NEUTRAL	8	18%	45	71%	0	0%	53	48%
NEGATIVE	14	30%	5	8%	0	0%	19	17%
TOTAL	46	100%	63	100%	1	100%	110	100%

$$X^2 = 29.91, P<.01$$
$$v = .52$$

The data indicate among other things that those police officers with a moderator adaptation are very likely (71%) to have neutral interaction. Suprisingly, respondents with a police adaptation are more likely to have positive (52%) than negative (30%) interaction with probation and they are least likely to have a neutral (18%) interaction. No data are available which shed light on this reversal from what one would have expected the relationship to have been.

The findings concerning the relationship among probation respondents between conflict adaptation and police-probation interaction are presented in Table VII-10.

TABLE VII-10

CONFLICT ADAPTATION AND POLICE-PROBATION INTERACTION STYLES, PROBATION RESPONDENTS, NASSAU COUNTY

INTERACTION STYLE	CONFLICT ADAPTATION							
	POSITIVE ADAPTATION		MODERATOR ADAPTATION		PROBATION ADAPTATION		TOTAL	
	N	%	N	%	N	%	N	%
POSITIVE	14	100%	5	15%	7	14%	26	27%
NEUTRAL	0	0%	24	73%	5	10%	29	30%
NEGATIVE	0	0%	4	12%	37	76%	41	43%
TOTAL	14	100%	33	100%	49	100%	96	100%

X^2 = 96.15, P<.01

V = .71

It may be seen in Table VII-10 that for probation, there is a strong, significant and consistent relationship between adaptation type and interaction style. All 14 of the police adaptation respondents express posititive interaction, while most probation adapters (76%) indicate negative interaction. Most of those with a moderator adaptation (73%) have a neutral interaction style.

Thus, it can be stated that for both police and probation officers, a police adaptation is associated with a situation of positive interaction and a moderator adaptation is associated with a neutral situation. Among probation officers, those with probation adaptation are negative in their assessment of interagency interaction.

Another question of interest is whether the type of conflict adaptation style is associated with an identifiable manner of dealing with clients and offenders. In order to determine the existence of any such relationship, the interviewers were instructed to distinguish three types of client interaction. The first type is described as law enforcement and refers to a tough approach geared toward inducing fear and immediate compliance. The second type is personal adjustment and relates to what has been described as the social casework method - a helping, personal oriented approach in which the officer attempts to personally relate to the client. The third type, processing, refers to an approach that stresses organizational and institutional processes as a means of implementing more efficiency and effectiveness in dealing with client's programs.

The following tables (Tables VII-11 and VII-12) present the relationship between conflict adaptation style and the three types of client interaction.

TABLE VII-11

CONFLICT ADAPTATION AND POLICE-CLIENT INTERACTION

CLIENT INTERACTION	CONFLICT ADAPTATION							
	POLICE ADAPTATION		MODERATOR ADAPTATION		PROBATION ADAPTATION		TOTAL	
	N	%	N	%	N	%	N	%
LAW ENFORCEMENT	41	89%	7	11%	0	0%	48	44%
PERSONAL ADJUSTMENT	0	0%	0	0%	1	100%	1	1%
PROCESSING	5	11%	56	89%	0	0%	61	55%
TOTAL	46	100%	63	100%	1	100%	110	100%

X^2 = 66.54, P <.01
V - .78

TABLE VII-12

CONFLICT ADAPTATION AND PROBATION-CLIENT INTERACTION

CLIENT INTERACTION	CONFLICT ADAPTATION							
	POLICE ADAPTATION		MODERATOR ADAPTATION		PROBATION ADAPTATION		TOTAL	
	N	%	N	%	N	%	N	%
LAW ENFORCEMENT	14	100%	3	9%	0	0%	17	18%
PERSONAL ADJUSTMENT	0	0%	4	12%	41	84%	45	47%
PROCESSING	0	0%	26	79%	8	16%	34	35%
TOTAL	14	100%	33	100%	49	100%	96	100%

X^2 = 105.27, P<01.
V = .74

As presented in Table VII-11, 89% of the police respondents with a police adaptation express a law enforcement approach to client interaction. Among those with a moderator adaptation, however, only 11% express a law enforcement approach and 89% express a processing approach. Among probation respondents, shown in Table VII-12, 84% of those with a probation adaptation style indicate a personal adjustment approach, wereas 79% of those with a moderator adaptation express a processing approach.

In brief then, the processing approach is very evident among moderators (comprising 89% of police and 79% of probation moderators), the personal adjustment approach is obvious among probation adaptation officers (comprising 84% of probation-adaptation officers), and the law enforcement approach is manifestly present with police adapters among probation officers as well as with police adapters among police officers (comprising 89% of police-adaptation police officers and 100% of police-adaptation probation officers).

Finally, in discussion with probation and police officials during the administration of the field survey instrument, it became apparent that a number of officers felt that the courts were responsible for some of the conflicts that might occur between police and probation. Consequently, an attempt was made to examine whether conflict adaptation style might be associated with a particular perception of the courts.

In determing a classification for perceptions of the courts, three categories (which had come to my attention as a result of previous discussions with police and probation officers) were utilized. The first, termed "jail shy", refers to the attitude (often expressed as "The courts have become jail shy since Attica") that the courts are far too permissive and lenient with offenders. The second category, described as the "revolving door", refers to an attitude that the courts are basically ineffective in that offenders go through them in a steady procession (like a revolving door) without anything of substance being accomplished. The third category, termed "O.K.", refers to an attitude that is neither strongly positive nor strongly critical. In other words, the courts are looked upon, from the perspective of the respondent, as minimally accomplishing what they are supposed to do.

The following tables (Tables VII-13 and VII-14) present the relationships between conflict adaptation and the respondents' evaluations of the courts.

TABLE VII-13

CONFLICT ADAPTATION AND POLICE EVALUATION OF THE COURTS

CONFLICT ADAPTATIONS

COURT EVALUATION	POLICE ADAPTATION N	%	MODERATOR ADAPTATION N	%	PROBATION ADAPTATION N	%	TOTAL N	%
JAIL SHY	35	76%	9	14%	0	0%	44	40%
REVOLVING DOOR	11	24%	33	52%	0	0%	44	40%
O.K.	0	0%	21	34%	1	100%	22	20%
TOTAL	46	100%	63	100%	1	100%	110	100%

X^2 = 47.21, P<.01

V = .66

TABLE VII-14

CONFLICT ADAPTATION AND PROBATION EVALUATION OF THE COURTS

COURT EVALUATION	CONFLICT ADAPTATION							
	POLICE ADAPTATION		MODERATOR ADAPTATION		PROBATION TOTAL			
	N	%	N	%	N	%	N	%
JAIL SHY	12	86%	0		3	6%	15	16%
REVOLVING DOOR	2	14%	25	76%	4	8%	31	32%
O.K.	0	0%	8	24%	42	86%	50	52%
TOTAL	14	100%	33	100%	49	100%	96	100%

X^2 = 103.65, P<.01
V = .73

As evidenced in Table VI-13, 76% of police respondents with a police adaptation consider the courts to be "jail shy" as compared to only 14% of moderators. Among probation respondents, Table VII-14 indicates that 86% of probation officers with a police adaptation also consider the courts to be "jail shy". However, among those with a probation adaptation style, only 6% regard the courts to be "jail shy", and 86% consider the courts to be "O.K." The moderators among probation respondents, however, are somewhat more critical in that 76% consider the courts to be functioning as a revolving door."

Clearly, a similar estimation of the courts exists according to conflict adaptation style on the part of police and probation respondents. Police adapters perceive the courts as lenient, moderators see them as ineffective, and probation adapters accord them general minimal acceptability.

SUMMARY

It has been shown that behavioral measures (based on data derived from a conflict adaptation typology applied to the organizational-perceptual vignettes) reflecting work related attitudes and activities of police and probation officers do exist. Furthermore, these measures are ones that demonstrate distinguishing characteristics associated with the three conflict adaptations: police, probation and moderator. These characteristics are as follows:

1. In reference to the category of assignment, police officers in juvenile and community relations assignments along with probation officers in the Family Division are the most orientated toward a moderator position. While the probation adaptation is practically nonexistent among the police, the police adaptation is strongest among police officers with narcotic assignments and among a small group of Adult Division probation officers.
2. Concerning inter-agency contact, it is possible to ascertain two kinds of contact situations, consisting of police moderators (juvenile and community relations officers) with probation moderators (Family Division Officers); and narcotic officers and detectives with a small number of probation officers with a police adaptation (located in the Adult Division).
3. In the area of police-probation interaction, for both police and probation officers, a police adaptation is associated with a situation of positive interaction and a moderator adaptation is associated with a neutral situation. Among probation officers, those with a probation adaptation are negative in their assessment of interagency interaction.
4. On the subject of officer-client interaction, the following may be stated: the processing approach is very evident among moderators, the personal adjustment approach is obvious among probation adapters, and the law enforcement approach is manifestly present among police-adaptation probation officers as well as among police-adaptation police officers.
5. Attitudes toward the judiciary are as follows: officers with a police adaptation perceive the courts as "jail shy," those with a probation adaptation see them as basically "O.K.," and moderator oriented officers are somewhat more critical in their description of the courts as "revolving doors."

in their description of the courts as "revolving doors."

6. There is a marked similarity between the three conflict adaptations reported in this study and probation typologies described by Daniel Glaser, Walter Barkdull and Ted Palmer.

One may conclude that a remarkable consistency is evident among the sample of interviewees: consisting of officers who were identified by their signature on the instrument. Among the police, the additional characteristic of being attached to an assignment more prone towards higher contact with probation officers than other categories of assignment was present.

Most notably, the probation and moderator adaptations were strong among probation officers (comprising 51% and 34% of their number, while the moderator adaptation was predominate among the police with a representation of 57%). The moderator adaptation was most evident among probation officers in the Family Division and police officers in community relations and juvenile assignments. While there is substantially no probation adaptation present among the police, a police adaptation consisting of 15% of the probation sample is strikingly evident among probation officers situated in the Adult Division.

From the interviewees it is possible to ascertain two kinds of contact situations according to conflict adaptation. The first situation consists of police moderators primarily in juvenile assignments with probation moderators in the Family Division. The other situation consists of police officers in narcotic and detective assignments, and police-adaptation probation officers from Adult Division. The police-adaptation probation group, as the cases indicate, display a most distinctive and unexpected mode of behavior.

It is interesting to observe that a police adaptation is associated with a positive estimate of police-probation interaction, whereas a probation adaptation is associated with a negative estimate.

While law enforcement concerns characterize the police adaptation approach towards offenders, and the personal adjustment approach characterizes the probation adaptation approach, the moderator orientation is concerned with coordination, follow-up procedures and program development on a systems basis.

Lastly, in reference to the courts, the police adaptation interviewees want to see more incarceration of offenders whereas the moderators are critical of the revolving door, non-system operations of the courts.

A most crucial distinction was evident concerning the rationale for increased contact and coordination between police and probation departments. One group, the police adaptation interviewees, want to encourage more coordinated law enforcement approaches; whereas the moderators stress more coordination for the purpose of system development. Furthermore, even the police moderators are very critical of increased contact between probation officers and specialized police officers with "narrow" law enforcement concerns. In addition, these police moderators are extremely opposed to allowing the "SWAT approach" engaged in by police adapters within probation to continue to exist.

In light of these interview findings, one might comment upon O'Leary and Newman's description of subprocesses in the criminal justice system[17] to the effect that the decision network is also composed of conflict adaptations within subprocesses that effect the entire process. The ultimate purpose of typological approaches, in the words of a foremost expert on this subject, Professor Marguerite O. Warren, is that of "producing improved management and treatment methods for the practitioner."[18] It is my hope that these proffered conflict adaptation classifications might contribute to this purpose.

NOTES

[1]. Daniel Glaser, The Effectiveness of a Prison and Parole System (New York: The Bobbs-Merrill Co., 1964), p. 430.

[2]. Ibid.

[3]. Walter L. Barkdull, "Probation: Call It Control - And Mean It," Federal Probation 40,No. 4 (December 1976): 6.

[4]. Ibid.

[5]. Ibid.

[6]. Ted Palmer, Types of Probation Officers and Types of Youth on Probation: Their Views and Interactions, Youth Studies Center, University of Southern California, 1963, p. 91.

[7]. Ibid. p. 101

[8]. Ibid., p. 92

[9]. Ibid, p. 96

[10]. Ibid, p. 96

[11]. Ibid., p. 103.

[12]. Ibid, p. 104.

13. John F. Ahern, Police in Trouble (New York: Hawthorne, 1972); William Brown, "Local Policing - A Three Dimensional Task Analysis," Journal of Criminal Justice 3, No. 1 (Spring 1975): 1-55; George D. Eastman and James A. McCain, "Police Managers and Their Perceptions of Higher Education," Journal of Criminal Justice 1, No. 2 (Summer 1973): 113-124; B. L. Garmire, "The Police Role in Ruban Society," in The Police and the Community, edited by R. F. Steadman (Baltimore, Maryland: John Hopkkins University Press, 1972); John C. Meyer and Winthrop E. Taylor, "Analyzing the Nature of Police Involvements: A Research Note Concerning the Effects of Forms of Police Mobilization," Journal of Criminal Justice 3, No. 2 (Summer 1975): 141-145; Ellen Mintz and Georgette Sandler, "Instituting a Full-Service Orientation to Policing," The Police Chief 16, No. 6 (June 1974): 44-50; President's Commission on Law Enforcement and Administration of Justice, Task Force Report: The Police (Wash., D.C.: U.S. Gov't Printing Office, 1967), pp. 122-124; James Q. Wilson, Varieties of Police Behavior (Cambridge, Harvard University Press, 1968).

[14] See William Brown, "Local Policing - A Three Dimensional Task Analysis," Journal of Criminal Justice 3, No. 1 (Spring 1975): 1-15.

[15] Ibid, p. 14

[16] Hans Toch, "The Care and Feeding of Typologies and Labels," Federal Probation 34, No. 3 (September 1970): 19.

[17] Vincent O'Leary and Donald J. Newman, "Conflict Resolution in Criminal Justice," Journal of Research in Crime and Delinquency 7, No. 2 (July 1970): 99-119.

[18] Marguerite Q. Warren, "Classification of Offenders As An Aid to Efficient Management and Effective Treatment," Journal of Criminal Law, Criminology and Police Science 62, (June 1971): 258.

CHAPTER 8

IMPLICATIONS FOR THE FUTURE OF THE CRIMINAL JUSTICE SYSTEM

This study has demonstrated that it is possible to identify conflict between operatives and their agencies in criminal justice operations. It has also laid the groundwork for the design of conflict resolution techniques bearing upon inter-organizational structuring and long-term planning on a system basis. Similarly, it creates a basis for more detailed research and organizational development planning for the purpose of conflict management among criminal justice agencies.

We described how thirty-one police and probation officials were brought together for a workshop at which conflicts and differences between them and their respective agencies were identified and scaled. In addition, we were able to more from the laboratory to the field and identify and further specify interaction patterns as well as demographic and attitudinal variables associated with conflict.

While there was no measurement of the amount or pattern of contact among the personnel of the agencies represented by the thirty-one police and probation officials at the Albany Conference, it was generally agreed that the police did not have very much contact with probation. Although there existed evidence of the presence of varying demensions of conflict between police and probation participants at Albany, the relationship of contact to conflict was not examined.

It was decided that the laboratory results called for further measurement in the field of operational conflict and an examination of the general patterning of the amount, situations, loci, and context of contact. Furthermore, it was felt that the relationship of contact to conflict should be studied, and the distinguishing of additional demographic and occupational variables associated with conflict should be undertaken.

As a result of the field survey in three regions (Nassau County, New York; Albuquerque, New Mexico; and San Jose, California), the following findings were obtained about the relationship between conflict and contact:

1. The police have far less contact with probation than does probation with the police.
2. Increased work-related contact is associated with low conflict for the police, while there is no significant relationship between work-related contact and conflict for probation officers.
3. The findings with respect to the police suggest that not only is low contact linked to high conflict, but two types of contacts, information verification and probation helping police, increase the risks of conflict. No such pattern emerged with respect to probation officers.
4. Over half of both police and probation officers report that the locus of most contacts is the telephone conversation.

After discovering the general patterning of the amount, situations, loci, and context of contact, it was possible to distinguish additional demographic and occupational variables associated with conflict.

5. Increased contact for police juvenile specialists is associated with low conflict, whereas increased contact for probation juvenile officers is associated with more conflict.
6. For both police and probation, youth (under 30) is related to high conflict and much experience (16 or more years) is related to low conflict.
7. It can be stated with caution (since the numbers are small) that while Hispanic probation officers experience low conflict, Hispanic police officers experience high conflict.
8. For police, it was discovered that an increase in both work-related and off-duty contact with probation officers is associated with lower conflict. Among probation officers, it was shown that when work-related contacts remain high and personal contacts also are high, then conflict is likely to be high.

In reference to dissensus, findings from the Albany Conference suggested that police and probation officials held strong differences in attitude regarding legal processes, approaches toward offenders, tolerance of deviance, faith-in-people, and in the status and esteem of the two positions.

The Albany Conference indicated the following:

1. The police were far less liberal than probation officers.
2. Both police and probation attributed higher status to the probation task as compared to the police task.

3. With respect to esteem, the police saw themselves as fully professional and worthy of self-respect as probation officers.

What was not possible at Albany was to chart the extent to which such differences existed in the real world and to relate these differences in value to independent measures of conflict. In the field survey, the following were discovered:

1. The police are far less liberal on political-legal issues than are probation officers.
2. There is a tendency for the police with high contact to be more liveral and probation with high contact to be less liberal.
3. Both police and probation attribute higher status to the probation task than to the police task.
4. With respect to esteem, the police saw themselves as worthy of more professional respect (esteem) than probation.
5. More conservative police express more conflict than do more liberal probation officers.

In reference to the question as to whether differential status and esteem accorded the other occupational role is related to the amount of reported inter-role conflict, the following were shown:

6. Among police, the accordance of low status (and secondarily the accordance of low esteem or professional respect) to probation is significantly related to high inter-role conflict.
7. Among probation officers, the ascription of low esteem to the police (and secondarily the ascription of low status) is significantly related to high inter-role con flict.

Concerning organizational conflict and perceptual distortion, organizational vignettes were designed at Albany for laboratory testing to determine whether there were significant differences between police and probation on organizational decisions involving inter-agency interaction, and whether perceptual distortion existed, and, if so, was it more evident among one group than another.

At the Albany Converence, it was found that there were marked discrepancies between the two groups on a number of organizational issued. Both police and probation expressed organizational conflict on inter-agency decisions reflecting police prerogative and probation autonomy issues. Data at the Albany Conference shows that probation officials were more inaccurate in predicting police responses than were the police in predicting probation responses.

In studying whether these differences would hold up in the field, factor analyses performed on the responses from the field data, as was indicated in Chapter 3, identified two scales: a police prerogative and a probation autonomy scale. These scales were incorporated into the analysis of the field data.

1. It was discovered that in addition to organizational conflict, perceptual distortion also existed; and, as occurred at Albany, perceptual distortion was more pronounced among probation than police officers. The field data shows the same direction (with greater magnitude) of organizational conflict and perceptual distortion that was discovered at the Albany Conference.

2. In addition to the presence of organizational conflict, a particular pattern of perceptual distortion because became evident such that each group over estimated the other group's opposition to issues affecting one's own group. In other words, the police over estimate probation opposition to police prerogative issues, and probation officers, to a greater extent, over estimate police opposition to probation autonomy decisions.

The next question examined in the field was whether a relationship existed between operational conflict and views held about police prerogative or probation autonomy issues.

3. It was discovered that a significant relationship between probation autonomy and conflict existed. Among the police, those who accorded low probation autonomy also expressed higher conflict.

The conflict adaptation typology was developed as a result of analyzing the responses of hundreds of officers on the vignettes following the administration, collection and tabulation of the final instrument.

In respect to conflict adaptation styles and typological classifications of police and probation officers, the following were discovered:

1. The use of the conflict adaptation formulation developed in this study distinguishes three adaptations: police, probation and moderator.
2. There are distinguishable characteristics displayed by each adaptation in refer-

ence to: police-probation interaction, client interaction and perceptions of the courts.

3. A striking similarity exists between these conflict adaptation styles and probation typologies reported by Daniel Glaser, Walter Barkdull and Ted Palmer.
4. The police classification dichotomy of control and service parallels the police (control) and moderator (service) adaptations of the police.

INTERVENTION IMPLICATIONS

A major purpose of this study was to chart conflict patterns. However, there are implications for action which flow from that charting - some of which we can explore. Some were suggested by O'Leary and Newman after the Albany Conference while others arose from the field study. For example, in reference to the findings on conflict and contact, it would appear that group interaction for the purpose of discussion might be undertaken with profit as a measure of conflict management. With increased group discussion, new procedures as to increasing communication, changing incentives and creating new norms of interaction, that might be applicable in dealing with inter-agency operational conflict could be openly discussed and examined.

The fact that among both police and probation officers, the young are the ones who express the most operational conflict (see Tables IV-31, IV-32) could be openly discussed by the two agencies so as to discover some of the reasons for this situation. Perhaps such an inter-agency examination might provide more information as to whether the conflict expressed by youth is due to problems of connumication, incentives, autonomy, maturity or some other combination of influences and produce suggestions for resolving this problem

In a recent discussion with police and probation officers in Nassau County, their explanation as to the association of conflict and youth was that the young officers enters his career all "charged up" with the importance of "arrest" work in the case of police, or with the importance of "rehabilitation" work in the case of probation officers. With time, these officers asserted, the younger officers became more "mellowed" and are better able to appreicate the "whole picture." Perhaps, a systems perspective presenting the whole picture might be built into police and probation initiation training to expedite the equivelent of mellowing.

It is most desirable in attempting to resolve operational conflicts, to structure situations so that discrete agencies can see their relationship to each other and their common allegiance to certain long range goals.[2] There is much evidence to support the contention that the presence of superordinate goals, which are much desired by all and cannot be attained by the energies and resources of one group, are likely to foster cooperation between groups.[3] Interaction might be encouraged on a limited basis wherein the issues involved were superordinate goals valued by both police and probation agencies with decision making rules having been agreed to beforehand.[4]

Perhaps seminars might be held on a regular basis for police and probation officers where similar goals being worked toward by both groups might be highlighted and interagency committees established to plan for more cooperation and corrdination in these endeavors.

The suggestion has been made that before any kind of direct negotiations occur between groups experiencing conflict, members of the group should be exchanged.[5] The rationale for this suggestion is that by exchanging members, the contrasting needs and problems are clarified through day-to-day interaction and increased familiarity with the other group's activities.[6] Perhaps police and probation officers might be exchanged for a period of three months and then report to their own group before direct negotiations occur between their respective agencies.

O'Leary and Newman maintain that it may prove valuable to utilize the game theory approach in order to demonstrate the importance of cooperation and the cost of dysfunctional competition in achieving conflict resolution.[7] There are various mechanisms involving the structure and payoff conditions in gaming that can be applied to encourage conflicting groups to reach cooperative (win-win) solutions.[8] This approach could be implemented with police and probation through the development of gaming exercises that require intense interaction between them under conditions where each group's failure to cooperate is more costly to itself than refraining from conflict.

For example, gaming might be applied on the basis of category of assignment. This study indicates that increased contact for police juvenile specialists is associated with low conflict (see Table IV-26). The following case description by a probation officer might serve as a rationale for utilizing a gaming situation for increased interaction between police juvenile specialists and a number of probation officers in various assignment categories.

> "I personally use the police as a resource. Now, I'm talking about juvenile aid police for they are not looking for arrests, like the others, but rather for assistance. In investigation, I use thcm as a source for all kinds of information about the kid - including their feelings about the client. I ask them for their feelings about the client's family and his environment. In supervision, I would use them as another resource. I would leave a list of my clients with the police. They would call me and I would go down to the JAB (Juvenile Aid Bureau) and try to work it out with the police."

Accordingly, the various situations of interaction associated with high and low conflict could be identified. After identification, the circumstances surrounding the low conflict interaction of police juvenile specialists could, in further gaming exercises, be applied to high conflict interactions. Thereby, the gaming exercises could be used to specify circumstances likely to be associated with low conflict among police-probation encounters in a variety of assignment categories.

It has been observed that stress on solving immediate crises between police and probation has too often left basic disputes unresolved.[9] Intergroup laboratory and problem solving exercises can be useful in approaching some of these problems. The purpose of these laboratory problem solving approaches are maifold: to acquire skills in group membership,[10] to inspire new conderns centered on equity, oppenness, collaboration, empathy, and insight,[11] to generate new values, [12] to stimulate group participation in planning changes, [13] to provide participants with the opportunity to analyze and evaluate group behavior,[14] and to instill a process of continual diagnosis and modification of work relationships.[15]

Another contribution to the study of operative change in criminal justice agencies is Agencies of Change by Hans Toch, Douglas Grant and Raymond Galvin. This study is excellent in presenting a process that engenders peer directed change in individuals displaying a problem with violence. In a case description of the Action Review Panel (a non-directive peer review process developed by one of the officer participants in the project study), the problem of a young policeman, Officer Chico Bond, in dealing with Mexican-Americans is dealt with.

This problem is of particular interest here since our data indicate that Hispanic police express high conflict (see Table IV-42) and that police and probation officers whose primary offender contact is with Hispanics express the most conflict (See Tables IV-47 and IV-48). The action review panel diagnosed Chico Bond's problem as follows: a feeling of being challenged by Hispanic youths aggravated by his own slight physical stature, inducing reactive fear upon others, a tendency to box other people in with orders, a consequent breakdown in ability to communicate verbally, a resultant mutual misunderstanding-violence.[16] The change agent approach has been described as "experiental behavior intervention"[17] in that the client, drawing upon his experience, employs a communications approach that integrates cognitive, affective and behavioral components of adaptive functioning.[18]

This study indicates that the situations of contact concerning information verification and the probation officer helping the police officer were associated with high conflict (see Tables IV-8 and IV-9) for the police at all frequency levles of contact. The following case descriptions reflect the feelings of many police officers:

> "The feeling seems to be that we are out to get the kid, the POs to help him. So they hold back information."
>
> "On their part, at times, they are unwilling to share their information. I can think of one case where the PO betrayed our trust and confidence in

order to keep the confidence of the kid."

"It's strange to me that probation files are closed. It's a one-way street."

"The probation department's holding back information is hindering us. They never share information. And those who have, have been admonished."

Future applications of various problem solving techniques[19] in the area of police-probation planning should focus on the information exchange between police and probation wherein the police request information verification from probation officers. Workshops that teach police and probation officers how to build problem solving mechanisms into the subcultures of their respective organizations could be established.

It has been noted that few formally structured liasons presently exist for the purpose of enabling agents to assume a larger criminal justice system focus as compared to traditional narrow conerns.[20] The approach of utilizing the link-pin method of interconnection wherein any important message is reinforced by interactive discussion has been recommended as a means of clarifying a systematic flow of two-way communications such that each receiver becomes in turn a sender and part of the message.[21]

It is shown in the field study that the young and inexperienced among both police and probation officers express the most conflict (see Tables IV-31, IV-32 and IV-16, IV-17). Programs stressing increased collaboration and structured communication on a systems basis[22] would appear to be most suitable for dealing with the dysfunctions present among the young. For example, communication workshops that train agents in how to establish link-pin communication processes such that every receiver becomes a sender of a desired communication - thereby increasing collaborative interaction - might be established for both police and probation officers. In addition, the recognition of the possible conflict effects, in the form of divergent subcultural and professional expectations, associated with the situation of high work-related and personal contact for probation officers (see Table IV-39) might be presented to officers at an early stage in their careers.

Although third party intervention has been primarily applied in the labor-management conflict area, it has been suggested that this approach may prove desirable and helpful to the criminal justice system.[23] Extrapolating from the principles developed in third party intervention, and focusing our concern on operational conflict between police and probation agencies, the attributes for third party intervention would be as follows:

1. High professional expertise regarding police and probation processes.
2. Low power over the fate of police and probation officers.
3. High control over the confrontation setting and processes.
4. Moderate knowledge about the principals, issues, and background factors.
5. Neutrality or balance with respect to substantive outcome, personal relation ships, and conflict-resolution methodology.[24]

Ideally, a third party interventionist would be one who would provide symmetry in motivational forces and situational power, synchronization in achieving compatible definitions of problems, proper sequencing of differentiation and integration activities, support for openness, adequate dialogue language.[25]

The study demonstrates that probation officers in juvenile assignments experience conflict with increasing interaction with the police (see Table IV-27). The role of a third party interventionist might be that of providing support for openness and a compatible definition of the problem by impressing upon the police department that this does constitute a matter of serious concern even though the police, in general, have very little interaction with probation.

In reference to dissensus involving value differences related to operational conflict, the assistance of a group leader who can place opponents in the place of their opposition and provide feedback has been suggested.[26] The techniques that might be employed in this endeavor include role reversal programs as well as the "Roger's rule" procedure wherein opponents are asked to state to the satisfaction of the other party what the person's point of view appears to be on the matter under contest.[27]

In addition, since it has been shown that among the police, conservatism contributes to conflict (see Table V-3) and that the police tend to become less conservative with increased probation contact (see Table V-6), an attempt to reduce the influence of dissensus on operational conflict might be made by asking those police with high contact and low conservatism to explain the liberal perspective on political-legal issues to the more conservative police.

Where there exists a wide evaluative discrepancy between groups of individuals, the process of a critical trial has been recommended where the differences are brought to the surface very early.[28] The free discussion that has been suggested should be left completely open and should not be subjected to the constraints of any task accuracy feedback structure.[29] Technology has been employed, in the form of a quantitative-pictorial visual interactive display unit visually demonstrating values and the weights of the components of values, to make individuals aware of their own views and the views of others.[30]

The suggestion of bringing dissensus to the surface by means of free discussion and the employment of technological devices that increase awareness of the components of dissensus would appear to be most apropos for the overwhelming majority of police who have little contact with probation and small encouragement to reexamine their own attitudes on political-legal issues.

In reference to status and esteem differentials between police and probation officers, the suggestion that organizations should strive to enlarge jobs would appear to be germane to reducing these differentials. The enlargement of jobs referred to is not limited to the doing or motor abilities, but includes expanded use of the individual's intellectual and interpersonal abilities.[31] Furthermore, in the course of reducing status and esteem differentials, it has been maintained that a likely effect of heightened feelings of status and esteem would be an increase in the generation of valid information.[32]

The study shows that the police who accord low status to probation express high operational conflict (see Table V-10), and that probation officers who attribute low esteem to the police officer express high operational conflict (see Table V-11).

In reference to the attribution of low status to probation by police, David Macpherson,

Probation Director in the LosAngeles County Probation Department, maintains that the most important activity in which a probation agency can be engaged is to probide leadership in the direction of vital social change.[33] Perhaps, if the potential for probation to function more as an alternative means of social control[34] as well as a catalyst for social change in communities[35] implemented, this enlargement of the probation function would raise the status of probation among many law enforcement personnel.

In dealing with the problem of an assignment of low esteem to the police on the part of some probation officers, decisions that enlarge the police officer's job and foster active participation in the planning and implementation of change[36] would seem to be constructive. It would appear that a number of opportunities to elicit the professional input of the police regarding client referral, inter-agency corrdination, follow-up procedures and feedback could be developed far more extensively. As in Britain, the police might be given greater professional autonomy in being allowed to submit material for presentence reports and recommendations concerning the correction of offenders.[37]

In order to deal with organizational conflict, it has been suggested that role playing be utilized to assist the contestants in sorting out the relevant issues.[38] Richard Beckhard maintains that the discussion of differences in a neutral setting is a valuable tool in reducing interagency conflict, particularly that arising from perceptual distortion of differences in interests.[39]

Perhaps a conjoint training system[40] bringing police and probation officers together might help lessen the perceptual distortion shown in the study wherein each group over estimates the group's opposition to the priorities of one's own group (see Tables VI-6 and VI-7).

In reference to the relationship of low acceptance of probation autonomy in decision makig and operational conflict (see Table VI-5), recommendations concerning collaborative problem solving[41] might be utilized. For example, in managing organizational and perceptual conflict, John Adams suggests that an OD (organization development) specialist be used to initiate or support a coherent plan for normative change involving the client group in planning and implementation.[42] Morton Deutsch maintains that such a process of intervention should involve the following:

"1. removal of blocks and distortions in the communication process;
2. keeping the issues limited and clearly focused;
3. determining possibilities by curbing unrealistic aspirations and encouraging the taking of responsibility and 'owning' of solutions;
4. making the agreement seem prestigeful to the groups represented."[43]

The implementation of this process in effecting organizational change away from organizational conflict and perceptual distortion, according to Ronald and Mary Havelock, should also include the following characteristics:

"1. Effective planning must be integrated, system oriented, continuous, continuously oriented and revised, and democratic.
2. The usefulness of innovations must be tested and determined on the consumer line by the user system.
3. Objectives should be stated in behavioral terms presenting a clear view of the desired future stateof affairs at an early stage in change strategy.
4. The conditions under which an innovation appears to work well should be clarified, cross-validated, and specified as to its cost benefits in comparison with alternative solutions.
5. Reciprocal feedback should be utilized that distinguished task feedback and interpersonal or socio-emotional feedback.
6. Collaborative relations with a variety of resource systems need to be developed.
7. Change requires a certain degree of error embracement.
8. Anticipated profit (reward) is a major incentive for diffusers and users of innovations.
9. A succession of successful changes that build toward a large goal are more likely to last than a large, dramatic change that was not built up out of internalized success.
10. There should be an appeal to cherished values.
11. The confronting change agent must also be supportive."[44]

The study suggests that these principles of OD interventionism might best be applied to police officers in the organizational interaction decision area involving autonomy. It would be quite feasible to focus on a limited, clear issue: the accordance of low probation autonomy and operational conflict, and to direct the enunciated change strategies towards those police officers who have been identified as attributing low autonomy to probation.

The advantage of the conflict adaptation typology is that it enables one to specify subsystem interactions. According to Roger Fisher, this ability to "fractionate conflict," to define immediate issues in a more limited and precise fashion, is most desirable in any attempt at conflict management.[45]

Through the utilization of the conflict adaptation typology, it is possible to identify particular contact patterns such as police moderators interacting with probation moderators, and police adapters among the police interacting with police adapters within the probation ranks. Karl Weick observed that the way an organization functions depends on the relationship that exists among processes rather than among groups.[46] William McWhinney and Everett Rogers maintain that interdependence[47] and communication[48] determine organizational structure. The conflict adaptation typology enables us to implement these observations by being better able to identify and, consequently, coordinate relationships among processes.

Ted Palmer, in attempting to overcome the notion that the probation officer can be all things to all clients, has done extensive work in studying the effects of matching clients with probation officers.[49] He distinguishes three types of probation officers, whose descriptions closely resemble the three conflict adaptations discovered in the field study (see Table VII-7), and describes the type client most suited to each type officer.[50]

The potential exists for building teams consisting of police and probation officers based on typological similarities. The study indicates that police and probation officers with a moderator adaptation seem to work quite well together. However, the study also shows that the police adapters among police and probation officers, although they work well together, produce a net effect of more aggressive law enforcement and apprehension activities that appear to be less than desirable in terms of overall system goals. Consequently, the employment of the conflict adaptation typology enables us to plan with more accuracy as to the effects as well as the constitution of different police-probation team combinations.

In attempting to arrive at an operative consensus as to what goals and tasks might be delegated to criminal justice agencies, the situation of police-probation interaction is in many respects a model one. Police and probation officers must operate in a matrix wherein both the control and service needs of society meet.

At present, however, both police[51] and probation officers[52] operate in a situation of contradictory and ambiguous role demands that contribute to fatigue, stress and tension. Louis Radelet asks,

> "Are the police to be social workers with guns or gunmen in social work, facilitators of social change or defenders of the faith?" [53]

The modus operandi for the choice between law enforcement and community service is provided by Chief Bernard Garmire of the Miami Police Department. He states:

> "If we provide only service to the community, we could ultimately have anarchy; if we provide only law enforcement, we could have benign repression at best - a police state at the worst. The task is to strike the right balance."[54]

Athough there is a general acknowledgment of the legitimacy of service demands as well as law enforcement functions, the nature of what constitutes rehabilitation is presently moot. Starting with the revelations of Thomas Szasz in Psychiatric Justice, the rehabilitative treatment approach has been increasingly critiqued as a pseudomedical model that denigrates an individual by treating him or her as less than a person capable of rational choice.[55] John Conrad states:

> The removal of the assumptions which the belief in rehabilitation has engendered will make possible a system which will be more modest in aims, more rational in its means, and more just in its disposition."[56]

A widely suggested alternative to the clinical approach is that of further integration of criminal justice operations with the community.[57] The American Bar Association states:

> "The basic idea underlying a sentence to probation is very simple. Sen tencing is in large part concerned with avoiding future crimes by helping the defendant learn to live productively in the community which he has offended against. Probation proceeds on the theory that the best way to pursue this goal is to orient the criminal sanction toward the community setting in those cases where it is compatible with the other objectives of sentencing."[58]

The next statement describes the move away from rehabilitation to reintegration:

> "Probation and parole as a form of casework has largely vanished; the major focus of the correctional worker lies in establishing in the inmate a community interest and establishing in the community an inmate interest. A majority of social workers about the city have recovered from their archaic clinical hangup, and spend more time in contacting churches, lodges, unions, civic groups, farm co-ops and PTA's, in recruiting community volunteers for service inside and outside the walls."[59]

It would appear, then, that what are being held up as goals of the system are not especially esoteric or complex. "The problems," Frederic Kellogg asserts, "derive from the failure to rationalize the activities of each stage in accordance with those goals."[60] The emphasis is upon coordination and integration of services via closer agency-community integration, expanded use of paraprofessionals, volunteers, and team processes for the purpose of ongoing change in participant decision making and organizational functions and structures.[61]

In attempting to rationalize means with goals, one is presented with tasks that are somewhat complex. Since the days of Saul Alinsky (the early Chicago criminologist who evolved into a broker for community power politics), the relationship between social change and criminal justice has become more evident whether one subscribes to radical criminology analysis or not. Yet, this awareness does not provide us with the answer, but, rather, it presents more questions as to the implementation of "alternative means of social control"[62] and new methods of "punishment in freedom."[63]

There is an increasing pressure being placed on criminal justice operations by concerned and representative community groups.[64] In an attempt to overcome the varying and often conflicting demands placed upon law enforcement and correctional agencies[65] increased use of volunteers has been strongly recommended.[66] Some sources, such as Ivan Scheier, the Director of the National Information Center on Volunteers in Courts, have very seriously implied that we need a West Point for volunteerism.[67] Perhaps special programs with volunteers representing the Hispanic community might help alleviate the situation reported upon in this study of higher conflict among police and probation officers whose primary offender contact occurs with Hispanics.

In order to more effectively implement conflict management between police and probation officers, the suggestion was pro-offered by officers with moderator conflict adaptations that seminars and other mechanisms encouraging information exchange and mutual problem solving should be established.

The following program, described as the Texas Plan, although developed as a probation training project, could just as well be applied to police and probation officers. The core elements of this plan are as follows:

> "1. Team-building and maximum participation among the participants, which brings the officers in the region closer together in the solution of their common problems and in the sharing of resources.
> 2. Committment and involvement of judges from both adult and juvenile courts.
> 3. The use of professional group facilitators.
> 4. Joint workshops for adult and juvenile officers - but separate programs within the workshops.
> 5. A carefully planned learning design which blends content and process . . ."[68]

The processes of intervention for the purpose of team building and the development of new work relationships[69] might help bring about the following idea presented by a police officer with a moderator conflict adaptation:

> "Perhaps an annex of annexes located in the community should

be set up to help break down any barriers between POs, the police and probationers. This would help all of us move from theories to a practical human relationship approach.

> Kids are being pushed from here to there and back again. We need more time, POs need more time, and we need to work closer together to be effective. These forms that we've got interfere with what they were meant to do - which is more effective corrdination."

Nevertheless, although there have been successful endeavors in getting police and social workers to work together[70] and in police coordination with some community service needs; [71] once again, one is faced with more questions than answers. For example, we may legitimately ask who, what, or where is the community? Albert Reiss, Jr., in his study, The Police and the Public, comments, "Community frequently means conflicting rather than common interests."[72] After determining that an identifiable community does exist, questions still remain as to what are the community's goals, by what standards should they be evaluated, and how does the community intend to implement them?

Acknowledging that the fear of misapplication is the beginning of wisdom, nevertheless, the demands of multiple role expectations, agency coordination, community integration and individual and system change remain.

Although there have been conspicuous successes in change motivation processes with individuals displaying a particular problem,[73] it is admitted that change maintenance is far more difficult.[74] The task of change maintenance becomes crucial in any long-term planning and system building. Although the research component may supply continuous feedback and guidance for the individual and the peer group as they move away from a problem,[75] the task of inter-organizational structuring and change towards a system solution to problem solving remains.

In reference to this larger, change-to task (as contrasted to an individual change-from motivation process), the change team concept has been recommended as helping on organization develop integrative conflict-reducing mechanisms to deal with the more differentiated organizational structure.[76] The task of the change team is as follows:

1. to identify areas in the organization in need of change:
2. to select innovative solutions;
3. to implement follow-through of solutions;
4. to develop commitment to changes:
5. to provide feedback based upon the state of the external environment and the degree of integration of the internal environment;
6. to encourage gateway innovations - small changes in the structure of an organization that set the stage for large scale innovations.[77]

For example, the problem of information verification, presented in Chapter 4, wherein the police recieve assistance from probation officers is one that involves fears on the part of probation officers of confidentiality being violated. The police, on the other hand, express resentment in that they feel that a real two way flow of information does not exist. In recent discussions with police and probation officers in Nassau County, the opinion was expressed that the conservative police see probation and the courts as "stacked against them in setting the criminal free." It was also stated that the liberal probation officer felt that the police are "out to get a probationer and hassle him."

As the two agencies move closer together towards problem solving, their capacity for generating new proposals for dealing with these issues and others could be increased by the introduction of Socratic consultation management assistance[78] wherein change team members would regularly consult with police and probation officers responsible for generating new work relationships.

It has been suggested that a necessary prerequisite of successful change involves the mobilization of forces against it.[79] It has also been recommended that at the earlier initiation stage of innovation, a more organic or less bureaucratic structure seems most appropriate; whereas, at the implementation stage, a more bureaucratic and centralized structure becomes appropriate.[80] In my recent discussions with police and probation line officers in Nassau County, it was strongly recommended that a professionally run (i.e. non-political) research and development department would offer the best hope for initiating innovation between their respective agencies.

Nevertheless, the road to change, while heavily mapped, is not without detours. Resistance is likely to develop as others in the agencies perceive their autonomy and security being threatened.[81]

In dealing with the problem of official resistance to change, a case described by Calvin Swank is most informative: Five patrolmen constituting a group with a mean age of twenty-eight and five years service were able to change an entire police department.[82] In the case, outside assistance from the informal power structure of the community was a prerequisite to any successful change.[83]

1. Contacting members of the press and directing them to specific problems in the police department and explaining who the responsible person was.
2. In the absence of informal contacts with the media, anonymous telephone calls were made to appropriate persons. (This, they believed, was not unethical so long as the information was correct and the public goad was served.)
3. In the initial stages, efforts were designed to gain support from politicians, fellow officers, civic organizations and the news media.
4. After substantial support was obtained, the group began to bargain - this being done through intermediaries.84

Although this strategy may conjur up images (favorable or unfavorable) of Saul Alinsky and Tammany Hall, it should be emphasized that this is not an illustration that the end justifies the means - only that some ends justify some means.

The goal of system change may require skills often overlooked by professionals advocating change; namely, sustaining change involves some tough (occasionally nasty) in-fighting and a type of community power politics that Saul Alinsky so skillfully orchestrated and of which much is predicated for the future.[85]

In an attempt at projecting future administrative structures, Louis Gawthrop suggests that change agents should be positioned in boundary spanning units.[86] These boundary spanning units are described as being composed of highly specialized work teams that develop meaningful interacting and interdependent relationships.[87] The change agents should contribute so self-actualized behavior (reflective of what psychologists such as Abraham Maslow and Hans Toch propound)[88] and a consequent expansion of the range of choice.

In addition, Fawthrop recommends the position of policy analyst. His role is that of providing an overall policy focus and an analytically devised set of program alternatives on a macro level.[89] Thus, with change agents maximizing horizontal integration in boundary spanning units and the policy analyst providing long term planning and coordination, the foundation for collegial, participative and innovative administration on a system basis is provided.

In conclusion, therefore, it has been demonstrated that techniques and strategies for resolving conflict and inducing change in the criminal justice system tend to reinforce one another at all levels and from varying perspectives. It has been documented that it is not only possible, but feasible, to encourage self-actualization and structure administration on the basis of analytic planning and flexibility. However, while the goals are not complex, the means are - for the realities of power supporting the status quo ante are involved.

If proponents of conflict resolution and change do their homework, the goals will be clear and the social science methods will be increasingly related, more exact and certain. Nevertheless, successful implementation will rest on the ability to combine interdisciplinary systems analysis with manipulation in the arena of community power politics.

NOTES

1. John L. Petelle, "The Role of Conflict in Discussion," in Small Group Communication, edited by Larry A. Samovar (Dubuque, Iowa: William C. Brown Co., 1970), p. 147; Kenneth W. Thomas, "Issues in Management of Conflict," in Management of Conflict, edited by Stewart Shapiro (Los Angeles: Institute of Industrial Relations, University of California, March 13, 1973), p. 11.

2. Vincent O'Leary and Donald J. Newman, "Conflict Resolution in Criminal Justice," Journal of Research in Crime and Delinquency 7, No. 2 (July 1970): 115.

3. Morton Deutsch, "The Effects of Cooperation and Competition upon Group Process," in Group Dynamics, edited by Dorwin Cartwright and Alvin Zander (New York: Harper and Row, 1968), p. 482; Douglas McGregor, The Human Side of Enterprise (New York: McGraw-Hill, 1960, p. 241; J. A. Robinson, Further Problems of Research on International Relations," in Intergroup Relations and Leadership, edited by M. Sherif (New York: Wiley and Sons, Inc., 1962), pp. 205-208; Muzafer Sherif and Carolyn Sherif, "Intergroup Relations," in An Outline of Social Psychology, edited by M. Sherif and C. Sherif (New York: Harper and Bros., 1956), pp. 280-332; Muzafer Sherif, "Superordinate Goals in the Reduction of Intergroup Conflict," American Journal of Sociology 43 (1958): 349-356.

4. Eric H. Neilson, "Understanding and Managing Intergroup Conflict," in Managing Group and Intergroup Relations, edited by Jay Lorsch and Paul Lawrence (Homewood, Illinois: Richard B. Irwin, 1972), p. 335.

5. Ibid., p. 338.

6. Ibid.

7. Vincent O'Leary and Donald J. Newman, p. 116.

8. George Cvetkovich, "Small Group Dynamics in Extended Judgment Situations," in Human Judgment and Social Interaction, edited by Leon Rappoport and David Summers (New York: Holt, Rinehart and Winston, 1973), p. 328; Rensis Likert and Jane Likert, New Ways of Managing Conflict (New York: McGraw-Hill, 1976), pp. 326-327; Eric H. Neilson, "Understanding and Managing Intergroup Conflict," in Managing Group and Intergroup Relations, edited by Jay Lorsch and Paul Lawrence (Homewood, Illinois: Richard B. Irwin, 1972), p. 339.

9. Vincent O'Leary and Donald J. Newman, p. 116.

10. Douglas McGregor, The Human Side of Enterprise (New York: McGraw-Hill, 1960), p. 242.

11. Hans Toch, Police, Prisons and the Problem of Violence (Rockville, Maryland:

National Institute of Mental Health, U.S. Dept. of Health, Education and Welfare, 1977), p. 82.

12. Norman R. F. Maier, Problem Solving and Creativity: In Individuals and Groups, (New York: McGraw-Hill, 1963), p. 247.

13. Lester Coch and John French, Jr., "Overcoming Resistance to Change," in Group Dynamics, edited by Dorwin Cartwright and Alvin Zander (New York: Harper & Row, 1968), p. 350.

14. Dean C. Barnlund and Franklyn S. Haiman, "A Philosophy and Method of Change," in Small Group Communication, edited by Robert S. Cathcart and Larry A. Samovar (Dubuque, Iowa: William C. Brown Co., 1970), p. 214.

15. Chris Argyris, Interpersonal Competence and Organizational Effectiveness (Homewood, Illinois: The Dorsey Press, 1962), p. 285.

16. Hans Toch et al., Agents of Change: A Study in Police Reform (New York: John Wiley and Sons, 1975), pp. 158-160.

17. George J. Steinfeld, "A Cognitive-Behavioral Analysis of Institutional Conflict and a Humanistic Solution,"International Journal of Criminology and Penology 3, No. 4 (November 1975): 342.

18. Ibid.

19. Morton Deutsch, The Resolution of Conflict (New Haven: Yale University Press, 1973), pp. 382-392; Leonard W. Doob, Resolving Conflict in Africa (New Haven: Yale University Press, 1970), pp. 167-172; A. D. Elbing, Behavioral Decisions in Organizations (Glenview, Ill.: Scott, Foresman, 1970), p. 317; Roger Fisher, "Fractionating Conflict," in Conflict Resolution, edited by Clagett Smith (Notre Dame, Indiana: University of Notre Dame Press, 1971), pp. 157-169; Donald Klein, "Some Notes on the Dynamics of Resistance to Change: The Defender Role," in Concepts for Social Change, edited by G. Watson (Wash., D.C.: NTL Institute for Applied Behavioral Science, 1967), p. 30; Paul R. Laurence and Jay W. Lorsch, Organization and Environment: Managing Differentiation and Integration, (Homewood, Ill.: Richard D. Irwin, 1967), p. 150: Edgar Schein, Organizational Psychology (Englewood Cliffs, New Jersey: Prentice-Hall, 1970), p. 120; John Thibaut, "The Development of Contractual Norms in Bargaining: Replication and Variation," Journal of Conflict Resolution 12, No. 1 (March 1968): 102-112; Hans Toch, Police, Prisons and the Problem of Violence (Rockville, Maryland: National Institute of

Mental Health, U.S. Dept. of Health, Education, and Welfare, 1977), p. 82; Richard E. Walton, "Interpersonal Confrontation and Basic Third Party Functions: A Case Study," Journal of Applied Behavioral Science 4, No. 3 (1967): 327-350; Richard E. Walton, "Third Party Roles in Interdepartmental Conflict," Industrial Relations 7, No. 1 (October 1967): 29-43; James Q. Wilson, "Innovations in Organization: Notes Toward a Theory," in Approaches to Organizational Design, edited by James D. Thompson (Pittsburgh: University of Pittsburgh Press, 1966), pp. 193-218; Gerald Zaltman, Robert Duncan and Jonny Holbek, Innovations and Organizations (New York: John Wiley and Sons, 1973).

20. Vincent O'Leary and Donald J. Newman, p. 118.

21. Douglas Brown, The Human Nature of Organizations (New York: American Management Associations, 1973), p. 65; Rensis Likert, New Patterns in Management (New York: McGraw-Hill, 1961).

22. Christ Argyris, Management and Organizational Development (New York: McGraw Hill, 1971), pp. 156-185; Douglas Brown, The Human Nature of Organizations (New York: American Management Associations, 1973), pp. 65-67; Rensis Likert and Jane G. Likert, New Ways of Managing Conflict (New York: McGraw-Hill, 1976); Anant R. Negandhi, Organizational Theory in an Open System (New York: Kennikat Press Corp., 1975); Everett M. Rogers and Rekha-Agarwala Rogers, Communication in Organizations (New York: Free Press, 1976); Kenneth W. Thomas, "Issues in Management of Conflict," in Management of Conflict, edited by Stewart Shapiro (Los Angeles: Institute of Industrial Relations, University of California, March 13, 1973), pp. 5-22; Karl E. Weick, The Social Psychology of Organizing (Reading, Mass.: Addison-Wesley Pub. Co., 1969), p. 108; Abraha Zaleznik and David Moment, The Dynamics of Interpersonal Behavior (New York: John Wiley and Sons, 1964), pp. 347-348.

23. Vincent O'Leary and Donald J. Newman, p. 118.

24. Eric H. Neilson, "Understanding and Managing Intergroup Conflict," in Managing Group and Intergroup Relations, edited by Jay Lorsch and Paul Laurence (Homewood, Illinois: Richard B. Irwin, 1972), p. 335; Richard Walton, Interpersonal Peacemaking: Confrontations and Third Party Consultation (Reading, Mass.: Addison-Wesley Pub. Co., 1969), p. 150.

25. Richard Walton, Interpersonal Peacemaking: Confrontations and Third Party Consultation (Reading, Mass.: Addison-Wesley Pub. C., 1969), pp. 144-146.

26. Neeley Gardner, Group Leadership (Washington, D.C.: National Training and Development Service, 1974), pp. 32-33.

27. Ibid., p. 33.

28. Kenneth R. Hammond, "The Cognitive Conflict Paradigm," in Human Judgment and Social Interaction, edited by Leon Rappoport and David Summers (New York: Holt, Rinehart and Winston, 1973), p. 201.

29. Henry McCarthy, "Some Situational Factors Improving Cognitive Conflict Reducation and Interpersonal Understanding," Journal of Conflict Resolution 21 (June 1977): 217-234.

30.Kenneth R. Hammond and Berndt Brehmer, "Quasi-Rationality and Distrust: Implications for International Conflict," in Human Judgment and Social Interaction, edited by Leon Rappoport and David Summers (New York: Holt, Rinehart and Winston, 1973), pp. 385-386.

31. Chris Argyris, Integrating the Individual and the Organization (New York: Wiley, 1964), p. 274.

32. Christ Argyris, Management and Organizational Development (New York: McGraw-Hill, 1971), p. 21.

33. David Macpherson, "Probation and Corrections in the Seventies," Federal Probation 35. No. 1 (March 1971): 15.

34. See Inkeri Anttila, "Probation and Parole: Social Control or Social Service?" International Journal of Criminology and Penology 3, No. 1 (Feb. 1975): 82-84.

35. Yona Cohen, "Staff Supervision in Probation," Federal Probation, 40, No. 3 (September 1976): 18; Paul Takagi, "Administrative and Professional Conflicts in Modern Corrections," The Journal of Criminal Law and Criminology 64, No. 3 (September 1973):

318; Charles Horejsi, "Training for the Direct-Service Volunteer in Probation," Federal Probation 37, No. 3 (September 1973): 41; Ira Schwartz, "Volunteers and Professionals: A Team in the Correctional Process," Federal Probation 35, No. 3 (September 1971): 49.

36. Chris Argyris, Integrating the Individual and the Organization (New York: Wiley, 1964), p. 274; Jay W. Lorsch and Alan Sheldon, "The Individual in the Organization: A Systems View," in Managing Group and Intergroup Relations, edited by Jay W. Lorsch and Paul R. Lawrence (Homewood, Ill.: Richard D. Irwin, Inc., 1972), pp. 161-182.

37. Wayne P. Jackson, "Treatment of the Offender in the United Kingdom," Federal Probation, 35, No. 3 (June 1971): 56.

38. Neely Gardner, p. 33.

39. Richard Beckhard, "The Confrontation Meeting," Harvard Business Review 45, No. 2 (1967): 149-153.

40. Alvin W. Cohn, "Training in the Criminal Justice Nonsystem," Federal Probation 38, No. 2 (June 1974): 37.

41.Richard Beckhard, "The Confrontation Meeting," Harvard Business Review 45, No. 2 (1967): 149-153; Robert R. Blake, Jane Mouton and Herbert Shepard, "An Intergroup Problem-Solving Approach to Mergers," in Managing Intergroup Conflict in Industry, edited by Blake, Shepard and Mouton (Houston, Texas: Gulf Publishing Co., 1964), pp. 146-152; Elise Boulding, "Further Reflections on Conflict Management," in Power and Conflict in Organizations, edited by Robert Kahn and Elise Boulding (New York: Basic Books, Inc., 1964), pp. 146-150; Lester Coch and John French, Jr., "Overcoming Resistace to Change," in Group Dynamics, edited by Dorwin Cartwright and Alvin Zander (New York: Harper & Row, 1968), pp. 336-350; Norman Maier, Problem Solving and Creativity: In Individuals and Groups (Belmont, California: Brooks Cole Pub. Co., 1970) p. 240; Herbert A. Shepard, "Responses to Situations of Competition and Conflict," in Power and Conflict in Organizations, edited by Robert Kahn and Elise Boulding (New York: Basic Books, 1964), pp. 127-135; James C. Taylor, Technology and Planned Organizational Change (Ann Arbor, Mich.: Institute for Social Research, The University of Michigan, 1971), p. 124.

42. John D. Adams, Organizational Development and Change (Washington, D.C.: National Training and Development Service, 1974), pp. 4-6.

43. Morton Deutsch, The Resolution of Conflict (New Haven: Yale University Press, 1973), pp. 383-86.

44. Ronald Havelock and Mary Havelock, Training for Change Agents, (Ann Arbor: Michigan Institute for Social Research, 1973), pp. 16-37.

45. Roger Fisher, "Fractionating Conflict," in Conflict Resolution, edited by Clagett

Smith (Notre Dame, Indiana: University of Notre Dame Press, 1971), p. 169.

46. Karl E. Weick, The Social Psychology of Organizing (Reading, Mass." Addison-Wesley Pub. Co., 1969), p. 108.

47. William McWhinney, "Organizational and Community Open System Planning," in Management of Conflict, edited by Stephen Shapiro (Los Angeles: Institute of Industrial Relations, University of California, March 13, 1973), p. 49.

48. Everett M. Rogers and Rekha-Agarwala Rogers, Communication in Organizations (New York: Free Press, 1976), pp. 106, 147.

49. Ted Palmer, "An Overview of Matching in the Community Treatment Project," presented at the Annual Meeting of the Western Psychological Association of San Diego, California, March 30, 1968, p. 2.

50. See Ted Palmer, "Matching Worker and Client in Corrections," Social Work 18, No. 2 (March 1973): 95-103; "Types of Treaters and Types of Juvenile Offenders," reprinted from Youth Authority Quarterly 18, No. 3 (Fall 1965): 1-9.

51. Louis A. Radelet, The Police and The Community: Studies (Beverly Hills: Glencoe Press, 1973), p. 289.

52. Yona Cohen, "Staff Supervision in Probation," Federal Probation 40, No. 3 (September 1976): 18; Nelson Watson and James Sterling, Police and Their Opinions (Wash., D.C.: International Association of Chiefs of Police, 1969), p. 1

53. Louis A. Radelet, p. 288.

54. Ibid. p. 292

55. See George I. Diffenbaucher, "Settling for Humanization: Evidence of Despair or of Facing Reality?" Federal Probation 40, N. 1 (March 1976): 28; M. Kay Harris, "Criminal Justice: Rehabilitation or Punishment?" Remarks for the Mid-Winter Workshop of The Metropolitan Washington Chapter of The National Assocation of Social Workers, Wash. D.C., (Jan. 1975): 6-7.

56. John Conrad, "Corrections and Simple Justice," The Journal of Criminal Law, Criminology and Police Science 64, No. 2 (June 1973): 217.

57. See American Bar Association: Standarards Relating to Probation (New York: Institute of Judicial Administration, 1970), p. 1; American Bar Association, Standards Relating to the Urban Police Function (New York: Institute of Judicial Administration, 1970); Dale G. Hardman, "Corrections and The Community: A View Through a Crystal Ball," Federal Probation 34, No. 1 (March 1970): 24; Ellen Mintz and Georgetta Sandler, "Instituting a Full-Service Orientation to Policing," The Police Chief 16, No. 6 (June

1974): 44-50; The President's Commission on Law Enforcement and Administration of Justice, Task Force Report: The Police (Wash., D.C.: U.S. Gov't. Printing Office, 1967), pp. 122-124.

58. American Bar Association, Standards Relating to Probation (New York: Institute of Judicial Administration, 1970), p.1.

59. Dale G. Hardman, "Corrections and The Community: A View Through a Crystal Ball," Federal Probation 34, No. 1 (March 1970): 24.

60. Frederic R. Kellogg, "Organizing the Criminal Justice System: A Look at Operative Objectives," Federal Probation 40, No. 2 (June 1976): 54.

61. Robert E. Keldgord and Robert O. Norris, "New Directions for Corrections," Federal Probation 35, No. 1 (March 1971): 9.

62. David Macpherson, p. 15.

63. Inkeri Anttila, pp. 82-84.

64. Milton Luger and Joseph Lobenthal, "Cushioning Future Shock in Corrections," Federal Probation 38, No. 2 (June 1974): 22.

65. Yona Cohen, "Staff Supervision in Probation," Federal Probation 40, No. 3 (September 1976): 18, Paul Takagi, "Administrative and Professional Conflicts in Modern Corrections," The Journal of Criminal Law and Criminolgy 64, No. 3 (September 1973): 318.

66. Charles Horejsi, "Training for the Direct-Service Volunteer in Probation," Federal Probation 37, No. 3 (September 1973): 41; Ira Schwartz, "Volunteers and Professionals: A Team in the Correctional Process," Federal Probation 35, No. 3 (September 1971): 49.

67. Ivan Scheier, "The Professional and the Volunteer in Probation: An Emerging Relationship," Federal Probation 34, No. 2 (June 1970): 18.

68. Libby Bertinot and Jack Taylor, "A Basic Plan for Statewide Probation Training," Federal Probation 38, No. 2 (June 1974): 31.

69. John D. Adams, Organizational Development and Change (Wash., D.C.: National Training and Development Service, 1974), pp. 3-8; Chris Argyris, Interpersonal Competence and Organizational Effectiveness (Homewood, Illinois: The Dorsey Press, 1962): W. Warner Burke and Harvey A. Hornstein, The Social Technology of Organization Development (La Jolla, California: University Associates, Inc., 1972), p. xviii.

70. See Harvey Treger, "Breakthrough in Preventive Corrections: A Police-Social Work Team Model," Federal Probation 36, No. 4 (December 1972): 53-58.

71. See Louis A. Radelet, The Police and The Community: Studies (Beverly Hills: Glencoe Press, 1973).

72. Albert Reiss, Jr., The Police and The Public (Nerw Haven: Yale University Press, 1971), p. 209.

73. Hans Toch et. al., Agents of Change: A Study in Police Reform (New York: John Wiley and Sons 1975), p. 346.

74. Ibid., p. 348.

75. Ibid., p. 349.

76. Gerald Zaltman, Robert Duncan and Johny Holbek, Innovations and Organizations (New York: John Wiley and Sons, 1973), p. 155.

77. Ibid, pp. 43-71.

78. John D. Adams, p. 8.

79. Donald Klein, "Some Notes on the Dynamics of Resistance to Change: The Defender Role," in Concepts for Social Change, edited by G. Watson (Wash., D.C.: NTL Institute for Applied Behavioral Science, 1967), 1967), p. 30.

80. Gerald Zaltman, p. 155.

81. Goodwin Watson, "Resistance to Change," in Police Community Relations, edited by Alvin Cohn and Emilio Viano (New York: J. B. Lippincott, 1976), p. 560.

82. Calvin Swank and James Parsons, "Police Organizations and the Art of Effecting Change," Internaional Journal of Criminology and Penology 2, No. 3 (August 1974): 291-293.

83. Ibid, p. 293.

84. Ibid, p. 292.

85. Milton Luger and Joseph Lobenthal, p. 22.

86. Louis C. Gawthrop, Administrative Politics and Social Change (New York: St. Morton's Press, 1971), p. 100.

87. Ibid., p. 98

88. See Abraham Maslow, Eupsychian Management (Homewood, I11.: The Dorsey Press, 1965); Hans Toch et al., Agents of Change: A Study of Police Reform (New York: John Wiley and Sons, 1975).

89. Louis C. Gawthrop, p. 95.

APPENDIX A

DATA FROM THE ALBANY CONFERENCE ON CRIMINAL JUSTICE

TABLE 1

CHARACTERISTICS OF PARTICIPANTS

AGE

Years	Probation	Police	Total
41 - 50	5	10	15
51 - 60	7	5	12
61 - 65	4	-	4

LENGTH OF SERVICE WITH PRESENT AGENCY

Years	Probation	Police	Total
1 - 5	1	1	2
6 - 10	5	1	6
11 - 15	5	-	5
Over 15	5	13	18

HIGHEST LEVEL OF EDUCATION COMPLETED

Grade	Probation	Police	Total
Some College	-	9	9
B. A. Degree	-	1	1
Some Graduate	5	2	7
Graduate Degree	11	3	14

ADMINISTRATIVE LEVEL

	Probation	Police	Total
Chief or Director	5	1	6
Deputy Chief or Director	8	8	16
Bureau Chief	2	4	6
Inspector or Supervisor	1	2	3

TABLE 1

FEELINGS CONCERNING CURRENT LEGAL PROCESSES

QUESTIONS	MEAN SCORES			
	POLICE (N=15)		PROBATION (N=16)	
	Actual Answer	Adjusted Score	Actual Answer	Adjusted Score
2. Today's laws let people get away with crime quite easily.	* +.07	**(-.07)	-1.31	**(+1.31)
11. Sometimes it is fair to let people off probation early.	+2.23	(+2.23)	+2.75	(+2.75)
19. People in this community wish that courts and the police were harder on offenders.	+2.15	(-2.15)	+2.00	(-2.00)
27. The present system of state and federal laws has undermined my authority to a dangerous extend.	-.23	(+.23)	-1.62	(+1.62)
35. A number of pressure groups have been successful in getting legislation and court decisions that severely restrict the actions you can take.	+.30	(-.30)	-.81	(+.81)
42. Generally speaking, police officers today have enough legal authority to get their jobs done efficiently.	-.69	(-.69)	+1.56	(+1.56)
47. Generally speaking, probation officers today have enough legal authority to get their jobs done efficiently.	+.38	(+.38)	+1.75	(+1.75)
ADJUSTED MEAN SCORE		-.05		+1.11

*Scores can range from +3.0 to -3.0

**The positive or negative signs in columns one and three were reversed for the adjusted score whenever a question was asked in a negative form.

TABLE 2

APPROACHES TOWARD THE OFFENDER

QUESTIONS	MEAN SCORES			
	POLICE (N=15)		PROBATION (N=16)	
	Actual Answer	Adjusted Score	Actual Answer	Adjusted Score
4. A patrolman should generally try to make offenders feel as though they were really law-abiding but had just made this one mistake.	-.38	(-.38)	-.56	(-.56)
13. A probation officer should generally try to make offenders feel as though they were really law-abiding but had just made this one mistake.	+1.15	(+1.15)	.00	(.00)
20. An offender should be sent to prison as punishment for his crime.	-1.46	(+1.46)	-2.43	(+2.43)
28. An offender should be sent to prison as an example in order to stop others from committing crimes.	-.84	(+.84)	-2.06	(+2.06)
36. There should be a greater emphasis on psychological treatment for offenders.	+1.00	(+1.00)	+1.37	(+1.37)
43. In our correctional policies, we should place greater emphasis on community treatment programs (half-way houses) and less on sending offenders to prison.	-.07	(-.07)	+2.81	(+2.81)
ADJUSTED MEAN SCORE		+.66		+1.35

TABLE 3

TOLERANCE TOWARD DEVIANCE

QUESTIONS	MEAN SCORES			
	POLICE (N=15)		PROBATION (N=16)	
	Actual Answer	Adjusted Score	Actual Answer	Adjusted Score
8. A high school principle should have the right to send boys with long hair home.	+.69	(.69)	(-.69)	(+.93)
16. A homesexual couple should not be allowed to cohabit in your community.	+.77	(-.77)	-1.00	(+1.00)
24. Prostitution shold be legalized and, if controlled, should be allowed to operate openly in a restricted area.	-1.38	(-1.38)	+.06	(+.06)
32. The criminal law already covers too much behavior.	-.37	(.37)	-.06	(-.06)
39. A former child molester who has served his time should be allowed to join my local bowling club.	+.39	(+.39)	+1.00	(+1.00)
44. Suicide should not be considered illegal.	+.15	(+.15)	+.63	(+.63)
48. If your son starts to imitate hippies, you should insist that he clean up and get a haircut.	+.84	(-.84)	-.13	(+.13)
51. Welfare recipients should not be able to receive subsidized rents for housing in middle class areas.	-.54	(+.54)	-1.18	(+1.18)
54. The legal rights of a conscientious objector should be decreased.	-.15	(+.15)	-1.68	(+1.68)
57. Student demonstrators should be subject to more discipline.	+2.23	(-2.23)	+1.37	(-1.37)

TABLE 3 (continued)

QUESTIONS	MEAN SCORES			
	POLICE (N=15)		PROBATION (N=16)	
	Actual Answer	Adjusted Score	Actual Answer	Adjusted Score
59. Penalties for smoking marijuana should be increased	-.61	(+.61)	-1.68	(+1.68)
61. If an ex-convict moved next door to me, I would move.	-1.53	(+1.53)	-2.12	(+2.12)
ADJUSTED MEAN SCORE		-.24		+.74

TABLE 4

FAITH IN PEOPLE

QUESTIONS	MEAN SCORES			
	POLICE (N=15)		PROBATION (N=16)	
	Actual Answer	Adjusted Score	Actual Answer	Adjusted Score
7. Most people can be trusted.	+1.92	(+1.92)	+2.18	+2.18
15. Most people are inclined to look out for themselves, at all costs, rather than try to help others.	+ .13	(-.31)	- .25	+.25
23. If you don't watch yourself, people will take advantage of you.	+ .38	(.38)	- .87	(+.87)
31. No one is going to care much about what happens to me.	-1.46	(+1.46)	-1.87	(+1.87)
38. I feel very much I belong in my community.	+1.69	(+1.69)	+1.68	(+1.68)
		+ .87		+1.37

TABLE 5

STATUS PERCEPTIONS

QUESTIONS	MEAN SCORES			
	POLICE (N=15)		PROBATION (N=16)	
	Actual Answer	Adjusted Score	Actual Answer	Adjusted Score
10. I would be proud if my son became a probation officer.	+.70		+1.44	(+1.44)
14. I would be proud if my son became a policeman	+1.00	(+1.00)	+.44	
18. Most people think probation officers work at the job they do because they were not good enough to get another job.	-2.38		-2.00	(+2.00)
26. Most people think policemen work at the job they do because they were not good enough to get another job.	- .77	(+.77)	-1.37	
34. A probation officer would most likely be accepted by the local country club.	+1.46		.69	(+.69)
41. A policeman would most likely be accepted by the local country club.	+ .54	(+.54)	+.37	
46. Most of the duties of a policeman can be learned by anyone of average intelligence in a six month period.	-1.15	(+1.15)	-.37	
50. Most of the duties of a probation officer can be learned by anyone of average intelligence in a six month period.	- .38		-1.18	(+1.18)
53. A court is not likely to accept the expertise of a police officer.	-1.92	(+1.92)	-1.75	

TABLE 5

STATUS PERCEPTIONS

QUESTIONS	MEAN SCORES			
	POLICE (N=15)		PROBATION (N=16)	
	Actual Answer	Adjusted Score	Actual Answer	Adjusted Score
10. I would be proud if my son became a probation officer.	+.70		+1.44	(+1.44)
14. I would be proud if my son became a policeman.	+1.00	(+1.00)	+.44	
18. Most people think probation officers work at the job they do because they were not good enough to get another job.	-2.38		-2.00	(+2.00)
26. Most people think policemen work at the job they do because they were not good enough to get another job.	-.77	(+.77)	-1.37	
34. A probation officer would most likely be accepted by the local country club.	+1.46		+.69	(+.69)
41. A policeman would most likely be accepted by the local country club.	+.54	(+.54)	+.37	
46. Most of the duties of a policeman can be learned by anyone of average intelligence in a six month period.	-1.15	(+1.15)	+.37	
50. Most of the duties of a probation officer can be learned by anyone of average intelligence in a six month period.	-.38		-1.18	(+1.18)
53. A court is not likely to accept the expertise of a police officer.	-1.92	(+1.92)	-1.75	

TABLE 5 (continued)

QUESTIONS	MEAN SCORES			
	POLICE (N=15)		PROBATION (N=16)	
	Actual Answer	Adjusted Score	Actual Answer	Adjusted Score
56. A court is not likely to accept the expertise of a probation officer.	-2.30		-2.50	(+2.50)
60. Police professionalism is pretty much the same no matter who is at the top of the department.	-1.61	(-1.61)	-2.00	
62. A probation officer's professionalism is pretty much the same no matter who is at the top of the department.	-1.38		-1.81	(-1.81)
58. A probation officer is more professional than a police officer.	- .54	(+.54)	+.01	(+.01)
ADJUSTED MEAN SCORE		+.62		+.82

TABLE 6

PERCEPTIONS OF ROLE TRANSFERABILITY

QUESTIONS	MEAN SCORES			
	POLICE (N=15)		PROBATION (N=16)	
	Actual Answer	Adjusted Score	Actual Answer	Adjusted Score
3. The average policeman is capable of performing the duties of a probation officer.	-.84	(-84)	-2.06	(-2.06)
12. The average probation officer is capable of performing the duties of a policeman.	-.46	(-.46)	-1.50	(-1.50)
ADJUSTED MEAN SCORES		-.65		-1.78

TABLE 7

COMMUNITY ACCEPTABILITY

QUESTIONS	MEAN SCORES			
	POLICE (N=15)		PROBATION (N=16)	
	Actual Answer	Adjusted Score	Actual Answer	Adjusted Score
9. My department has the respect of most poor people in my community.	+.84	(+.84)	+1.37	(+1.37)
17. People generally cooperate with me in my work.	+2.07	(+2.07)	+2.06	(+2.06)
25. It is important that I be liked by the people in the community with whom I come in contact.	+1.15	(+1.15)	+1.18	(+1.18)
33. I feel very much that I belong in my community.	+2.30	(+2.30)	+2.06	(+2.06
40. My function is widely understood by the community.	+.69	(+.69)	-1.87	(-1.87)
45. People in my community want more probation officers.	+1.07		+.37	(+.31)
49. People in my community want more police officers.	+2.23	(+2.23)	+2.31	
52. Most people in my community would be proud to have their sons become probation officers.	+1.07		+.68	(+.68)
55. Most people in my community would be proud to have their sons become police officers.	+.15	(+.15)	+.56	____
ADJUSTED MEAN SCORE				

TABLE 8

OPERATIONAL SITUATIONS

QUESTION SUMMARY	MEAN SCORES		
	Police Score (N=15)	Probation Score (N=16)	Difference
1. Police request revocation of probationer for rule violation when new crime can't be proved.	2.72*	4.06*	1.34
2. Probation department requests police chief to require policemen to report any probation violation.	3.00	3.00	.00
3. Police contend probation department request for a list of names of persons on probation.	2.20	4.33	2.13
4. Probation department refuses police department request for a list of names of persons on probation.	3.45	1.40	2.05
5. Probation department refuses police request to hold probationer in custody pending investigation.	2.63	2.00	.63
6. Police department wants information, which youth conselors may gather, shared with them.	1.99	3.41	1.42
7. Police department requests 16 - year-old youth be held in detention.	2.81	3.26	.45
8. Police department believes it should be given right to make recommendations to judge.	2.72	4.53	1.81

TABLE 8 (continued)

QUESTION SUMMARY	MEAN SCORES		
	Police Score (N=15)	Probation Score (N=16)	Difference
9. Probation department will not allow probationers to act as informer for police.	3.90	3.60	.30
10. Probation department refuses police request for access to a probationer's case file.	4.45	2.60	1.85
11. It is proposed that police and probation agencies be combined into a single agency.	5.09	4.60	.49
12. Police department argues that a man with serious prior record should not receive probation.	3.18	5.00	1.82

*The higher the score the greater the disagreement with the question.

TABLE 9

PREDICTIONS OF RESPONSES TO
ORGANIZATIONAL PROBLEMS

Questions	POLICE PREDICTIONS (N=15)		PROBATION PREDICTIONS)N=16	
	Mean Errors on Police Items	Mean Errors on Probation Items	Mean Errors on Probation Items	Mean Errors on Police Items
1	.6	.3	.6	1.2
2	.6	.8	.5	2.0
3	.2	.3	.4	.5
4	.1	.9	.3	1.0
5	.1	.5	.6	.4
6	.1	.5	.6	.4
7	.8	1.6	.7	2.4
8	.3	.1	1.3	.1
9	1.0	1.0	.9	1.6
10	.1	.3	.3	.3
11	.6	1.8	2.0	.5
12	.4	.2	.4	.4
TOTAL OF MEAN ERRORS	4.9	7.8	8.0	11.5

TABLE 10

PERCEIVED ORGANIZATIONAL CONFLICT
BETWEEN GROUPS

		MEAN PERCEPTIONS	
Questions	Actual Differences in Responses	Police Estimation of Differences (N=15)	Probation Estimation of Differences (N=16)
1	1.3	2.3	2.6
2	0	1.7	1.7
3	2.1	2.4	3.2
4	2.0	2.0	3.8
5	.6	2.2	3.4
6	1.4	2.2	2.2
7	.5	2.0	2.9
8	1.8	2.8	3.1
9	.3	2.2	3.0
10	1.8	2.7	3.4
11	.5	.5	.6
12	1.8	2.4	3.1
TOTAL DIFFERENCES	14.1	25.2	33.0

TABLE 11

PERCEIVED DISTANCE BETWEEN OWN ANSWERS AND ESTIMATED ANSWERS OF GROUPS

	POLICE (N=15)		PROBATION (N=16)	
Questions	Distance Between Own and Estimated Police Response	Distance Between Own and Estimated Probation Response	Distance Between Own and Estimated Probation Response	Distance Between Own and Estimated Police Response
1	1.0	1.0	.8	2.7
2	1.2	1.5	1.7	1.6
3	1.1	2.9	1.2	3.0
4	2.0	2.0	.8	3.6
5	1.7	2.0	1.1	2.6
6	.7	2.1	1.0	2.4
7	1.2	1.2	1.7	2.8
8	.4	2.4	1.2	2.6
9	1.0	1.5	1.0	1.8
10	.5	2.4	1.3	2.2
11	.6	.6	.8	2.6
12	1.4	1.5	1.2	2.6
TOTAL ESTIMATED DIFFERENCES	12.8	21.1	14.0	29.1

APPENDIX B

PILOT INSTRUMENT AND ANALYSIS

TABLE OF CONTENTS

APPENDIX B

SECTION 1. PRELIMINARY INSTRUMENT
Administered to 550 Police
and 184 Probation Officers

CRIMINAL JUSTICE SURVEY I

Administered by Ted Ryan, Project Director for
Criminal Justice Agencies Study, at the
National Institute of Law Enforcement and
Criminal Justice
U. S. Dept. of Justice

This questionnaire is one phase of a national survey directed at exploring the relations between criminal justice agencies. Your answers will constitute an important part of this total national picture. Your cooperation in answering all questions will be greatly appreciated. Please take as much time as you need to answer carefully the survey.

Instructions: When you have finished the questionnaire, enclose it in a sealed envelope.

BIOGRAPHICAL DATA

1. Age: Under 25____, 25-29 ____, 30-34 ____, 35-39 ____, 40-44 ____, 45-49 ____, 50 and over ____.

2. Marital Status: Single ____, Married ____, Separated or divorced ____, Widowed ____.
3. Sex: Male ____, Female ____.

4. Number of Children: None ____, 1 ____, 2 ____, 3 ____, 4 ____, 5 ____ 6 or more ____.

5. Ethnic Origin: White ____, Negro or Black ____, Puerto Rican ____, Mexican American ____, Oriental ____, Other ____.

EDUCATIONAL BACKGROUND

6. Grammar School: Public only ____, Parochial only ____, Public and Parochial ____.

7. High School Graduate: Yes ____, No ____, or equivalency certificate ____.

8. What is the highest level of education which you have attained?

   Less than 8 years ____
   Some High School ____
   High School or Equivalency Diploma ____
   Less than 1 year of college ____
   1-3 years of college ____
   4 year College degree ____
   Attended Graduate School ____
   Obtained a graduate degree ____

9. Within the past year, have you taken any courses which count toward a high school, college, or University degree? Yes ____ No ____

10. Total years of Police experience (only municipal, county, state, federal or other public agency):

    Less than 1 ____, 1-3 ____, 4-6 ____, 7-10 ____, 11-15 ____, 16-20____ 21-25 ____ 26 or more ____.

11. Please check the category or categories assignment:

For Police: Patrol ____, Detective ____, Juvenile ____, Training (Staff) ____,
Communications ____, Traffic____, Headquarters ____,
Other (specify) ________________________________.

For Probation: Juvenile Division of Family Court ____
Another division of Family Court ____
Adult Division ____
Other (specify) ____, __________________________

12. Present Rank

For Police: Patrolman ____
Corporal ____
Sergeant ____
Lieutenant ____
Technician ____
Captain ____
Bureau/Division Commander ____
Assistant Chief ____
Chief ____
Other (specify) ____ __________________

For Probation: Caseworker ____
Senior Caseworker ____
Supervisor ____
Other (specify) ____ ____________________

13. Is your work: Supervisory ____, Field Work ____, Administrative but not non-supervision ____, Other (specify) ____ ________________.

14. Organizational Fraternal and Social memberships (e.g. Elks, K of C, PBA etc.) Please list:

Organizational: ____

____

____

Fraternal: ____

____

Social ____

____

____

POLICE PROBATION CONTACT

Instructions: Many of the questions in the following section refer to probation officers. When the word "probation" officer is used, it refers to an individual who is responsible for supervising offenders who have been brought in on an offense, but placed on probation instead of being sent to prison. A "probation" officer is not a parole officer. A parole officer supervises offenders after they have been released from prison.

When we mention the average police or probation officer, we mean the police or probation officer in the community where you work.

15. In your work during the past year, how often did you have contact with probation officers?

None at all ______

Less than once a month ______

Once or twice a month ______

Three or four times a month ______

More than once a week ______

16. In your police experience before the past year, how much contact did you have with probation officers?

N None at all ______

Less than once a month ______

Once or twice a month ______

Three or four times a month ______

More than once a week ______

Had no previous police work ______

17. In your current police work, how many probation officers do you have contact with?

None at all __________

Most of my contacts are with one probation officer __________

Most of my contacts are with two or three probation officers __________

Most of my contacts are with four or more probation officers __________

18. In your police work, what type probation officer do you have most contact with?

For Police:

Probation officer from Adult Division __________

Probation officer from Family Division __________

About 50-50 contact with each __________

No contact with either __________

Other(s), please specify: ______________ __________

In your probation work, what type police officer do you have most contact with?

For Probation:

Juvenile or Youth Division Officer __________

Detective __________

Captain __________

Lieutenant __________

Sergeant __________

Patrolman __________

Other(s), please specify: ______________ __________

19. At what location (s) have most of your contacts with probation officers taken place? (Place an "M" where most contact has occurred. Place a check mark where other contacts have taken place.)

None at all	________
On the street	________
In the police station house	________
In the Family Court	________
In the Adult Court	________
In a Probation Office not located in a criminal court building	________
Over the telephone	________
Other (s), please specify: ____________	________

20. In what kinds of situation (s) have most of your contacts with probation officers occurred? (Place an "M" where most contact has occurred. Place a check mark where other contacts have taken place.)

For Police:

None at all	________
When you were filing a complaint on behalf of another party	________
Filing a complaint when you were the complainant	________
When the probation officer was helping you in a police-related task	________
When you were helping the probation officer in a probation-related task	________
When you and the probation officer were working together to solve a crime	________
Other(s), please specify: ____________	________

For Probation:

None at all ______________

When the police officer was helping you in a probation-related task ______________

When you were helping the police officer in a police-related task ______________

When you and the police officer were working together to solve a crime ______________

Other(s), please specify: ____________________ ______________

11. Outside of your job as a police officer, how many probation officers do you ever have personal contact with?

None ______________

1 or 2 ______________

3-5 ______________

6 or more ______________

22. Considering the amount of contact you now have or last have had with probation officers, do you think that in the future you will have

A lot less contact ______________

Somewhat less contact ______________

About the same contact ______________

A lot more ______________

Instructions: The following statements are matters of opinion. Some of them you may agree with and others you may not agree with. Please indicate the extent to which you agree or disagree with each of the following statements. Use the following numerical scale and after each item circle the appropriate number.

-3	-2	-1	+1	+2	+3
Disagree Very Much	Disagree Pretty Much	Disagree A Little	Agree A Little	Agree Pretty Much	Agree Very Much

	Disagree					Agree
23. The majority of judges have gone too far in protecting rights of criminal offenders.	-3	-2	-1	+1	+2	+3
24. Most of what passes for rehabilitation is a farce and should be replaced with tougher measures	-3	-2	-1	+1	+2	+3
25. Most people think that policemen work at the job they do because they would have a hard time getting another job which pays as much	-3	-2	-1	+1	+2	+3
26. There is a need to reduce conflict between police and probation officers in our area (where you work).	-3	-2	-1	+1	+2	+3
27. The law has been far too lenient in its treatment of conscientious objectors.	-3	-2	-1	+1	+2	+3
28. The death penalty is barbaric, and should be abolished	-3	-2	-1	+1	+2	+3
29. Street demonstrations by homosexual groups such as "gay lib" should be banned as an offense against public moraility.	-3	-2	-1	+1	+2	+3
30. There is a need to improve cooperation between police and and probation officers in our area.	-3	-2	-1	+1	+2	+3
31. It doesn't take anything more than the average intelligence of the man in the street to make a good pro-						

	bation officer.	-3	-2	-1	+1	+2	+3
32.	The right of a citizen to protest against any policy of the U.S. government (be it foreign or domestic) must be vigilantly protected.	-3	-2	-1	+1	+2	+3
33.	On a personal level, police and probation officers generally get along quite well together in our area.	-3	-2	-1	+1	+2	+3
34.	Penalties for smoking marijuana should be increased.	-3	-2	-1	+1	+2	+3
35.	Marriages between persons of different races should be socially acceptable.	-3	-2	-1	+1	+2	+3
36.	It would be desirable to require new policemen to complete two years of college before they are eligible for promotion.	-3	-2	-1	+1	+2	+3
37.	It doesn't take more than the average intelligence of the man in the street to make a good policeman.	-3	-2	-1	+1	+2	+3
38.	Young people should be taught more discipline and respect for authority in the school.	-3	-2	-1	+1	+2	+3
39.	Adults should be allowed to read or see anything they want to in the way of explicit sexual materials.	-3	-2	-1	+1	+2	+3
40.	In the course of carrying out their jobs in our area, probation and police officers seem to have lots of conflicts.	-3	-2	-1	+1	+2	+3

41. Certain religious groups whose beliefs do not permit them to salute the flag should either be forced to conform or else be abolished. -3 -2 -1 +1 +2 +3

42. Most people think that probation officers work at the job they do because they would have a hard time getting another job which pays as much. -3 -2 -1 +1 +2 +3

43. There are very few conflicts existing between the police and probation department in our area. -3 -2 -1 +1 +2 +3

44. Any country which tolerates as much dissent as the U.S. has recently experienced is headed for disaster. -3 -2 -1 +1 +2 +3

45. The action of the National Guard in shooting four Kent State students was a shameful and completely unnecessary response. -3 -2 -1 +1 +2 +3

46. A situation of serious conflict exists between the police and probation department in our area. -3 -2 -1 +1 +2 +3

47. Any demonstrator who makes obscene gestures and remarks at any law enforcement officer deserves to be clubbed. -3 -2 -1 +1 +2 +3

48. Those individuals who openly acknowledge their homosexuality should have the same opportunities for employment and housing as guaranteed by law to other citizens. -3 -2 -1 +1 +2 +3

49. Drawing on my own work experience, I think that in our area there is a great amount of conflict between police and probation officers. -3 -2 -1 +1 +2 +3

SECTION 2. DATA ANALYSIS DESCRIPTION

The following analysis were prepared from the responses to the Phase I questionnaire:

I. Initial Group Rescriptive Statistics

(1) Means $(\overline{x})$, standard deviations (s), and variance (o^2) according to group (i.e. police and probation).

(2) Pearson (r), Kuder Richardson (r_{11}), and rkk (the reliability coefficient of a K item test determined from the intercorrelations of items on the test) tests.

II. Descriptive Statistics

(1) Pearson's (r) correlation analysis for all cells (i.e. cells were constructed according to the various combinations of conflict and contact).

(2) Z Transformation tests of the significance of Pearson (r) correlations for groups and cells.

(3) Means $(\overline{x})$, standard deviations (s), and variances (o^2) according to cell for scaleable items.

(4) Distribution on all items (non-scaleable and scaleable) for groups and cells.

III. Significance Tests for Comparison

Chi Square (X^2) analysis of the distribution of items concerning key points of interests and important variables. Other means of analysis were considered (t tests, multivariate analysis of variance, discriminate function analysis); but it was felt that chi^2 analysis would provide the most complete information within the strictest interpretation of allowable statistical assumptions. Chi^2, however, may be supplemented with t testing to determine with greater statistical sensitivity significant group mean difference.

IV. Factor Analysis

A factorial analysis consisting of a factor loading matrix and a factor score matrix incorporating a varimax rotation procedure was employed by means of a factor loading matrix, one is able to determine whether or not hypothesized scales (conflict, conservative - liberal) actually exist by measuring whether the items hypothesized to fall on that scale actually do. Factor analysis functions, in this study, as a test of the validity of scale hypotheses as well as a test indicator of the reliability of a scale in terms of its internal consistency.

The factor score matrix employed in this study enables the researcher to study the relative contribution of each item to the factor (i.e. the relative weight given to each item for that factor).

While various tests of reliability result in actual numbers representing the degree of internal homogeneity of a scale, alone they are insufficient as a full correlation matrix analysis. Thus, factor analysis was employed in conjuction with inter-item correlation analysis.

SECTION 3. ABSTRACT OF DEMOGRAPHIC AND ATTITUDINAL DATA

The following information is an abstract of the demographic and attitudinal data contained in Appendix A. The Nassau County respondents consist of 550 police officers who are predominantly less educated and more experienced than the 184 probation officers. Thirty-four percent of the police have more than fifteen years experience whereas only seven percent of the probation group has that much experience. The largest age grouping for the police is in the 40-44 age category and for the probation group it lies in the 25-29 age category. Both groups are overwhelmingly white, male, married (averaging 2 to 3 children) and public school educated with a significant minority (over 29% for both groups) having parochial school backgrounds. In the probation department, there is a significant minority (18.5%) of female respondents. Whereas most probation officers have attended graduate school and no longer take courses, most police officers have some college education and are currently taking courses.

On the general conservative attitude dimension, 65.3% of the police scored highly conservatively and 1.7% scored in a high liberal manner. The probation group consisted of a 12.5% conservative and 46.1% liberal constituency. Approximately 15% in both groups estimated some directly perceived conflict to exist with the largest category in each group perceiving the least conflict. Whereas 81% of probation officers have high contact (at work and of a personal nature) with the police, only 17.8% of the police have high contact with probation officers.

The police group consists of a majority of patrolmen with a sizeable number of detectives and probation group consists primarily of low ranking officers. For both groups, most interaction occurs over the telephone. When contact does occur, the primary situation is that of the police helping probation. The majority of officers in both groups are engaged in field work. For the police group, there is no concentrated interaction with the probation department, whereas probation officers have very high contact with police specialists, i.e., juvenile officers, detectives, and lieutenants.

SECTION 4.

GROUP RESPONSES TO PHASE I QUESTIONNAIRE: ANALYSIS BY MEANS OF GROUP MEAN DIFFERENCE (X), STANDARD DEVIATION(S), AND PERCENTAGE DISTRIBUTIONS ON NONE-SCALEABLE ITEMS

	POLICE (N=550)	PROBATION (N=184)
1. AGE	$\overline{x}$ 38.2 yrs.	$\overline{x}$ 37.8 yrs.
under 25	10.7%	8.2%
25-29	16.9%	*31.9%
30-34	15.3%	14.1%
35-39	15.8%	9.8%
40-44	*22.7%	10.3%
45-49	12.5%	10.3%
50 and over	6.0%	15.2%
2. MARITAL STATUS:		
single	8.5%	22.3%
married	*86.7%	*69.6%
divorced or separated	3.3%	6.0%
widowed	1.1%	1.6%
3. SEX:		
male	96.4%	79.9%
female	2.7%	18.5%
4. CHILDREN	$\overline{x}$ 2	$\overline{x}$ 3
5. ETHNIC ORIGIN:		
white	96.2%	89.7%
black	1.3%	6.0%
6. GRAMMER SCHOOL:		
public	*55.8%	*63.6%
parochial	18.0%	18.5%
both	23.6%	10.9%
7. HIGH SCHOOL GRADUATE:		
yes	83.1%	91.8%
no	4.7%	1.1%
Equiv.	11.6%	1.1%

*represents largest category

	POLICE	PROBATION
1. HIGH LEVEL OF EDUCATION:	$\bar{x}$ less than one. year of college	$\bar{x}$ attended Graduate School
less than 8 yrs.	1.5%	1.1%
some High School	5.1%	.5%
H.S. or Equiv. Dip.	21.6%	.9%
less than 1 year of college	27.3%	.5%
1-3 years of college	*41.1%	.0%
4 year College Degree	2.2%	27.2%
Attended graduate school	.9%	*48.4%
Obtained a graduate degree	.0%	21.7%
9. TAKEN COURSES IN PAST YEARS:		
yes	63.3%	31.0%
no	36.4%	66.8%
10. TOTAL YEARS EXPERIENCE:		
	$\bar{x}$ 11-15 yrs.	$\bar{x}$ 4-6 yrs.
less than 1 year	4.2%	6.0%
1-3 years	14.2%	*29.9%
4-6 years	13.5%	28.3%
7-10 years	13.6%	20.7%
11-15 years	20.4%	7.1%
16-20 years	*20.9%	3.3%
21-25 years	11.6%	3.3%
26 or more	1.5%	.5%

11. CATEGORY OF ASSIGNMENT:

POLICE		PROBATION	
Patrol	*59.3%	Adult Division	*45.7%
Detective	26.0%	Juvenile Division	33.2%
Headquarters	8.9%	Other Div. of Family Court	13.6%
Juvenile	2.4%	Other (research and staff,	

POLICE		PROBATION	
Other (plainclothes and clerical)	3.4%	intake, narcotics, court liaison)	6.0%
12. RANK			
Patrolman	*52.5%	Caseworker-P.O.	*45.0%
Detective	23.3%	Senior Case-worker	26.0%
Sergeant	14.7%	Supervisor	15.0%
Lieutenant	5.1%	Other (administrator counselor, consultant, training)	12.0%
13. NATURE OF WORK:			
Field work	*57.1%		*40.2%
Supervisory	22.9%		28.3%
Administrative	16.4%		26.6%
Other (investigation and identification)	3.6%	Other (court liaison, counseling, intake, investigative)	4.9%
14. GROUP MEMBERSHIPS:			
$\overline{x}$	1.4%	$\overline{x}$ 1.9	
15. CONTACT DURING PAST YEAR:			
none at all	*45.8%		8.7%
less than once a month	36.0%		10.3%
once or twice a month	10.5%		17.9%
three or four times a month	4.2%		21.2%
more than once a week	3.1%		*41.8%
x less than once a month		x three or four times a month	
16. CONTACT BEFORE PART YEAR:			
none at all	36.4%		10.3%
less than at present	13.1%		14.7%
about same as present	*33.8%		*47.8%
more than at present	15.8%		23.9%
no previous (police or probation) work	.5%		2.7%

*represents largest category

POLICE		PROBATION	
x same as at present		x same as at present	
17. CONTACT WITH HOW MANY PROBATION OFFICERS:		CONTACT WITH HOW MANY POLICE OFFICERS:	
none at all	*53.8%		15.8%
1	7.1%		7.6%
2-3	22.9%		14.1%
4 or more	15.6%		*59.8%
$\bar{x}$	1	$\bar{x}$	2-3
18. CONTACT WITH TYPE PROBATION OFFICER:		CONTACT WITH TYPE POLICE OFFICER:	
Adult Division	29.1%	Juvenile	35.3%
Family Division	12.01%	Detective	33.7%
50-55	12.0%	Lieutenant	27.2%
Neither	43.6%		
19. CONTACT ACCORDING TO LOCATION:			
none at all	31.6%		4.3%
on the street	4.7%		1.1%
in police station house	12.2%		16.8%
in Family Court	4.4%		19.0%
in Adult Court Probation Office	.5%		1.6%
in a criminal court building	.7%		1.1%
Probation office not located in a criminal court building	.7%		2.7%
Over the telephone	*43.6%		*51.1%
20. CONTACT according to SITUATION:			
none at all	34.9%		5.4%
police helping probation	*33.5%		*73.4%
probation helping police	14.0%		7.6%
working together to solve a crime	3.6%		2.7%
Other (when probation officer needed information,		Other (joing counseling, joint planning, information	

* represents largest category

The following questions were coded as follows:

		x	coded
Disagree Very Much	-3	1	0-1
Disagree Pretty Much	-2	2	1-2
Disagree A Little	-1	3	2-3
Neutral	(+1 -1 or zero response	4	3-4
Agree A Little	+1	5	4-5
Agree Pretty Much	+2	6	5-6
Agree Very Much	+3	7	6-7

POLICE PROBATION

---

23. The majority of judges have gone too far in protecting the rights of criminal offenders.

	police		probation
$\overline{x}$ = Neutral	(3.5)	$\overline{x}$	Agree Pretty Much (5.9)

24. Most of what passes for rehabilitation is a farce and should be replaced with tougher measures.

	police		probation
$\overline{x}$ = Agree A Little	(5.4)	$\overline{x}$	Disagree A Little (3.0)

25. Most people think that policemen work at the job they do because they would have a hard time getting another job which pays as much.

	police		probation
$\overline{x}$ = Disagree A Little	(2.8)	$\overline{x}$	Disagree Pretty Much (2.4)

26. There is a need to reduce conflict between police and probation officers in our area (where you work).

	police		probation
$\overline{x}$ = Disagree A Little	(3.1)	$\overline{x}$	Disagree A Little (3.4)

27. The law has been far too lenient in its treatment of conscientious objectors.

	police		probation
$\overline{x}$ = Agree A Little	(5.0)	$\overline{x}$	Disagree A Little (2.8)

28. The death penalty is barbaric, and should be abolished.

	police		probation
$\bar{x}$ = Disagree Pretty Much	(2.0)	$\bar{x}$	Neutral (4.3)

29. Street demonstrations by homosexual groups such as "gay lib" should be banned as an offense against public morality.

	police		probation
$\bar{x}$ = Agree A Little	(4.5)	$\bar{x}$	Disagree A Little (2.6)

30. There is a need to improve cooperation between police and probation officers in our area.

	police		probation
$\bar{x}$ = Neutral	(3.9)	$\bar{x}$	Neutral (4.2)

31. It doesn't take anything more than the average intelligence of the man in the street to make a good probation officer.

	police		probation
$\bar{x}$ = Disagree A Little	(2.5)	$\bar{x}$	Disagree Pretty Much (1.7)

32. The right of a citizen to protest against any policy of the U. S. government (be it foreign or domestic) must be vigilantly protected.

	police		probation
$\bar{x}$ = Agree A Little	(5.0)	$\bar{x}$	Agree Pretty Much (5.6)

33. On a personal level, police and probation officers generally get along quite well together in our area.

	police		probation
$\bar{x}$ = Agree Pretty Much	(5.5)	$\bar{x}$	Agree Pretty Much (5.9)

34. Penalties for smoking marijuana should be increased.

	police		probation
$\bar{x}$ = Agree A Little	(4.5)	$\bar{x}$	Disagree Pretty Much (2.3)

POLICE	PROBATION

35. Marriages between persons of different races should be socially acceptable.

	police		probation	
$\bar{x}$ = Neutral	(3.9)	$\bar{x}$	Agree Pretty Much	(5.7)

36. It would be desirable to require new policemen to complete two years of college before they are eligible for promotion.

	police		probation	
$\bar{x}$ = Neutral	(3.8)	$\bar{x}$	Agree Pretty Much	(5.6)

37. It doesn't take more than the average intelligence of the man in the street to make a good policeman.

	police		probation	
$\bar{x}$ = Disagree Pretty Much	(2.5)	$\bar{x}$	Disagree Pretty Much	(2.4)

38. Young people should be taught more discipline and respect for authority in the school.

	police		probation	
$\bar{x}$ = Agree Pretty Much	(6.3)	$\bar{x}$	Agree A Little	(5.1)

39. Adults should be allowed to read or see anything they want to in the way of explicit sexual materials.

	police		probation	
$\bar{x}$ = Neutral	(4.2)	$\bar{x}$	Agree Pretty Much	(5.5)

40. In the course of carrying out their jobs in our area, probation and police officers seem to have lots of conflicts.

	police		probation	
$\bar{x}$ = Disagree A Little	(2.8)	$\bar{x}$	Disagree Pretty Much	(2.4)

41. Certain religious groups whose beliefs do not permit them to salute the flag should either be forced to conform or else be abolished.

	police		probation	
$\bar{x}$ = Disagree A Little	(2.9)	$\bar{x}$	Disagree Pretty Much	(1.8)

POLICE	PROBATION

42. Most people think that probation officers work at the job they do because they would have a hard time getting another job which pays as much.

	police		probation
$\bar{x}$ = Disagree A Little	(2.5)	$\bar{x}$	Disagree Pretty Much (2.1)

43. There are very few conflicts existing between the police and probation department in our area.

	police		probation
x = Agree A Little	(5.1)	$\bar{x}$	Agree A Little (5.3)

44. Any country which tolerates as much dissent as the U.S. has recently experienced is headed for disaster.

	police		probation
$\bar{x}$ = Neutral	(4.3)	$\bar{x}$	Disagree Pretty Much (2.4)

45. The action of the National Guard in shooting four Kent State students was a shameful and completely unnecessary response.

	police		probation
$\bar{x}$ = Disagree A Little	(2.6)	$\bar{x}$	Agree A Little (4.5)

46. A situation of serious conflict exists between the police and probation department in our area.

	police		probation
$\bar{x}$ = Disagree Pretty Much	(2.2)	$\bar{x}$	Disagree Pretty Much (1.7)

47. Any demonstrator who makes obscene gestures and remarks at any law enforcement officer deserves to be clubbed.

	police		probation
$\bar{x}$ = Disagree A Little	(2.8)	$\bar{x}$	Disagree Pretty Much (2.0)

48. Those individuals who openly acknowledge their homosexuality should have the same opportunities for employment and housing as guaranteed by law to other citizens.

	police		probation
$\bar{x}$ = Neutral	(4.2)	$\bar{x}$	Agree Pretty Much (5.7)

49. Drawing on my own work experience, I think that in our area there is a great amount of conflict between police and probation officers.

	police		probation
$\bar{x}$ = Disagree Pretty Much	(2.1)	$\bar{x}$	Disagree Pretty Much (1.7)

SECTION 5.

OPERATIONAL CONFLICT SCALE, POLICE-PROBATION DISTRIBUTION, (TABLE 1) AND FACTOR (TABLE 2 & 3) ANALYSIS

Directly Perceived Conflict Scale

26. There is a need to reduce conflict between police and probation officers in our area (where you work).

30. There is a need to improve cooperation between police and probation officers in our area.

33. On a personal level, police and probation officers generally get along quite well together in our area.

40. In the course of carrying out their jobs in our area, probation and police officers seem to have lots of conflicts.

43. There are very few conflicts existing between the police and probation department in our area.

46. A situation of serious conflict exists between the police and probation department in our area.

49. Drawing on my own work experience, I think that in our area there is a great amount of conflict between police and probation officers.

*rkk reliability is .81 for police and .87 for probation

TABLE 1

POLICE AND PROBATION DISTRIBUTION ON CONFLICT SCALE

Respondents from Nassau Count	-3 Disagree Very Much	-2 Disagree Pretty Much	-1 Disagree A Little	+1 Agree A Little	+2 Agree Pretty Much	+3 Agree Very Much
Police						
(by number)	161	156	152	62	11	8
(by percentage)	29.3	28.4	27.6	11.3	2.0	1.5
Probation						
(by number	67	55	34	21	5	2
(by percentage)	36.4	29.9	18.5	11.4	2.7	1.1

Police n = 550
Probation n = 184

CONFLICT (numerically)

	HIGH	LOW
Police	81	161
Probation	28	67

CONFLICT (by percentage)

	HIGH	LOW
Police	14.8	29.3
Probation	15.2	36.4

High = +1, +2, +3
Low = -3

FACTORIAL ANALYSIS INCORPORATING A VARIMAX ROTATION PROCEDURE

TABLE 2. FACTOR LOADING MATRIX

	Police	Probation
(26)	.655	.748
(30)	.652	.717
(33)	.505	.738
(40)	.700	.785
(43)	.640	.837
(46)	.741	.644
(49)	.737	.736

TABLE 3. FACTOR SCORE MATRIX (I.E. WEIGHTING OF THE ITEMS WITH THE FACTOR)

	Police	Probation
(26)	.22	.18
(30)	.25	.19
(33)	.14	.17
(40)	.23	.18
(43)	.21	.19
(46)	.21	.15
(49)	.21	.17

SECTION 6.

CONTACT VARIABLE AND POLICE - PROBATION DISTRIBUTION (TABLE 4)

TABLE 4. POLICE AND PROBATION DISTRIBUTION ON CONTACT VARIANCE

CONTACT ITEM

15. In your work during the past year, how often did you have contact with police officers?

Respondents from Nassau County	None at all	Less than once a mo.	Once or twice a month	Three or four times a month	More than once a month
Police					
(by percentage)	46.2	36.0	10.5	4.2	3.1
(by number	254	198	58	23	18
Probation					
(by percentage)	8.7	10.3	17.9	21.2	41.8
(by number	16	19	33	39	77

Police n = 550
Probation n = 184

CONTACT (numerically)

	HIGH	LOW
Police	98	452
Probation	149	35

CONTACT (by percentage)

	HIGH	LOW
Police	17.8	82.2
Probation	81.0	19.0

Low = None at all
Less than once a month
High = Once or twice a month
Three or four times a month
More than once a week

Section 7:

CONSERVATIVE - LIBERAL QUESTIONS AND CONSERVATIVE SCALE, POLICE-PROBATION DISTRIBUTION ON THE SCALE (TABLE 5), POLICE - PROBATION DISTRIBUTION ON SAMPLE LIBERAL QUESTIONS (TABLE 6), GROUP MEAN RESPONSES FOR CONSERVATIVE - LIBERAL ITEMS (TABLE 7), PEARSON'S r CORRELATION ANALYSIS OF CONSERVATIVE - LIBERAL QUESTIONS FOR BOTH GROUPS (TABLE 8).

CONSERVATIVE - LIBERAL QUESTIONS

Conservative Questions

* 23. The majority of judges have gone too far in protecting rights of criminal offenders.

* 24. Most of what passes for rehabilitation is a farce and should be replaced with tougher measures.

* 27. The law has been far too lenient in its treatment of conscientious objectors.

29. Street demonstrations by homosexual groups such as "gay lib" should be banned as an offense against public morality.

* 34. Penalties for smoking marijuana should be increased.

* 38. Young people should be taught more discipline and respect for authority in the school.

41. Certain religious groups whose beliefs do not permit them to salute the flag.
should either be forced to conform or else be abolished.

* 44. Any country which tolerates as much dissent as the U.S. has recently experienced is headed for disaster.

Liberal Questions

28. The death penalty is barbaric, and should be abolished .

32. The right of a citizen to protest against any policy of the U.S. government (be it foreign or domestic) must be vigilantly protected.

35. Marriages between persons of different races should be socially acceptable.

39. Adults should be allowed to read or see anything they want to in the way of explicit sexual materials.

* 45. The action of the National Guard in shooting four Kent State students was a shameful and a completely unnecessary response.

48. Those individuals who openly acknowledge their homosexuality should have the same opportunities for employment and housing as guaratneed by law to other citizens.

---

* represents questions that form a general conservative scale for both police and probation groups. rkk reliability is .69 for police and .81 for probation.

TABLE 5.

POLICE-PROBATION DISTRIBUTION ON THE GENERAL CONSERVATIVE SCALE

rESPONDENTS FROM Nassau County	HIGHLY LIBERAL RESPONSES			HIGHLY CONSERVATIVE RESPONSES		
	-3 Disagree Very Much	-2 Disagree Pretty Much	-1 Disagree A Little	+1 Agree A Little	+2 Agree Pretty Much	+3 Agree Very Much
Police						
(by number)	1	8	59	123	189	170
(by percentage)	.2	1.5	10.7	22.4	34.4	30.9
Probation						
(by number)	33	52	44	32	20	3
(by percentage)	17.9	28.3	23.9	17.4	10.9	1.6

Police n = 550
Probation n = 184

Group Percentages of High Conservative and High Liberal Responses

	HIGH Conservative %	HIGH Liberal %
Police	65.3%	1.7%
Probation	12.5%	46.1

TABLE 6.
POLICE-PROBATION DISTRIBUTION ON SAMPLE LIBERAL QUESTIONS

Respondents from Nassau County	Ques No.	-3 Disagree Very Much	-2 Disagree Pretty Much	-1 Disagree A Little	0 Neutral	+1 Agree A Little Much	+2 Agree Pretty Much	+3 Agree Very Much
Police	35.	20.2	10.4	15.1	2.5	26.0	12.0	13.8
Probation		3.3	5.4	5.4	1.6	20.7	17.4	46.2
Police	39.	14.9	12.4	17.3	.9	19.1	16.1	18.7
Probation		4.9	7.6	10.3	2.2	14.1	13.6	47.3
Police	48.	13.8	10.9	15.3	2.2	25.5	16.4	16.0
Probation		5.4	.5	6.5	2.2	17.9	24,5	42.9

TABLE 7. GROUP MEAN RESPONSES FOR CONSERVATIVE-LIBERAL ITEMS

-3 Disagree Very Much	-2 Disagree Pretty Much	-1 Disagree A Little	0 Neutral	+1 Agree A Little	+2 Agree Pretty Much	+3 Agree Very Much
0-1	1-2	2-3	3-4	4-5	5-6	6-7

Respondents from Nassau County	Conservative Items $\overline{x}$	Liberal Items $\overline{x}$
Police	Agree a little 4.9	Neutral 3.7
Probation	Disagree a little 2.9	Agree Pretty Much 5.2

TABLE 8.

PEARSON'S (r) INTER-ITEM CORRELATION ANALYSIS OF THE CONSERVATIVE LIBERAL QUESTIONS FOR THE POLICE AND PROBATION GROUPS

Respondents from Nassau County	Conservative Itmes with conservative items	Liberal Items with liberal items	Liberal items with conservative items
Police	.228	.164	.131
Probation	.338	.315	.291

APPENDIX C

FINAL QUESTIONNAIRE

TABLE OF CONTENTS

APPENDIX C

SECTION 1.

FINAL INSTRUMENT

CRIMINAL JUSTICE SURVEY

Administered by Ted Ryan

This questionnaire is onc phase of a national study and your answers will constitute an important part of this total national picture. Your cooperation in answering all questions will be greatly appreciated. Please take as much time as you need to answer carefully the survey.

Request: I would appreciate your name in order to enable me to more exactly sample (according to high and low contact respondents) at a later date.

Your Name: ____
(Please print)

DEMOGRAPHIC VARIABLES FOR FINAL INSTRUMENT

1. AGE: Under 25 ____, 25-29 ____, 30-34 ____, 35-39 ____, 40-44 ____, 45-49 ____, 50 and over ____.

2. ETHNIC ORIGIN: White ____, Negro or Black ____, Spanish-American ____, Other (specify) ____, ______________________________.

3. RELIGION: Protestant ____, Catholic ____, Jewish ____, None ____. Other (specify) ____, ______________________________.

4. What is the highest level of education which you have attained?

   less than 8 years ____
   some high school ____
   high school or equivalency diploma ____
   less than 1 year of college ____
   1-3 years college degree ____
   4 year college degree ____
   attended graduate school ____
   obtained a graduate degree ____

5. Within the past year, have you taken any job related courses?

   Yes ____ No ____

6. What type offender do you most often come in contact with?

   White ____, Negro or Black ____, Spanish-American ____,
   No particular type ____, Other (specify)____, __________________.

7. To me, the most important part of my job is:

   performing community services ____
   enforcing the law ____
   Other (specify) ____, ____________________.

8. Total years of police or probation service experience (only municipal, county, state, federal or other public agency):

   less than 1 ____, 1-3 ____, 4-6 ____, 7-10 ____, 11-15 ____, 16-20 ____, 21-25 ____, 26 or more ____.

9. Specialized unit of assignment: (Check one if it applies to you).

(Police) narcotics ____
morals-vice ____
Other (specify) ______

(Probation) none ____
intake ____
research and staff ____
Other (specify) ______

10. (Police) Category of assignment (if you are a patrolman or a detective assigned to juvenile (youth division) work, or a headquarters assignment, check only that assignment and not the patrol or detective lines.

Check one:

patrol ____, detective ____, juvenile ____, headquarters ____,
Other (specify) ____, ____________________.

(Probation) Category of assignment:

Juvenile Division of Family Court ____
Another Division of Family Court ____
Adult Division ____
Other (specify) ____, ____________________.

11. (Police) Present Rank:

Patrolman ____
Detective (investigator) ____
Corporal ____
Sergeant ____
Detective Sergeant ____
Lieutenant ____
Detective Lieutenant ____
Administrator (Captain or above) ____

(Probation) Present Position:

Probation officer trainee ____
Permanent probation officer ____
Senior probation officer ____
Supervisor ____
Principal probation officer (senior supervisor) ____
Probation administrator or above ____

12. Nature of work:

Supervisory ____, Field work ____, Administrative but non-supervision____.

POLICE-PROBATION CONTRACT VARIABLES FOR FINAL INSTRUMENT

Instructions: (for police) Many of the questions in the following section refer to probation officers. When the word "probation" officer is used, it refers to an individual who is responsible for supervising offenders who have been brought in on an offense, but placed on probation instead of being sent to prison. A "probation" officer is not a parole officer. A parole officer supervises offenders after they have been released from prison.

When we mention the average police or probation officer, we mean the police or probation officer in the community where you work.

13. (Police) In your work during the past year, how often did you have contact with probation officers?

(Probation) In your work during the past year, how often did you have contact with police officers?

None at all ____
Less than once a month ____
Once or twice a month ____
Three or four times a month ____
More than once a week ____

14. (Police) In your current police work, how many probation officers do you have contact with?

(Probation) In your current probation work, how many police officers do you have contact with?

None at all ____
One ____
Two or three ____
Four or more ____

15. (Police) In your police work, what type probation officer do you have the most contact with?

Probation officer from Adulty Division ____
Probation officer from Family Division ____
About 50-60 contact with each ____
On the street ____

(Probation) In your probation work, what type police officer do you have most contact with?

Juvenile or Youth Division Officer ____
Detective ____
Lieutenant ____
Patrolman ____
Other (specify) ____, ________________.

16. (Police) At what location(s) have most of your contacts with probation officers taken place?

None at all ____
On the street ____
In the police station house ____
In the Family Court ____
In a probation office ____
Over the telephone ____
Other (s), please specify ____, ____________________.

17. (Police) In what kinds of situation(s) have most of your contacts with probation officers occurred?

None at all ____
When you were helping the probation officer in a probation-related task ____
When the probation officer was helping you in a police-related task ____
When you and the probation officer were working together to solve a crime ____
Information verification ____
Other (s), please specify ____ ______________________.

18. (Police) Outside of your job as a police officer, how many probation officers do you ever have personal contact with?

(Probation) Outside of your job as a probation officer, how many police officers do you ever have personal contact with?

None ____
1 or 2 ____
3-5 ____
6 or more ____

19. Jones admits drinking excessively for several days, but denies possessing or using drugs. He states he did not know of the prior arrest of Brown. The police admit they cannot prove the narcotics charge and ask the probation office to recommend revocation of probation for Jones on the basis of violation of probation rule for association and drinking.

My opinion about the police request is:

	1 Strongly agree	2 Somewhat agree	3 Slightly agree	4 Slightly Disagree	5 Somewhat Disagree	6 Strongly Disagree
My opinion:						
Police opinion:						
Probation opinion:						

20. The legislature is considering new penal and criminal law revisions. One proposal is for the police department to be given the right to make recommendations directly to the court on whether individuals should be granted probation or not. The probation department opposes this proposal, contending that recommendations should be made only on the basis of a balanced weighing of all the facts by professionally trained probation staff. The police department argues that the probation department should continue to submit their reports, but that it should be able also to make its views known directly to the sentencing judge.

My opinion about the police request is:

	1 Strongly agree	2 Somewhat agree	3 Slightly agree	4 Slightly Disagree	5 Somewhat Disagree	6 Strongly Disagree
My opinion:						
Police opinion:						
Probation opinion:						

21. The probation department is starting a new program of working with offenders in groups and gangs. In order for the program to be effective, the probation department argues that youths will have to learn to trust the probation officers. Gang members will be told that anything the probation officers learn will be held in strictest confidence. The police contend information about illegal acts should not be withheld by the probation department. The probation department argues that it is important for them to be able to work with the youthful gangs and to withhold such information. The police contend it must be shared.

My opinion about the police department's view is:

	1 Strongly agree	2 Somewhat agree	3 Slightly agree	4 Slightly Disagree	5 Somewhat Disagree	6 Strongly Disagree
My opinion:						
Police opinion:						
Probation opinion:						

22. Police Officer Phelps is working on a forgery case. He has some leads which indicate that Harry Kelp, a probationer may be involved. Phelps asked Probation Officer Garrison if he could read the file of Kelp to see if there is any information in his background which may help him settle this case. The probation officer says he is willing to tell Phelps anything if he will let him know what kind of information he wants. Phelps contends that he is not sure of the kind of information he needs and it would be helpful if he could read the file without having it screened first by Probation Officer Garrison. Garrison refuses to turn the file over for Officer Phelps' inspection, stating that certain information is not relevant and should not be made available.

My opinion about the probation officer's action is:

	1 Strongly agree	2 Somewhat agree	3 Slightly agree	4 Slightly Disagree	5 Somewhat Disagree	6 Strongly Disagree
My opinion:						
Police opinion:						
Probation opinion:						

23. The police Department asked the Adult Probation Department to provide them with an up-to-date list including an address, some background information and a photograph of everyone placed on probation. The purpose is to let selective policemen, especially detectives, know who is on probation in various areas of the city in the event of the commission of a crime. The Probation Department says it will be glad to give information to police on specific individuals but are opposed to giving the Police Department such a blanket list. It contends that it is unfair to the offender and could lead to unnecessary harassment.

My opinion about the probation department's position is:

	1 Strongly agree	2 Somewhat agree	3 Slightly agree	4 Slightly Disagree	5 Somewhat Disagree	6 Strongly Disagree
My opinion:						
Police opinion:						
Probation opinion:						

24. The police department has arrested John Jones at the scene of an assualt on an elderly man who was struck from behind. Jones has a prior record of assault and is on probation for manslaughter. No one had a direct view of the assailant. Jones was picked up within a few minutes of the assault in the next block running away. The police contend that they need time to find persons who might have witnessed the assault. They ask the probation department to place a "hold" on the defendant so he will be held in custody until the investigation is completed. The probation department contends that there are no known violations of probation against this man and refuse to place a hold against him.

My opinion about the probation department's action is:

	1 Strongly agree	2 Somewhat agree	3 Slightly agree	4 Slightly Disagree	5 Somewhat Disagree	6 Strongly Disagree
My opinion:						
Police opinion:						
Probation opinion:						

25. Ernie, age 16, is brought in by the police and charged with assault with a deadly weapon. According to the officer, he and two friends crashed a party, disrupted the proceedings by bullying and making insulting advances towards girls. In the ensuing fight, Ernie used a broken coke bottle to seriously gash the host's arm. Ernie insists that he was invited to the party and did nothing objectional there. He justified the use of the weapon by the fact that five boys jumped him because he was "making out" with the girls.

Eight months ago, Ernie and the same two friends were placed on probation after they stole a car to drive to a party. Progress reports indicate very satisfactory improvement. He has avoided further difficulty, reenrolled in school and maintained a passing grade while working part-time in a gas station. The police insist that Ernie be held in detention until his case is heard before the juvenile court judge two days later. The probation department released him the same evening instructing him to return for the hearing.

My opinion about the probation department's action is:

	1 Strongly agree	2 Somewhat agree	3 Slightly agree	4 Slightly Disagree	5 Somewhat Disagree	6 Strongly Disagree
My opinion:						
Police opinion:						
Probation opinion:						

26. When a probationer violates any of the conditions of his probation, the police department is asked by the probation department to put him in custody for a review of his case by the court. This review may result in continuance or probation or commitment to an institution. The Police Department argues that if the probation has committed new violations of the law they will arrest him. Otherwise, the probation department should have the responsibility for taking persons into custody who are simply charged with violation or probation rules. The Probation Department argues that arrest is a police function, and they should not be required to arrest probationers. The Police Department refuses.

My opinion about the police department's position is:

	1 Strongly agree	2 Somewhat agree	3 Slightly agree	4 Slightly Disagree	5 Somewhat Disagree	6 Strongly Disagree
My opinion:						
Police opinion:						
Probation opinion:						

27. The police department has been trying to make an important narcotics arrest in the local community. Joe Jones, probationer, tells his probation officer that he has been asked to act as an informer. In order for him to do it, it would be necessary to hang out in taverns, associate with narcotics and be in touch with those who traffic in narcotics. A telephone call from Captain Jensen of the Police Department confirms the request. The probation officer tells Jones and Captain Jensen that the conditions of Jones' probation forbid him to associate with narcotics users and to hang out in taverns. Even though he is acting as an informer for the police department, he will be given no protection. Revocation of probation will follow for violations of the rules.

My opinion about the probation department's position is:

	1 Strongly agree	2 Somewhat agree	3 Slightly agree	4 Slightly Disagree	5 Somewhat Disagree	6 Strongly Disagree
My opinion:						
Police opinion:						
Probation opinion:						

28. The police department tells the Probation Officer that Frank O'Neill, a probationer, is suspected of possessing stolen goods obtained from a burglary. The police do not have enough information presently to secure a search warrant, but urge the Probation Department to issue a warrant for investigation of probation violation so that a search might take place. The Probation Department argues that their policy does not permit them to arrest probationers under these circumstances. The Police Department argues that the probationer has violated his

probation on several occasions by drinking and this could be used as a basis for arresting a probationer. Material from the burglary could be found during a valid search. The Probation Department refuses.

My opinion about the probation department's position is:

	1 Strongly agree	2 Somewhat agree	3 Slightly agree	4 Slightly Disagree	5 Somewhat Disagree	6 Strongly Disagree
My opinion:						
Police opinion:						
Probation opinion:						

Instructions: The following statements are matters of opinion. Some of them you may agree with and others you may not agree with. Please indicate the extent to which you agree or disagree with each of the following statements. Use the following numerical scale and after each item circle the appropriate number.

1	2	3	4	5	6
Strongly agree	Somewhat agree	Slightly agree	Slightly Disagree	Somewhat Disagree	Strongly Disagree

	Agree	Disagree
29. It's a good idea for prisoners to have their own union.	1 2 3	4 5 6
30. We need to have stricter penalties in order to enforce our laws.	1 2 3	4 5 6
31. Most criminals need treatment programs - not punishment.	1 2 3	4 5 6
32. There is a need to reduce conflict between police and probation officers in our area (where you work)	1 2 3	4 5 6
33. Most people think that policemen work at the job they do because they would have a hard time getting another job which pays as much.	1 2 3	4 5 6

34.	The death penalty constitutes cruel and unusual punishment.	1 2 3 4 5 6
35.	It should be necessary to prove that a confession is voluntary in order to have it admitted into evidence.	1 2 3 4 5 6
36.	There are very few conflicts existing between the police and probation department in our area.	1 2 3 4 5 6
37.	Too much permissiveness is helping to destroy this country.	1 2 3 4 5 6
38.	Interracial dating should be socially acceptable.	1 2 3 4 5 6
39.	It doesn't take anything more than the average intelligence of the man in the street to make a good probation officer.	1 2 3 4 5 6
40.	There is a need to improve cooperation between police and probation officers in our area.	1 2 3 4 5 6
41.	The law has been far too lenient in its treatment of conscientious objectors.	1 2 3 4 5 6
42.	The rights of Black Muslims must be as vigilantly protected as the rights of any other religious group.	1 2 3 4 5 6
43.	Any demonstrator who makes obsence gestures and remarks at a law enforcement officer deserves to be clubbed.	1 2 3 4 5 6
44.	A situation of serious conflict exists between the police and probation department in our area.	1 2 3 4 5 6
45.	Those individuals who openly acknowledge their homosexuality should have the same opportunities for employment and housing as guaranteed by law to other citizens.	1 2 3 4 5 6
46.	It doesn't take more than the average intelligence of the man in the street to make a good policeman.	1 2 3 4 5 6
47.	On a personal level, police and probation officers generally get along quite well together in our area.	1 2 3 4 5 6

48.	The approach taken by the authorities in the Attica disturbance indicated a gross disregard for human life.	1	2	3	4	5	6
49.	Most of what passes for rehabilitation is too soft and should be replaced with tougher measures.	1	2	3	4	5	6
50.	The action of the National Guard in shooting four Kent State students was a shameful and completely unnecessary response.	1	2	3	4	5	6
51.	The Minister who married two homosexuals ought to be barred from the ministry.	1	2	3	4	5	6
52.	Most people think that probation officers work at the job they do because they would have a hard time getting another job which pays as much.	1	2	3	4	5	6
53.	In the course of carrying out their jobs in our area, probation and police officers seem to have lots of conflict.	1	2	3	4	5	6
54.	The police should be allowed to detain any person who they have reasonable cause to believe may commit a serious crime.	1	2	3	4	5	6
55.	In order to deal more effectively with the crime problem, we should use more chain gang techniques in our correctional approaches.	1	2	3	4	5	6
56.	The police should not have to be bothered with going through the process of getting search warrants.	1	2	3	4	5	6
57.	Drawing on my own work experience, I think that in our area there is a great amount of conflict between police and probation officers.	1	2	3	4	5	6

APPENDIX C

SECTION 2.

CODING, SCORE RANGES AND INTERPRETATIONS, AND GROUPINGS

A. Grouping

Table 1 (on page 17 and 18)

B. Coding

Table 2 Coding

Items 13, 14, 18 Operational Conflict Scale and Attitudinal Variables

1.	Item 13.	In your work during the past year, how often did you have contact with (police or probation) officers?	
	Coding	1. None at all 2. Less than once a month	Low
		3. Once or twice a month 4. Three or four times a month	Medium
		5. More than once a week	High
2.	Item 14.	In your current police (probation) work, how many probation (police) officers do you have contact with?	
		1. None at all	Low
		2. One	Medium
		3. Two or three 4. Four or more	High

3. Item 18. Outside of your job as a police (probation) officer, how many probation (police) officers do you ever have personal contact with?

1. None	Low
2. One or two	Middle
3. Three to five	
4. Six or more	High

4. Operational Conflict Scale: Items 32, 36, 40, 44, 47, 53, 57.

Coding		
	1. Disagree very much	
	2. Disagree pretty much	Low
	3. Disagree a little	
	4. Neutral	Middle
	5. Agree a little	
	6. Agree pretty much	High
	7. Agree very much	

5. Attitudinal Variables and status and esteem items were computed above and below the midpoint, 4.0, split.

6. Orginization-Perceptual Scales (the Police Prerogative Scale and Probation Autonomy Scale) were computed with an above and below the midpoint, 3.5, split.

C. Score Ranges and Interpretations

Table 3

GROUPING

TABLE 1

DEMOGRAPHIC VARIABLES AND GROUPING USED FOR STATISTICAL ANALYSIS

	POLICE GROUPING						PROBATION GROUPING					
ITEM	1	2	3	4	5	6	1	2	3	4	5	6
1. Age	Under 30	30-44 45	over				Same	as	Police			
2. Ethnic Group	White	Black	Spanish American				"	"	"			
3. Religion	Cath-olic	Cath-olic	Jewish	None			"	"	"			
4. Educa-tion	H.S.or less	Some College	4 yr. degree or grad.				less than 4 yr degree	4 yr. degree	Grad.			
5. Taking Job Re-lated Courses	Yes	No					Same	as	Police			
6. Type Offender Contact	White	Black	Spanish American				Same	as	Police			
7. Job Percep-tion	Comm. service	Enfor-cing Law	Both				Same	as	Police			
8. Years Exper-ience	Less than 6	7-15	more than 16				Same	as	Police			
9. Special-ized Assign-ment	Nar-cotics	Morals-Vice	Other				None	Nar-cotics	Intake	Res-earch		

TABLE 1 (contiued)

ITEM	POLICE GROUPING 1	2	3	4	5	6	PROBATION GROUPING 1	2	3	4	5	6
10. Category of assignment	Patrol	Detective	Juvenile	H.Q.			Juvenile	Another Div. of Family Crt	Adult			
11. Rank	Patrolman Detective Corporal	Sergeant Detective Sergeant	Lieutenant or above				Trainee or Permanent P.O.	Senior P.O. Supervisor	Principal P.O. Administrator			
12. Nature of work	Supervisory	Field work	Administrative				Same	as	Police			
13. Amount of Contact	None or less than 1/mo.	1-4 per mo.	more than 1/ week				Same	as	Police			
14. Number of People Contact	None	1	More than 1				Same	as	Police			
15. Type Person in Contact	Adult Division PO	Family Division PO	Half with each	None			Jevenile Officer	Detective	Lieutenant	Patrolman		
16. Contact Location	None	Street House	Police Station	Family Court	Probation Office	Telephone	same	as	Police			
17. Contact Situations	None	Probation Task	Police Task	Solve Crime	Information ver.		same	as	Police			
18. Personal Contact	None	1 or 2	More than 2				same	as	Police			

TABLE 3

SCORE RANGES AND INTERPRETATION

Variable	Questionnaire (Items)	Possible Range of Score	Meaning of Low Score
Operational Conflict	32, 36, 40, 44 47, 53, 57	7 - 49	SUBJECT feels a high degree of police-probation conflict exist in his area
Conservative I	30, 35, 42, 49, 56 31, 37, 43, 50, 53	10-70	SUBJECT favors stricter legal penalties for crimes than now exist
Conservative II	29, 34, 41, 48, 54	5-35	SUBJECT takes a liberal stand on human rights issues
Conservative III	38, 45, 51	3-21	SUBJECT takes a liberal stand on sex related social issues
Police Status	33	1-7	SUBJECT attributes low status to police
Probation Esteem	39	1-7	SUBJECT holds probation officers in low esteem
Police Esteem	46	1-7	SUBJECT holds police officers in low esteem
Probation Status	52	1-7	SUBJECT attributes low status to probation officers
Police Orientation	19-28	0-50	Absolute difference between 1 and 2 across 10 items. Low score means organizational police orientation and high score means disagreement with police department

TABLE 3 (continued)

Probation Orientation	19-28	0-50	Absolute difference between 1 and 2 across 10 items. Low score means organizational probation orientation and high score means disagreement with probation department.
Perceptual Conflict	19-28	0-50	Absolute difference between 2 and 3 across 10 items.

APPENDIX C

SECTION 3.

RELIABILITY ESTIMATES

Spearman Brown reliability estimates (N 1,457)

Operational Conflict Scale (Questions 32, 36, 40, 44, 47, 53 and 57).	.89
Conservatism I (political Legal) Scale (Questions 30, 35, 42, 49, 56, 31, 37, 43, 50 and 55).	.85
Conservatism II (Social Control) Scale (Questions 29, 34, 41, 48 and 54).	.79
Conservatism III (Sexual) Scale (Questions 38, 45 and 51).	.70
Police Preogative Scale (Questions 19, 20, 21 and 26)	.79
Probation Autonomy Scale (Questions 22, 23, 24 and 28).	.78

Chronbach Alpha reliability estimates of operational conflict scale:

Nassau County, New York	
Police (N 598)	.87
Probation (N 216)	.95
Albuquerque, New Mexico	
Police (N 180)	.96
Probation (N 145)	.86

SECTION 4.

FACTOR COMPOSITION OF RESPONSES TO VIGNETTES BASED ON ACTUAL RESPONSES, SIX AGENCIES

POLICE

ITEM NUMBER	NASSAU POLICE FACTORS (N=598)		ALBUQUERQUE POLICE FACTORS (N=180)		SAN JOSE POLICE FACTORS (N=286)	
	I.	II.	I.	II.	I.	II.
19.*	.088	.597*	.284	.460*	.642*	.110
20.*	.165	.587*	.367	.496*	.509*	.143
21.*	.070	.433*	.234	.665*	.483*	.031
22.**	.510**	.067	.347**	.076	.131	.504**
23.**	.526**	.137	.359**	-.077	.233	.586**
24.**	.399**	.003	.397**	.031	.279	.398**
25.	.323	-.018	.264	-.030	.085	.380
26.*	-.110	.267*	-.155	.287*	.054*	-.091
27.	.387	-.018	.381	.074	.329	.170
28.**	.460**	.086	.552**	.155	.373	.474**

PROBATION

ITEM NUMBER	NASSAU POLICE FACTORS (N=216)		ALBUQUERQUE POLICE FACTORS (N=32)		SAN JOSE POLICE FACTORS (N=145)	
	I.	II.	I.	II.	I.	II.
19.*	.370*	.164	.524*	-.003	.433*	.234
20.*	.295*	.185	.505*	.063	.463*	-.002
21.*	.279*	.216	.724*	-.063	.523*	.105
22.**	.090	.669**	.568	.454**	.086	.475**
23.**	.450	.453**	.419	.472**	.118	.581**
24.**	.140	.371**	-.144	.658**	-.041	.371**
25.	.564	.008	.658	.263	.516	.074
26.*	.026*	.138	.535*	.092	.309*	-.423
27.	.067	.197	.076	.804	-.414	.250
28.**	.647	.133*	.515	.520**	.151	.386**

NOTES: A single asterisk identifies an item comprising the Police Prerogative Scale.

A double asterisk identifies an item comprising the Probation Autonomy Scale.

SECTION 5.

FACTOR COMPOSITION OF RESPONSES TO VIGNETTES BASED ON PERCEPTION OF POLICE RESPONSE, SIX AGENCIES

POLICE

ITEM NUMBER	NASSAU POLICE FACTORS (N=598)		ALBUQUERQUE POLICE FACTORS (N=180)		SAN JOSE POLICE FACTORS (N=286)	
	I.	II.	I.	II.	I.	II.
19.*	.120	.559*	.145	.638*	.200	.379*
20.*	.174	.496*	.204	.566*	.181	.346*
21.*	.031	.443*	-.158	.490*	.181	.438*
22.**	.537**	.025	.359**	-.056	.496**	-.037
23.**	.597**	.123	.365**	-.042	.530**	.213
24.**	.526**	.021	.518**	-.023	.528	.137
25.	.387	-.080	.378	-.189	.343	.227
26.*	-.108	.380*	-.095	.274*	.005	-.125*
27.	.345	.358	.355	.054	.115	.372
28.	.452**	.114	.610**	.149	.504**	.205

PROBATION

ITEM NUMBER	NASSAU POLICE FACTORS (N=216)		ALBUQUERQUE POLICE FACTORS (N=32)		SAN JOSE POLICE FACTORS (N=145)	
	I.	II.	I.	II.	I.	II.
19.*	.207	.388*	.284	-.217	.260	.480*
20.*	.176	.453*	-.425	.100*	.158	.596*
21.*	.007	.372*	.057	-.285*	.018	.373*
22.**	.689**	.046	.689**	-.060	.453**	.128
23.**	.559**	-.005	.667**	.183	.764**	-.043
24.**	.529**	.194	.622**	.316	.471**	.345
25.	.303	.170	.867	.280	.268	.492
26.*	.049	.145*	.518	-.485*	-.049	.218*
27.	.011	.225	.166	.671	.287	.006
28.**	.442**	.329	.434**	.672	.327**	.092

NOTES: A single asterisk identifies an item comprising the Police Prerogative Scale. A double asterisk identifies an item comprising the Probation Autonomy Scale.

SECTION 6.

FACTOR COMPOSITION OF RESPONSES TO VIGNETTES
BASED ON PERCEPTION OF PROBATION
RESPONSE, SIX AGENCIES

POLICE

ITEM NUMBER	NASSAU POLICE FACTORS (N=598)		ALBUQUERQUE POLICE FACTORS (N=180)		SAN JOSE POLICE FACTORS (N=286)	
	I.	II.	I.	II.	I.	II.
19.*	.022	.274*	-.016	.382*	.145	.323*
20.*	.170	.577*	.026	.591	.069	.565*
21.*	.069	.604*	.165	.243*	.134	.533*
22.**	.640**	.103	.609**	-.127	.534**	.132
23.**	.646**	-.046	.573**	.043	.581**	.033
24.**	.611**	.101	.607**	.108	.442**	.136
25.	.431	.254	.292	.174	.502	.147
26.*	.288	.373*	.108	-.118	.085	.322*
27.	.375	.227	.312	.013	.292	.197
28.**	.391**	.239	.534**	-.022	.475**	.156

PROBATION

ITEM NUMBER	NASSAU POLICE FACTORS (N=216)		ALBUQUERQUE POLICE FACTORS (N=32)		SAN JOSE POLICE FACTORS (N=145)	
	I.	II.	I.	II.	I.	II.
19.*	.135	.252*	.477	.526*	.171	.413*
20.*	.219	.236*	.004	.212*	-.011	.312*
21.*	.265	.221*	.058	.532*	.040	.622*
22.**	.357**	.096	.206**	.142	.636**	.136
23.**	.846**	-.053	.698**	.205	.568**	.127
24.**	.110*	.428	.409**	-.472	.456**	.171
25.	.298	.235	.736	-.079	.086	.440
26.*	.080	.313*	.111	-.006*	-.343	.330*
27.	.202	.449	.509	-.565	.342	-.186
28.**	.286**	.436	.508**	-.108	.449**	.045

NOTES: A single asterisk identifies an item comprising the Police Prerogative Scale.
A double asterisk identifies an item comprising the Probation Autonomy Scale.

SECTION 7.

TABLE IV-9

PERCENTAGE OF POLICE OFFICERS WITH HIGH CONFLICT BY NATURE OF CONTACT SITUATION AND AMOUNT OF CONTACT, OFFICERS WITH CONTACT ONLY

Amount of Overall Contact	Situation of Contact								Police (N=613)	
	Police helping Probation		Probation Helping Police		Working Together		Information Verification		Multiple	
	%	N	%	N	%	N	%	N	%	N
High	10%	(21)	0%	(4)	33%	(3)	43%	(14)	19%	(16)
Medium	26%	(54)	59%	(22)	33%	(6)	47%	(45)	29%	(34)
Low	39%	(155)	46%	(37)	40%	(10)	48%	(159)	52%	(29)

NOTE: N appearing in parenthesis refers to the denominator on which the percentages are based.

X^2 = 12.19, $P < .05$

V = .14

TABLE IV-12

DEGREE OF CONFLICT AND THE NATURE OF THE LOCATION OF CONTACT FOR POLICE OFFICERS

Conflict	Location of Contact													
	Street		Station House		Family Court		Probation Office		Telephone		Multiple		Row	
	N	%	N	%	N	%	N	%	N	%	N	%	N	%
High	20	59%	35	41%	11	44%	17	45%	139	39%	35	38%	257	40%
Low	14	41%	51	59%	14	56%	21	55%	220	61%	58	62%	378	60%
Column Total	34	100%	86	100%	25	100%	38	100%	359	100%	93	100%	635	100%

NOTE: 40% of police officers express no location of contact.

X^2 = 5.94, $P < .3$

V = .10

TABLE IV - 13

DEGREE OF CONFLICT AND THE NATURE OF THE LOCATION OF CONTACT FOR PROBATION OFFICERS

Conflict	Location of Contact													
	Street		Station House		Family Court		Probation Office		Telephone		Multiple		Row	
	N	%	N	%	N	%	N	%	N	%	N	%	N	%
High	1	33%	18	49%	7	33%	11	41%	83	48%	37	44%	157	46%
Low	2	67%	19	51%	14	67%	16	59%	89	52%	47	56%	187	54%
Column Total	3	100%	37	100%	21	100%	27	100%	172	100%	84	100%	344	100%

NOTE: 12% of probation officers express no location of contact.

X^2 = 2.42, $P < .7$
V = .08

APPENDIX D

SUPPLEMENTAL CASE DESCRIPTIONS ACCORDING TO CONFLICT ADAPTATION STYLE

TABLE OF CONTENTS

APPENDIX D

SECTION 1. Case Descriptions of Probation and Police Officers with a Police Adaptation Style

Police Adaptation Probation Officers

The extreme emphasis on law enforcement concerns can be illustated in the following case:

> "Two officers saw a car being driven in an erratic manner, and they decided to go after the driver. They almost cornered him in a gas station, but he drove away almost hitting one of them in the process. They chased him for almost an hour with speeds up to one-hundred miles per hour. They didn't catch him and he got away 'that's how good a driver he was.' Later, they finally caught him."

Police Adaptation Police Officers

> "I feel that some POs are bending over backwards for the kid. They don't think like us.
>
> No one is there to kick them Ps (probationers) in the ass!
>
> I don't see how they could straighten any kid out. The kid knows that this Thursday he has to be clean. The day before he cleans himself up. The other days he goes bananas. You have to attach a chain to him."

> "The probationer seems to have absolutely no respect for the probation officer. The universal feeling is to beat out the PO... this shithead.
>
> We have contact with the ilk of society. Some of these are on probation. And they tell me that probation is a bunch of bullshit. At C. W. Post College, I meet some of the guys that are actually on probation and they always speak derogatorily of it. And also about the POs. They laugh at it.
>
> I think every probation officer should have police experience to gain what I call a street sense. You don't have to be arbitrary or harsh. But POs have to be able to recognize bullshit. The POs admit that they lack this street sense when we talked in casual conversation."

> " I believe that the PO should have some police experience first. They need to know about people on the street. What does he know about losers? He sits behind the desk and most of the persons we deal with are losers. This would be an aid to eliminate friction and problems."

The attitude of the police adapters towards the courts is strongly expressed in the following case accounts.

> "I am not a social worker at all. The sytem is overloaded with do-gooders. The police cannot take this attitude. They are a law enforcement agency."
>
> "The offenders have a cocky, flippant attitude and just laugh at the system."
>
> "The kid should be dealt with severely, even on a first offense. But today, when a kid is arrested, he is treated like a two-year-old, babied.
>
> There is no deterrent atmosphere and, therefore, the kid is not afraid the next time."
>
> "Maybe we should talk with the North Koreans to find out how to completely whitewash a guy's mind and start fresh.
>
> I feel we only help the probationer when we put them away so that they can get straigntened out."
>
> "A known criminal has to know fear and be threatened in order to shape up. You have to be the boss."

Police Adaptation Police and Probation Officers

The attitude of both police and probation officers towards the courts is best described as follows: "They've become jail shy since Attica." The following accounts are presented from police testimonies:

> "The Court is Freedom Land. We need five or six offenses before an offender goes to jail; except if you are a cop."
>
> "The courts are too lenient. It is damn frustrating when you take the chances, and this guy goes to court five times, and the courts let him off."

SECTION 2. Case Description of Police Officers with a Moderator Adaptation Style.

Police officers with a moderator orientation have a very favorable and cooperative attitude towards the probation task of reintegration of the client into society. The following police accounts indicate this attitude:

> "Probation is necessary. You can't send them to prison. Especially a person who is trying to help himself, it is hard to imprison him."

> "You cannot lock up someone simply because you have the power to do so. Lockup should be the last resort.

> I feel that a mistake should not be held over anyone's head. And just because a person is on probation, I am not going to pick on him."

As was the case with moderator probation officers, police officers with this moderator adaptation emphasize more of a systems approach for dealing with the client as compared to a strict law enforcement or supportive social casework approach. The following case descriptions represent this orientation:

> "I think probation is good and with more facilities and programs involving families we could find the means to rehabilitate."

> "The system has to give better controlled and better coordinated supervision. We don't really have the time and the right procedures to really work with probationees. The PO could help if we had the right kind of operations and programs."

> "We should have some seminars or something like that at which the work of this or that department could be explained to others who work with the same kind of problems. I need to know more about probation."

> "I would like us to work together. You have to work together. It bugs me. I realize a kid should be referred. The ultimate is not the arrest procedure. Some kind of help is needed. I hope some day we can work together, for the good of the offender and a better system of criminal justice."

> "You need a more developed system for helping to decide properly who should or should not go on probation."

These moderator police officers are also very prone to offer specific suggestions as to how this sytems approach might be initiated. The following case descriptions are indicative of this orientation:

> "Perhaps an annex of annexes located in the community should be set up to help break down any barriers between POs, the police and probationees. This would help all of us move from theories to a practical human relationship approach."

> "Kids are being pushed from here to there and back again. We need more time, POs need more time, and we need to work closer together to be effective. These forms that we've got interfere with what they were meant to do -- which is more effective coordination."

APPENDIX E

SECTION 1. Chi Square Analysis for Chapter Three (Conflict and Contact) Relationships.

SECTION 2. Chi Square Analysis for Chapter Four (Dissensus) Relationships dealing with Political-Legal Conservatism.

SECTION 3. Chi Square Analysis for Chapter Four (Dissensus) Relationships dealing with Status and Esteem.

SECTION 4. Chi Square Analysis for Chapter Five (Perceptual Conflict) Relationships dealing with Police Prerogatives and Probation Autonomy.

SECTION 1. Probation Contact

1 (1) Contact with Age

1 (2) Contact with Role Concept

1 (3) Contact with Specialized Assignment

1 (4) Contact with Category of Assignment

1 (5) Contact with Nature of Work

1 (6) Contact with Numbers in Contact

1 (7) Contact with Location of Contact

1 (8) Contact with Personal Contact

1 (9) Contact with Ethnicity of Offender

1 (10) Contact with Situation of Contact

SECTION 1. Police Contact

1 (11) Contact with Age

1 (12) Contact with Role Concept

1 (13) Contact with Category of Assignment

1 (14)	Contact with Nature of Work
1 (15)	Contact with Numbers in Contact
1 (16)	Contact with Rank
1 (17)	Contact with Location of Contact
1 (18)	Contact with Situation of Contact
1 (19)	Contact with Personal Contact
1 (20)	Contact with Education
1 (21)	Contact with Experience
1 (22)	Contact with Job Related Courses

SECTION 1. Probation Conflict

1 (23)	Conflict with Age
1 (24)	Conflict with Experience
1 (25)	Conflict with Rank
1 (26)	Conflict with Police Status
1 (27)	Conflict with Probation Status
1 (28)	Conflict with Probation Esteem
1 (29)	Conflict with Police Esteem

SECTION 1. Police Conflict

1 (30)	Conflict with Age
1 (31)	Conflict with Police Status
1 (32)	Conflict with Probation Status

1 (33) Conflict with Probation Esteem

1 (34) Conflict with Ethnicity of Police Officer

1 (35) Conflict with Ethnicity of Offender

1 (36) Conflict with Category of Assignment

1 (37) Conflict with Specialized Assignment

1 (38) Conflict with Nature of Work

1 (39) Conflict with Type of Officer in Contact

1 (40) Conflict with Experience

1 (41) Conflict with Rank

1 (42) Conflict with Contact

1 (43) Conflict with Numbers in Contact

1 (44) Conflict with Personal Contact

1 (45) Conflict with Location of Contact

1 (46) Conflict with Situation of Contact

SECTION 2. Probation Conservatism

2 (1) Conservatism with Contact

2 (2) Conservatism with Role Concept

2 (3) Conservatism with Category of Assignment

2 (4) Conservatism with Experience

2 (5) Conservatism with Rank

2 (6) Conservatism with Specialized Assignment

SECTION 2. Police Conservatism

SECTION 3. Probation on Police Status

SECTION 3. Probation on Police Esteem

3 (24) Police Esteem with Situation of Contact

3 (25) Police Esteem with Conflict

3 (26) Police Esteem with Specialized Assignment

SECTION 3. Probation on Probation Status

3 (27) Probation Status with Age

3 (28) Probation Status with Experience

3 (29) Probation Status with Conflict

SECTION 3. Police on Probation Status

3 (30) Probation Status with Conflict

3 (31) Probation Status with Age

3 (32) Probation Status with Experience

3 (33) Probation Status with Liberalism

3 (34) Probation Status with Rank

3 (35) Probation Status with Contact

3 (36) Probation Status with Numbers of Contact

3 (37) Probation Status with Category of Assignment

3 (38) Probation Status with Specialized Assignment

3 (39) Probation Status with Location of Contact

SECTION 4. Probation on Police Prerogatives

4 (40) Police Prerogatives with Liberalism

4 (41) Police Prerogatives with Probation Autonomy

4 (42) Police Prerogatives with Religion

4 (43) Police Prerogatives with Role Concept

4 (44) Police Prerogatives with Nature of Work

4 (45) Police Prerogatives with Experience

4 (46) Police Prerogatives with Situation of Contact

4 (47) Police Prerogatives with Personal Contact

SECTION 4. Police on Police Pregogatives

4 (48) Police Prerogatives with Liberalism

4 (49) Police Prerogatives with Probation Autonomy

4 (50) Police Prerogatives with Religion

4 (51) Police Prerogatives with Role Concept

4 (52) Police Prerogatives with Nature of Work

4 (53) Police Prerogatives with Police Status

4 (54) Police Prerogatives with Ethnicity of Officer

4 (55) Police Prerogatives with Education

4 (56) Police Prerogatives with Ethnicity of Offender

4 (57) Police Prerogatives with Rank

4 (58) Police Prerogatives with Category of Assignment

4 (59) Police Prerogatives with Type of Officer in Contact

Table 1 (1) Probation (N=370)

CONTACT	AGE			
	Low	Middle	High	Row Total
Low	26	28	24	78
Middle	65	65	27	157
High	66	47	22	135
Column Total	157	140	73	370

$X^2 = 9.95, P < .05$
$V = .12$

Table 1 (2) Probation (N=330)

CONTACT	ROLE CONCEPT			
	Community Service	Law Enforcement	Both	Row Total
Low	36	6	24	66
Middle	68	10	61	139
High	55	25	45	125
Column Total	159	41	130	330

$X^2 = 11.68, P < .02$
$V = .13$

Table 1 (3) Probation (N=312)

CONTACT	SPECIALIZED ASSIGNMENT				
	None	Narcotics	Intake	Research	Row Total
Low	51	3	4	10	68
Middle	93	16	9	11	129
High	73	15	22	5	115
Column Total	217	34	35	26	312

X^2 = 20.12, P <.01
V = .18

Table 1 (4) Probation (N=348)

CONTACT	CATEGORY OF ASSIGNMENT			
	Juvenile Division	Family Branch	Adult Division	Row Total
Low	14	17	32	63
Middle	68	9	73	150
High	46	8	81	135
Column	128	34	186	348

X^2 = 32.02, P <.01
V = .22

Table (5) Probation (N=360)

CONTACT	NATURE OF WORK			
Total	Supervisory	Field	Administrative	Row
Low	21	34	18	73
Middle	42	96	17	155
High	29	83	20	132
Colum Total	92	213	55	360

X^2 = 9.6, P <.05
V = .12

Table 1 (6) Probation (N=373)

CONTACT	NUMBERS IN CONTACT			
	Low	Middle	High	Row Total
Low	48	12	18	78
Middle	4	15	139	158
High	0	12	125	137
Column	52	39	282	373

X^2 = 199.03, P <.01
V = .52

Table 1 (10) Probation (N=367)

CONTACT SITUATION OF CONTACT

	None	Police Helping	Probation Helping	Working Together	Information Verification	Multiple	Row Total
Low	28	12	3	0	22	12	77
Middle	0	44	11	7	64	31	157
High	0	38	2	3	40	50	133
Column Total	28	94	16	10	126	93	367

X^2 = 134.33, $P < .01$
V = .43

Table 1 (11) Police (N=1,052)

CONTACT AGE

	Low	Middle	High	Row Total
Low	323	408	96	827
Middle	43	92	30	165
High	11	31	18	60
Column Total	377	531	144	1,052

X^2 = 29.76, $P < .01$
V = .12

Table 1 (12) Police (N-1,011)

CONTACT	ROLE CONCEPT			
	Community Service	Law Enforcement	Both	Row Total
Low	193	527	75	795
Middle	30	184	23	157
High	15	33	11	59
Column Total	238	664	109	1,011

X^2 = 9.39, P <.06
V = .09

Table 1 (7) Probation (N=371)

CONTACT	LOCATION OF CONTACT							
	None	Street	Station House	Family Court	Probation Office	Tele-phone	Multi-ple	Row Total
Low	28	1	8	5	3	28	4	77
Middle	0	1	13	7	12	96	29	158
High	0	1	15	9	12	48	51	136
Column Total	28	3	36	21	27	172	84	371

X^2 = 147.47, P <.01
V = .45

Table 1 (8) Probation (N=370)

CONTACT — PERSONAL CONTACT

CONTACT	Low	Middle	High	Row Total
Low	37	25	16	78
Middle	53	61	43	157
High	25	32	78	135
Column Total	115	118	137	370

X^2 = 44.54, $P < .01$
V = .25

Table 1 (9) Probation (N=366)

CONTACT — ETHNICITY OF OFFENDER

CONTACT	White	Black	Spanish	No Type	Row Total
Low	28	5	6	37	76
Middle	83	11	27	34	155
High	60	8	28	39	135
Column Total	171	24	61	110	366

X^2 = 20.58, $P < .01$
V = .17

Table 1 (13) Police (N=960)

CONTACT CATEGORY OF ASSIGNMENT

	Patrol	Detective	Juvenile	Head-quarters	Row Total
Low	512	132	11	94	749
Middle	28	62	37	27	154
High	1	7	32	17	57
Column Total	541	201	80	138	960

X^2 = 379.01, P <.01
V = .44

Table 1 (14) Police (N=1,020)

CONTACT NATURE OF WORK

	Supervisory	Field	Administrative	Row
Total				
Low	181	575	46	802
Middle	36	118	5	159
High	21	33	5	59
Column Total	238	726	56	1,020

X^2 = 8.84, P <.07
V = .07

Table 1 (15) Police (N=1,051)

CONTACT	NUMBERS IN CONTACT			
	Low	Middle	High	Row Total
Low	627	74	126	827
Middle	16	11	137	164
High	6	0	54	60
Column Total	649	85	317	1,051

X^2 = 417.53, P <.01
V = .45

Table 1 (16) Police (N=1,047)

CONTACT	RANK			
	Low	Middle	High	Row Total
Low	631	132	61	824
Middle	120	31	14	165
High	26	27	5	58

X^2 = 35.59, P <.01
V = .13

Table 1 (17) Police (N=1,051)

CONTACT LOCATION OF CONTACT

	None	Street	Station House	Family Court	Probation Office	Tele-phone	Multiple	Row Total
Low	418	32	60	16	20	246	36	828
Middle	1	2	17	6	13	90	35	164
High	0	0	7	3	5	22	22	59

X^2 = 264.83, P <.01
V = .36

Table 1 (18) Police (N=1,045)

CONTACT SITUATION OF CONTACT

	None	Police Helping	Probation Helping	Working Together	Information Verification	Mult-iple	Row Total
Low	432	155	37	10	159	29	822
Middle	4	54	22	6	45	34	165
High	0	21	4	3	14	16	58
Column Total	436	230	63	19	218	79	1,045

X^2 = 242.16, P <.01
V = .34

Table 1 (19) Police (N=1,047)

CONTACT	PERSONAL CONTACT			
	Low	Middle	High	Row Total
Low	614	168	40	822
Middle	97	48	20	165
High	38	10	12	60
Column Total	749	226	72	1,047

X^2 = 23.40, $P < .01$
V = .13

Table 1 (20) Police (N=1,052)

CONTACT	EDUCATION			
	Low	Middle	High	Row Total
Low	167	545	116	828
Middle	23	112	29	164
High	8	36	16	60
Column Total	198	693	161	1,052

X^2 = 10.80, $P < .05$
V = .07

Table 1 (21) Police (N=1,0480

CONTACT	EXPERIENCE			
	Low	Middle	High	Row Total
Low	345	299	179	823
Middle	41	70	54	165
High	9	31	20	60
Column Total	395	400	253	1,048

X^2 = 32.79, P <.01
V = .13

Table 1 (22) Police (N=1,047)

CONTACT	JOB-RELATED COURSES TAKEN		
	Yes	No	Row Total
Low	467	356	823
Middle	112	52	164
High	38	22	60
Column Total	617	430	1,047

X^2 = 8.05, P <.05
V = .09

Table 1 (23) Probation (N=376)

CONFLICT	AGE			
	Low	Middlle	High	Row Total
High	95	64	17	176
Low	65	78	57	200
Column Total	160	142	74	376

X^2 = 27.21, P <.01
V = .27

Table 1 (24) Probation (N=378)

CONFLICT	EXPERIENCE			
	Low	Middle	High	Row Total
High	120	53	3	176
Low	117	68	17	202
Column Total	237	121	20	378

X^2 = 9.96, P <.01
V = .16

Table 1 (25) Probation (N=375)

CONFLICT RANK

	Low	Middle	High	Row Total
High	98	70	5	173
Low	98	85	19	202
Column Total	196	155	24	375

X^2 = 7.42, P <.05
V = .14

Table 1 (26) Probation (N=393)

CONFLICT POLICE STATUS

	Low	High	Row Total
High	65	117	182
Low	47	164	211
Column Total	112	281	393

X^2 = 8.01, P <.01
V = .14

Table 1 (27) Probation (N=393)

CONFLICT	PROBATION STATUS		
	Low	High	Row Total
High	50	132	182
Low	32	179	211
Column Total	82	311	393

X^2 = 8.23, P <.01
V = .15

Table 1 (28) Probation (N=393)

CONFLICT	PROBATION ESTEEM		
	Low	High	Row Total
High	53	129	182
Low	32	179	211
Column Total	85	308	383

X^2 = 10.42, P <.01
V = .16

Table 1 (29) Probation (N=393)

CONFLICT	POLICE ESTEEM		
	Low	High	Row Total
High	73	109	182
Low	42	169	211
Column Total	115	278	393

X^2 = 18.31, P <.01
V = .26

Table 1 (30) Police (N=1,057)

CONFLICT	AGE			
	Low	Middle	High	Row Total
High	236	228	47	511
Low	142	306	98	546
Column Total	378	534	145	1.057

X^2 = 51.61, P <.01
V = .22

Table 1 (31) Police (N=1,064)

CONFLICT	POLICE STATUS		
	Low	High	Row Total
High	200	316	516
Low	172	376	548
Column Total	372	692	1,064

X^2 = 6.03, $P < .02$
V = .08

Table 1 (32) Police (N=1,064)

CONFLICT	PROBATION STATUS		
	Low	High	Row Total
High	218	298	516
Low	115	433	548
Column Total	333	731	1,064

X^2 = 54.79, $P < .01$
V = .23

Table 1 (33) Police (N=1,064)

CONFLICT	PROBATION ESTEEM		
	Low	High	Row Total
High	203	313	516
Low	159	389	548
Column Total	362	702	1,064

X^2 = 12.17, P <.01
V = .11

Table 1 (34) Police (N=1,045)

CONFLICT	ETHNICITY OF POLICE OFFICER			
	White	Black	Spanish	Row Total
High	463	11	29	503
Low	517	6	19	542
Colum Total	980	17	48	1,045

X^2 = 5.08, P <.08
V = .07

Table 1 (35) Police (N=1,045)

CONFLICT	ETHNICITY OF OFFENDER				
	White	Black	Spanish	None	Row Total
High	138	65	105	200	508
Low	182	77	54	224	537
Column Total	320	142	159	424	1,045

X^2 = 23.99, P <.01
V = .15

Table 1 (36) Police (N=965)

CONFLICT	CATEGORY OF ASSIGNMENT				
	Patrol	Detective	Juvenile	Headquarters	Row Total
High	312	75	29	53	469
Low	230	127	51	88	496
Column Total	540	202	80	141	965

X^2 = 39.81, P <.01
V = .20

Table 1 (37) Police (N=244)

CONFLICT SPECIALIZED ASSIGNMENT

	Narcotics	Morals-Vice	Other	Row Total
High	16	19	89	124
Low	6	16	98	120
Column Total	22	35	187	244

X^2 = 5.17, P <.10
V = .15

Table 1 (38) Police (N=1,025)

CONFLICT NATURE OF WORK

	Supervisory	Field	Administrative	Row Total
High	98	369	27	494
Low	143	359	29	531
Column Total	241	728	56	1,025

X^2 = 7.29, P <.05
V = .08

Table 1 (39) Police (N=1,045)

CONFLICT	TYPE OF OFFICER IN CONTACT					
	Adult	Family	50-50	None	Multiple	Row Total
High	104	82	29	287	1	503
Low	175	100	54	213	0	542
Column Total	279	182	83	500	1	1,045

X^2 = 37.93, P <.01
V = .19

Table 1 (40) Police (N=1,053)

CONFLICT	EXPERIENCE			
	Low	Middle	High	Row Total
High	240	190	79	500
Low	156	212	176	544
Column Total	396	402	255	1,053

X^2 = 54.82, P <.01
V = .23

Table 1 (39) Police (N=1,045)

CONFLICT TYPE OF OFFICER IN CONTACT

	Adult	Family	50-50	None	Multiple	Row Total
High	104	82	29	287	1	503
Low	175	100	54	213	0	542
Column Total	279	182	83	500	1	1,045

X^2 = 37.93, P <.01
V = .19

Table 1 (40) Police)N=1,053)

CONFLICT EXPERIENCE

	Low	Middle	High	Row Total
High	249	190	79	509
Low	156	212	176	544
Column Total	396	402	255	1,053

X^2 = 54.82, P <.01
V = .23

Table 1 (41) Police (N=1,052)

CONFLICT	RANK			
	Low	Middle	High	Row Total
High	403	80	23	506
Low	376	113	57	546
Column Total	779	193	80	1,052

X^2 = 19.54, P <.01
V =

Table 1 (42) Police (N=1,054)

CONFLICT	CONTACT			
	Low	Middle	High	Row Total
High	432	63	13	508
Low	397	102	47	546
Column Total	829	165	60	1,054

X^2 = 28.63, P <.01
V = .16

Table 1 (43) Police (N=1,054)

CONFLICT	NUMBERS IN CONTACT			
	Low	Middle	High	Row Total
High	361	43	102	506
Low	289	42	217	548
Column Total	650	85	319	1,054

X^2 = 47.85, P <.01
V = .21

Table 1 (44) Police (N=1,051)

CONFLICT	PERSONAL CONTACT			
	Low	Middle	High	Row Total
High	378	110	21	509
Low	374	116	52	542
Column Total	752	226	73	1,051

X^2 = 12.32, P <.01
V = .11

Table 1 (45) Police (N=1,054)

CONFLICT LOCATION OF CONTACT

	None	Street	Station House	Family Court	Probation Office	Tele-phone	Mul-tiple	Row Total
High	251	20	35	11	17	139	35	508
Low	168	14	51	14	21	220	58	546
Column Total	419	34	86	25	38	359	93	1,046

X^2 = 43.91, P <.01
V = .20

Table 1 (46) Police (N=1,049)

CONFLICT SITUATION OF CONTACT

	None	Police Helping	Probation Helping	Working Together	Information Verification	Mul-tiple	Row Total
High	258	77	30	7	105	28	505
Low	178	155	33	12	115	51	544
Column Total	436	232	63	19	220	79	1,049

X^2 = 48.13, P <.01
V = .21

Table 2 (1) Probation (N=374)

CONTACT	CONSERVATISM		
	High	Low	Row Total
Low	26	52	78
Middle	74	85	159
High	65	72	137
Column Total	165	209	374

X^2 = 4.91, P <.10
V = .15

Table 2 (2) Probation (N=336)

CONSERVATISM	ROLE CONCEPT			
	Community Service	Law Enforcement	Both	Row Total
High	63	28	60	151
Low	99	14	72	185
Column Total	162	42	132	336

X^2 = 4.91, P <.10
V = .15

Table 2 (3) Probation (N=354)

CONSERVATISM	CATEGORY OF ASSIGNMENT			
	Juvenile	Family	Adult	Row Total
High	45	14	106	165
Low	86	20	83	189
Column Total	131	34	189	354

X^2 = 7.78, $P < .05$
V = .21

Table 2 (4) Probation (N=378)

CONSERVATISM	EXPERIENCE			
	Low	Middle	High	Row Total
High	87	70	12	169
Low	150	51	8	209
Column Total	237	121	20	378

X^2 = 10.42, $P < .05$
V = .21

Table 2 (5) Probation (N=375)

CONSERVATISM	RANK			
	Low	Middle	High	Row Total
High	72	84	13	167
Low	124	71	11	208
Column Total	196	155	24	375

X^2 = 8.73, $P < .05$
V = .20

Table 2 (6) Probation (N=316)

CONSERVATISM	SPECIALIZED ASSIGNMENT				
	None	Narcotics	Intake	Research & Staff	Row Total
High	99	22	16	9	146
Low	122	12	19	17	170
Column Total	221	34	35	26	316

X^2 = 6.78, $P < .10$
V = .22

Table 2 (7) Probation (N=373)

CONSERVATISM	ETHNICITY OF PROBATION OFFICER			
	White	Black	Spanish	Row Total
High	157	1	6	164
Low	185	13	11	209
Column Total	342	14	17	373

X^2 = 6.01, P <.10
V = .16

Table 2 (8) Probation (N=368)

CONSERVATISM	TYPE OFFICER IN CONTACT WITH					
	Juvenile	Detective	Lieutenant	Patrolman	Other	Row Total
High	6	40	61	29	28	164
Low	29	67	49	27	32	204
Column Total	35	107	110	56	60	368

X^2 = 11.91, P <.05
V = .25

Table 2 (9) Probation (N=371)

CONSERVATISM	PERSONAL CONTACT			
	Low	Middle	High	Row Total
High	37	42	87	166
Low	78	76	51	205
Column Total	115	118	138	371

X^2 = 16.51, P <.01
V = 29.18

Table 2 (10) Police (N=1,054)

CONTACT	CONSERVATISM		
	High	Low	Row Total
Low	395	434	829
Middle	70	95	165
High	20	40	60
Column Total	485	569	1,054

X^2 = 5.63, P <.06
V = .07

Table 2 (11) Police (N=1,064)

CONFLICT	CONSERVATISM		
	High	Low	Row Total
High	283	233	516
Low	208	340	548
Column Total	491	573	1,064

X^2 = 29.83, $P < .01$
V = .17

Table 2 (12) Police (N=1,052)

CONSERVATISM	JOB RELATED COURSE TAKING		
	Yes	No	Row Total
High	256	228	484
Low	363	205	568
Column Total	619	433	1,052

X^2 = 7.68, $P < .05$
V = .12

Table 2 (13) Police (N=1,052)

CONSERVATISM	RANK			
	Low	Middle	High	Row Total
High	387	73	23	483
Low	392	120	57	569
Column Total	779	193	80	1,052

X^2 = 9.11, P <.05
V = .13

Table 2 (14) Police (N=1,025)

CONSERVATISM	NATURE OF WORK			
	Supervisory	Field	Administrative	Row Total
High	87	362	24	473
Low	154	366	32	552
Column Total	241	728	56	1,052

X^2 = 5.81, P <.05
V = .10

Table 2 (15) Police (N=1,045)

CONSERVATISM	OFFENDER CONTACT				
	White	Black	Spanish	Other	Row Total
High	137	80	82	180	479
Low	183	62	77	244	566
Column Total	320	142	159	424	1,045

X^2 = 11.61, P <.05
V = .15

Table 2 (16) Police (N=1,057)

CONSERVATISM	EDUCATION			
	Low	Middle	High	Row Total
High	110	304	70	484
Low	90	392	91	573
Column Total	200	696	161	1,057

X^2 = 5.89, P <.10
V = .11

Table 2 (17) Police (N=1,053)

CONSERVATISM	EXPERIENCE			
	Low	Middle	High	Row Total
High	203	173	97	483
Low	193	229	148	570
Column Total	396	402	245	1,053

X^2 = 5.79, P <.10
V = .11

Table 2 (18) Police (N=1,016)

CONSERVATISM	ROLE CONCEPT			
	Community Service	Law Enforcement	Both	Row Total
High	90	337	45	472
Low	149	330	65	544
Column Total	239	667	110	1,016

X^2 = 5.35, P <.10
V = .10

Table 2 (19) Police (N=244)

CONSERVATISM	SPECIALIZED ASSIGNMENT			
	Narcotics	Morals	Other	Row Total
High	12	20	65	97
Low	10	15	122	147
Column Total	22	35	187	244

X^2 = 4.71, P <.10
V = .20

Table 2 (20) Police (N=965)

CONSERVATISM	CATEGORY OF ASSIGNMENT				
	Patrol	Detective	Juvenile	Headquarters	Row Total
High	269	94	26	53	442
Low	273	108	54	88	523
Column Total	542	202	80	141	965

X^2 = 6.41, P <.10
V = .11

Table 3 (1) Probation (N=393)

POLICE STATUS	CONFLICT		
	High	Low	Row Total
Low	65	47	112
High	117	164	281
Column Total	182	211	393

X^2 = 8.01, P <.01
V = .14

Table 3 (2) Probation (N=376)

POLICE STATUS	AGE			
	Low	Middle	High	Row Total
Low	59	36	11	106
High	101	106	63	270
Column Total	160	142	74	376

X^2 = 13.02, P <.01
V = .1

Table 3 (3) Probation (N=378)

POLICE STATUS	EXPERIENCE			
	Low	Middle	High	Row Total
Low	81	21	3	105
High	156	100	17	273
Column Total	237	121	20	378

X^2 = 13.02, $P < .01$
V = .19

Table 3 (4) Probation (N=375)

POLICE STATUS	RANK			
	Low	Middle	High	Row Total
Low	67	33	5	105
High	129	122	19	270
Column Total	196	155	24	375

X^2 = 7.29, $P < .05$
V = .14

Table 3 (5) Probation (N=328)

POLICE STATUS	RELIGION			
	Protestant	Catholic	Jewish	Row Total
Low	33	33	18	84
High	102	117	25	244
Column Total	135	150	43	328

$X^2 = 7.08, P < .05$
$V = .15$

Table 3 (6) Probation (N=63)

POLICE STATUS	CATEGORY OF ASSIGNMENT AT LOW CONTACT			
	Juvenile	Family	Adult	Row Total
Low	6	1	10	17
High	8	16	22	46
Column Total	14	17	32	63

$X^2 = 5.93, P < .06$
$V = .31$

Table 3 (7) Police (N=1,064)

POLICE STATUS	CONFLICT		
	High	Low	Row Total
Low	200	172	372
High	316	376	692
Column Total	516	548	1,064

X^2 = 6.03, P <.02
V = .08

Table 3 (8) Police (N=1,064)

POLICE STATUS	POLICE PEROGATIVES		
	Low	High	Row Total
Low	164	208	372
High	252	440	692
Column Total	416	648	1,064

X^2 = 5.66, P <.02
V = .07

Table 3 (9) Police (N=965)

POLICE STATUS CATEGORY OF ASSIGNMENT

	Patrol	Detective	Juvenile	Headquarters	Row Total
Low	200	55	31	51	338
High	342	147	49	90	628
Column Total	542	202	80	141	965

X^2 = 6.81, P <.10
V = .08

Table 3 (10) Police (N=1,054)

POLICE STATUS LOCATION OF CONTACT

	None	Street	Station House	Family Court	Probation Office	Tele-phone	Other	Row Total
Low	154	13	38	9	18	105	29	366
High	265	21	48	16	20	254	64	688
Column Total	419	34	86	25	38	359	93	1,054

X^2 = 12.31, P <.06
V = .11

Table 3 (11) Probation (N=393)

PROBATION ESTEEM	CONFLICT		
	High	Low	Row Total
Low	53	32	85
High	129	179	308
Column Total	182	211	393

X^2 = 10.42, $P < .01$
V = .16

Table 3 (12) Probation (N=376)

PROBATION ESTEEM	AGE			
	Low	Middle	High	Row Total
Low	43	32	5	80
High	117	110	69	296
Column Total	160	142	74	376

X^2 = 12.44, $P < .01$
V = .18

Table 3 (13) Probation (N=378)

PROBATION ESTEEM	EXPERIENCE			
	Low	Middle	High	Row Total
Low	60	18	2	80
High	177	103	18	298
Column Total	237	121	20	378

X^2 = 6.81, $P < .05$
V = .13

Table 3 (14) Probation (N=372)

PROBATION ESTEEM	LOCATION OF CONTACT							
	None	Street	Station House	Family Court	Probation Office	Tele-phone	Other	Row Total
Low	5	0	9	3	1	47	14	79
High	23	3	28	18	26	125	70	293
Column Total	28	3	37	21	27	172	84	372

X^2 = 11.64, $P < .10$
V = .18

Table 3 (15) Probation (N=368)

PROBATION ESTEEM SITUATION OF CONTACT

	None	Probation Task	Police Task	Solve Crime	Information Verification	Other	Row Total
Low	5	30	3	0	26	14	78
High	23	65	13	10	100	79	290
Column Total	28	95	16	10	126	93	368

X^2 = 11.20, P <.05
V = .17

Table 3 (16) Police (N=1,064)

PROBATION ESTEEM CONFLICT

	High	Low	Row Total
Low	203	159	362
High	313	389	702
Column Total	516	548	1,064

X^2 = 12.17, P <.01
V = .11

Table 3 (17) Police (N=1,057)

PROBATION ESTEEM	AGE			
	Low	Middle	High	Row Total
Low	133	188	37	358
High	245	346	108	699
Column Total	516	548	145	1,057

X^2 = 12.17, P <.01
V = .11

Table 3 (18) Police (N=1,053)

PROBATION ESTEEM	EXPERIENCE			
	Low	Middle	High	Row Total
Low	152	139	65	356
High	244	263	190	697
Column Total	396	402	255	1,053

X^2 = 11.70, P <.01
V = .11

Table 3 (17) Police (N=1,057)

PROBATION ESTEEM	AGE Low	Middle	High	Row Total
Low	133	188	37	358
High	245	346	108	699
Column Total	378	534	145	1,057

X^2 = 5.23, $P < .10$
V = .07

Table 3 (18) Police (N=1,053)

PROBATION ESTEEM	EXPERIENCE Low	Middle	High	Row Total
Low	152	139	65	356
High	244	263	190	697
Column Total	396	402	255	1,053

X^2 = 11.70, $P < .01$
V = .11

Table 3 (19) Police (N=1,052)

PROBATION ESTEEM	RANK			
	Low	Middle	High	Row Total
Low	280	60	13	353
High	499	133	67	699
Column Total	779	193	80	1,052

X^2 = 13.27, $P < .01$
V = .11

Table 3 (20) Police (N=1,025)

PROBATION ESTEEM	NATURE OF WORK			
	Supervisory	Field	Administrative	Row
Total				
Low	71	262	14	347
High	170	466	42	678
Column Total	241	728	56	1,025

X^2 = 5.52, $P < .10$
V = .07

Table 3 (21) Police (N=244)

PROBATION ESTEEM	SPECIALIZED ASSIGNMENT			
	Narcotics	Morals	Other	Row Total
Low	12	14	56	82
High	10	21	131	162
Column Total	22	35	187	244

X^2 = 5.95, P <.06
V = .16

Table 3 (22) Police (N=1,064)

PROBATION ESTEEM	CONSERVATISM		
	High	Low	Row Total
Low	204	158	362
High	287	415	702
Column Total	491	573	1,064

X^2 = 22.38, P <.01
V = .15

Table 3 (23) Police (N=1,016)

PROBATION ESTEEM ROLE CONCEPT

	Community Service	Law Enforcement	Both	Row Total
Low	66	238	39	343
High	173	429	71	673
Column Total	239	667	110	1,016

X^2 = 5.28, P <.10
V = .07

Table 3 (24) Probation (N=368)

POLICE ESTEEM SITUATION OF CONTACT

	None	Probation Task	Police Task	Solve Crime	Information Verification	Other	Row Total
Low	8	34	5	2	38	15	102
High	20	61	11	8	88	78	266
Column Total	28	95	16	10	126	93	368

X^2 = 10.11, P <.10
V = .17

Table 3 (25) Probation (N=393)

POLICE ESTEEM	CONFLICT		
	High	Low	Row Total
Low	73	42	115
High	109	169	278
Column Total	182	211	383

X^2 = 18.31, P <.01
V = .22

Table 3 (26) Police (N=244)

POLICE ESTEEM	SPECIALIZED ASSIGNMENT			
	Narcotics	Morals	Others	Row Total
Low	10	16	53	79
High	12	19	134	165
Column Total	22	35	187	244

X^2 = 5.95, P <.06
V = .16

Table 3 (27) Probation (N=376)

PROBATION STATUS	AGE			
	Low	Middle	High	Row Total
Low	37	32	8	77
High	123	110	66	299
Column Total	160	142	74	376

X^2 = 5.30, $P < .10$
V = .12

Table 3 (28) Probation (N=378)

PROBATION STATUS	EXPERIENCE			
	Low	Middle	High	Row Total
Low	47	29	0	76
High	190	92	20	302
Column Total	237	121	20	378

X^2 = 6.17, $P < .05$
V = .13

Table 3 (29) Probation (N=393)

PROBATION STATUS	CONFLICT		
	High	Low	Row Total
Low	50	32	82
High	132	179	311
Column Total	182	211	393

X^2 = 8.23, P <.01
V = .15

Table 3 (30) Police (N=1,064)

PROBATION STATUS	CONFLICT		
	High	Low	Row Total
Low	218	115	333
High	298	433	731
Column Total	516	548	1,064

X^2 = 54.80, P <.01
V = .23

Table 3 (31) Police (N=1,057)

PROBATION STATUS	AGE			
	Low	Middle	High	Row Total
Low	134	163	31	328
High	244	371	114	729
Column Total	378	534	145	1,057

X^2 = 9.82, $P < .01$
V = .09

Table 3 (32) Police (N=1,053)

PROBATION STATUS	EXPERIENCE			
	Low	Middle	High	Row Total
Low	154	119	52	325
High	242	283	203	728
Column Total	396	402	255	1,053

X^2 = 27.91, $P < .01$
V = .16

Table 3 (33) Police (N=1,064)

PROBATION STATUS	CONSERVATISM		
	High	Low	Row Total
Low	194	139	333
High	297	434	731
Column Total	491	573	1,064

X^2 = 27.91, $P < .01$
V = .16

Table 3 (34) Police (N=1,052)

PROBATION STATUS	RANK			
	Low	Middle	High	Row Total
Low	258	47	18	323
High	521	146	62	729
Column Total	779	193	80	1,052

X^2 = 8.33, $P < .02$
V = .09

Table 3 (35) Police (N=1,054)

PROBATION STATUS	CONTACT			
	Low	Middle	High	Row Total
Low	272	37	18	327
High	557	128	42	727
Column Total	829	165	60	1,054

X^2 = 6.97, P <.05
V = .08

Table 3 (36) Police (N=1,054)

PROBATION STATUS	NUMBERS OF CONTACT			
	Low	Middle	High	Row Total
Low	222	24	80	326
High	428	61	239	728
Column Total	650	85	319	1,054

X^2 = 8.56, P <.02
V = .09

Table 3 (37) Police (N=965)

PROBATION STATUS	SPECIALIZED ASSIGNMENT				
	Patrol	Detective	Juvenile	Headquarters	Row Total
Low	187	55	22	34	298
High	355	147	58	107	667
Column Total	542	202	80	141	965

X^2 = 8.05, $P < .05$
V = .09

---

table 3 (38) Police (N=244)

PROBATION STATUS	SPECIALIZED ASSIGNMENT			
	Narcotics	Morals	Other	Row Total
Low	9	10	50	74
High	13	25	137	170
Column Totals	22	35	187	244

X^2 = 4.91, $P < .10$
V = .14

Table 3 (39) Police (N=1,054)

PROBATION STATUS	LOCATION OF CONTACT							
	None	Street	Station House	Family Court	Probation Office	Tele-phone	Other	Row Total
Low	154	22	27	7	13	93	22	328
High	265	22	59	18	25	266	71	726
Column Total	419	34	86	25	38	358	93	1,054

X^2 = 13.74, $P < .05$
V = .11

Table 3 (40) Probation (N=393)

POLICE PEROGATIVES	CONSERVATISM		
	High	Low	Row Total
Low	63	138	201
High	114	78	192
Column Total	177	216	393

X^2 = 30.05, $P < .05$
V = .28

Table 4 (41) Probation (N=393)

POLICE PEROGATIVES	PROBATION AUTONOMY		
	High	Low	Row Total
Low	141	60	201
High	96	96	192
Column Total	237	156	393

X^2 = 15.82, P <.01
V = .20

Table 4 (42) Probation (N=328)

POLICE PEROGATIVES	RELIGION			
	Protestant	Catholic	Jewish	Row Total
Low	65	67	28	160
High	70	83	15	168
Column Total	135	150	43	328

X^2 = 5.63, P <.06
V = .13

Table 3 (43) Probation (N=336)

POLICE PEROGATIVES	ROLE CONCEPT			
	Community Service	Law Enforcement	Both	Row Total
Low	88	13	68	169
High	74	29	64	167
Column Total	162	42	132	336

X^2 = 7.42, $P < .05$
V = .15

Table 4 (44) Probation (N=361)

POLICE PEROGATIVES	NATURE OF WORK			
	Supervisory	Field	Administrative	Row Total
Low	37	116	32	185
High	56	97	23	176
Column Total	93	213	55	361

X^2 = 8.58, $P < .02$
V = .15

Table 4 (45) Probation (N=378)

POLICE PEROGATIVES	EXPERIENCE			
	Low	Middle	High	Row Total
Low	136	51	8	195
High	101	70	12	183
Column Total	237	121	20	378

X^2 = 8.58, $P < .02$
V = .15

Table 4 (46) Probation (N=368)

POLICE PEROGATIVES	SITUATION OF CONTACT						
	None	Probation Task	Police Task	Solve Crime	Information Verification	Other	Row Total
Low	21	44	11	2	63	52	193
High	7	51	5	8	63	41	175
Column Total	28	95	16	10	126	93	368

X^2 = 13.82, $P < .02$
V = .19

Table 4 (47) Probation (N=371)

POLICE PEROGATIVES	PERSONAL CONFLICT			
	Low	Middle	High	Row Total
Low	66	68	58	192
High	49	50	80	179
Column Total	115	118	138	371

X^2 = 8.32, P <.02
V = .15

Table 4 (48) Police (N=1,064)

POLICE PEROGATIVES	CONSERVATISM		
	High	Low	Row Total
Low	160	256	416
High	331	317	648
Column Total	491	573	1,064

X^2 = 15.73, P <.01
V = .12

Table 4 (49) Police (N=1,064)

POLICE PEROGATIVES	PROBATION AUTONOMY		
	High	Low	Row Total
Low	266	150	416
High	281	367	648
Column Total	547	517	1,064

X^2 = 42.13, $P < .01$
V = .20

Table 4 (50) Police (N=992)

POLICE PEROGATIVES	RELIGION			
	Protestant	Catholic	Jewish	Row Total
Low	176	200	7	383
High	221	382	6	609
Column Total	397	582	13	992

X^2 = 11.18, $P < .01$
V = .11

Table 4 (51) Police (N=1,016)

POLICE PEROGATIVES	ROLE CONCEPT			
	Community Service	Law Enforcement	Both	Row Total
Low	109	231	51	391
High	130	436	59	625
Column Total	239	667	110	1,016

X^2 = 12.19, P <.01
V = .11

Table 4 (52) Police (N=1,025)

POLICE PEROGATIVES	NATURE OF WORK			
	Supervisory	Field	Administrative	Row Total
Low	110	263	29	402
High	131	465	27	623
Column Total	241	728	56	1,025

X^2 = 10.80, P <.01
V = .11

Table 4 (53) Police (N=1,064)

POLICE PEROGATIVES	POLICE STATUS		
	Low	High	Row Total
Low	164	252	416
High	208	440	648
Column Total	372	692	1,064

X^2 = 5.66, P <.02
V = .07

Table 4 (54) Police (N=1,045)

POLICE PEROGATIVES	ETHNICITY OF OFFICER			
	White	Black	Spanish	Row Total
Low	372	10	28	410
High	608	7	20	635
Column Total	980	17	48	1,045

X^2 = 10.75, P <.01
V = .11

Table 4 (55) Police (N=1,057)

POLICE PEROGATIVES	EDUCATION			
	Low	Middle	High	Row Total
Low	76	257	80	413
High	124	439	81	644
Column Total	200	696	161	1,057

X^2 = 9.07, P <.01
V = .09

Table 4 (56) Police (N=1,045)

POLICE PEROGATIVES	ETHNICITY OF OFFENDER				
	White	Black	Spanish	Other	Row Total
Low	108	42	80	177	407
High	212	100	79	247	638
Column Total	320	142	159	424	1,045

X^2 = 11.23, P <.01
V = .10

Table 4 (57) Police (N=1,052)

POLICE PEROGATIVES	RANK			
	Low	Middle	High	Row Total
Low	285	85	43	413
High	494	108	37	639
Column Total	779	193	80	1,052

X^2 = 11.23, P <.01
V = .10

Table 4 (58) Police (N=965)

POLICE PEROGATIVES	CATEGORY OF ASSIGNMENT				
	Patrol	Detective	Juvenile	Headquarters	Row Total
Low	234	54	33	59	380
High	208	148	47	82	585
Column Total	542	202	80	141	965

X^2 = 17.28, P <.01
V = .13

Table 4 (59) Police (N=1,044)

POLICE PEROGATIVES	TYPE OF OFFICER IN CONTACT				
	Adult	Family	50-50	None	Row Total
Low	81	85	39	203	408
High	198	97	44	297	636
Column Total	279	182	83	500	1,044

X^2 = 20.49, $P < .01$
V = .14

Table 4 (60) Police (N=1,054)

POLICE PEROGATIVES	LOCATION OF CONTACT							
	None	Street	Station House	Family Court	Probation Office	Tele-phone	Other	Row Total
Low	168	14	41	8	22	116	43	412
High	251	20	45	17	16	243	50	642
Column Total	419	34	86	25	38	359	93	1,054

X^2 = 17.99, $P < .01$
V = .13

Table 4 (61) Probation (N=393)

PROBATION AUTONOMY	CONSERVATISM		
	High	Low	Row Total
High	84	153	237
Low	93	63	156
Column Total	177	216	393

X^2 = 21.24, P <.01
V = .23

Table 4 (62) Probation (N=336)

PROBATION AUTONOMY	ROLE CONCEPT			
	Community Service	Law Enforcement	Both	Row Total
High	113	19	67	199
Low	49	23	65	137
Column Total	162	42	132	336

X^2 = 14.76, P <.01
V = .21

Table 4 (63) Probation (N=373)

PROBATION AUTONOMY	ETHNICITY OF OFFICER			
	White	Black	Spanish	Row Total
High	200	11	16	227
Low	142	3	1	146
Column Total	342	14	17	373

X^2 = 10.55, P <.01
V = .17

Table 4 (64) Probation (N=354)

PROBATION AUTONOMY	CATEGORY OF ASSIGNMENT			
	Juvenile	Family	Adult	Row Total
High	100	20	89	209
Low	31	14	100	145
Column Total	131	34	189	354

X^2 = 27.37, P <.01
V = .28

Table 4 (65) Probation (N=375)

PROBATION AUTONOMY	RANK			
	Low	Middle	High	Row Total
High	118	87	21	226
Low	78	68	3	149
Column Total	196	155	24	375

X^2 = 8.54, P <.02
V = .15

Table 4 (66) Probation (N=372)

PROBATION AUTONOMY	LOCATION OF CONTACT							
	None	Street	Station House	Family Court	Probation Office	Tele-phone	Other	Row Total
High	18	3	20	17	25	94	49	226
Low	10	0	17	4	2	78	35	146
Column Total	28	3	37	21	27	172	84	372

X^2 = 20.75, P <.01
V = .24

Table 4 (67) Probation (N=372)

PROBATION AUTONOMY	ETHNICITY OF OFFENDER				
	White	Black	Spanish	None	Row Total
High	106	8	42	68	224
Low	68	16	22	42	148
Column Total	174	24	64	110	372

X^2 = 8.18, P <.05
V = .15

Table 4 (68) Probation (N=368)

PROBATION AUTONOMY	TYPE OFFICER IN CONTACT					
	Juvenile	Detective	Lieutenant	Patrol	Other	Row Total
High	23	83	52	33	34	225
Low	12	24	58	23	26	143
Column Total	35	107	110	56	60	368

X^2 = 21.99, P <.01
V = .24

Table 4 (69) Probation (N=371)

PROBATION AUTONOMY	PERSONAL CONTACTS			
	Low	Middle	High	Row Total
High	77	73	73	223
Low	38	45	65	148
Column Total	115	118	138	371

X^2 = 5.39, $P < .07$
V = .12

TABLE 4 (70) Police (N=1,064)

PROBATION AUTONOMY	CONSERVATISM		
	High	Low	Row Total
High	212	335	547
Low	279	238	517
Column Total	491	573	1,064

X^2 = 24.13, $P < .01$
V = .15

Table 4 (71) Police (N=1,016)

PROBATION AUTONOMY	ROLE CONCEPT			
	Community Services	Law Enforcement	Both	Row Total
High	134	321	66	521
Low	105	346	44	495
Column Total	239	667	110	1,016

X^2 = 8.19, P <.02
V = .09

Table 4 (72) Police (N=1,045)

PROBATION AUTONOMY	ETHNICITY OF OFFICER			
	White	Black	Spanish	Row Total
High	490	12	35	537
Low	490	5	13	508
Column Total	980	17	48	1,045

X^2 = 12.17, P <.01
V = .11

Table 4 (73) Police (N=965)

PROBATION AUTONOMY — CATEGORY OF ASSIGNMENT

	Patrolmen	Detective	Juvenile	Headquarters	Row Total
High	252	101	50	83	486
Low	290	101	30	58	479
Column Total	542	202	80	141	965

X^2 = 12.05, P <.01
V = .11

Table 4 (74) Police (N=1,052)

PROBATION AUTONOMY — RANK

	Low	Middle	High	Row Total
High	380	103	57	540
Low	399	90	23	512
Column Total	779	193	80	1,052

X^2 = 15.05, P <.01
V = .12

Table 4 (75) Police (N=1,054)

PROBATION AUTONOMY	LOCATION							
	None	Street	Station House	Family Court	Probation Office	Tele-phone	Other	Row Total
High	206	19	57	14	25	167	54	542
Low	213	15	29	11	13	192	39	512
Column Total	419	34	86	25	38	359	93	1,054

X^2 = 17.17, P <.01
V = .13

Table 4 (76) Police (N=1,064)

PROBATION AUTONOMY	PROBATION ESTEEM		
	Low	High	Row Total
High	162	385	547
Low	200	317	517
Column Total	362	702	1,064

X^2 = 9.34, P <.01
V = .09

Table 4 (77) Police (N=1,064)

PROBATION AUTONOMY	CONFLICT		
	High	Low	Row Total
High	243	304	547
Low	273	244	517
Column Total	516	548	1,064

X^2 = 7.14, $P < .01$
V = .08

Table 4 (78) Police (N=1,054)

PROBATION AUTONOMY	CONTACT			
	Low	Middle	High	Row Total
High	412	95	37	544
Low	417	70	23	510
Column Total	829	165	60	1,054

X^2 = 5.99 , $P < .05$
V = .08

Table 4 (79) Police (N=1,057)

PROBATION AUTONOMY	AGE			
	Low	Middle	High	Row Total
High	172	282	89	543
Low	206	252	56	514
Column Total	378	534	145	1,057

X^2 = 11.47, $P < .01$
V = .10

Table 4 (80) Police (N=1,053)

PROBATION AUTONOMY	EXPERIENCE			
	Low	Middle	High	Row Total
High	178	217	147	542
Low	218	185	108	511
Column Total	396	402	255	1,053

X^2 = 8.61, $P < .01$
V = .09

Table 4 (81) Police (N=1,052)

PROBATION AUTONOMY	JOB RELATED COURSE TAKING		
	Yes	No	Row Total
High	344	200	544
Low	275	233	508
Column Total	619	433	1,052

X^2 = 8.61, P <.01
V = .09

TABLE 4 (82) Police (N=244)

PROBATION AUTONOMY	SPECIALIZED ASSIGNMENT			
	Narcotics	Morals	Other	Row Total
High	15	14	111	140
Low	7	21	76	104
Column Total	22	35	187	244

X^2 = 5.67, P <.06
V = .15

Table 4 (83) Police (N=1,025)

PROBATION AUTONOMY	NATURE OF WORK			
	Supervisory	Field	Administrative	Row Total
High	139	357	30	526
Low	102	371	26	499
Column Total	241	728	56	1,052

X^2 = 5.53, P <.07
V = .07

Table 4 (84) Police (N=1,051)

PROBATION AUTONOMY	PERSONAL CONTACT			
	Low	Middle	High	Row Total
High	378	114	47	539
Low	374	112	26	512
Column Total	752	226	73	1,051

X^2 = 5.39, P <.10
V = .07

BIBLIOGRAPHY

Adams, John D. — Organizational Development and Change. Wash., D.C.: National Training and Development Service, 1974.

Adorno, T.W.; Brunswick-Frenkel, Else; Levinson, Daniel J.; and Sanford, Nevitt R. — The Authoritarian Personality, New York: Harper & Row, 1950.

American Bar Association Project on Standards for Ciminal Justice. — Standards Relating to the Administration of Criminal Justice. Chicago, Ill.: American Bar Association, Institute of Judicial Administration 1974.

American Bar Association. — Standards Relating to Probation. Chicago, Ill.: American Bar Association, Institute of Judicial Administration, 1970.

American Bar Association. — Standards Relating to Urban Police Function. Chicago, Ill.: American Bar Association, Institute of Judicial Administration, 1972.

American Civil Liberties Union. — "Police Power and Citizens' Rights."

Anorasik, Frank, and McNamara, John. — "Optimizing Staff Performance in an Institutional Behavior Change System." Behavior Modification 1, No. 2 (April 1977): 235-248.

Anttila, Inkeri. — "Probation and Parole: Social Control or Social Service?" International Journal of Criminology and Penology 3, No. 1 (February 1975): 79-84.

Arcaya, Jose. — "The Multiple Realities Inherent in Probation Counseling." Federal Probation 37, No. 4 (December 1973): 58-63.

Argyle, M.; Gardner G.; and Coffee, F. — "Supervisory Methods Related to Productivity, Absenteeism and Labor Turnover." Human Re-tions 11 (1958): 23-40.

Argyris, Chris — Integrating the Individual and the Organization. New York: Wiley, 1964.

Argyris, Chris — Interpersonal Competence and Organizational Effectiveness. Homewood, Illinois: The Dorsey Press, 1962.

Argyris, Chris — Intervention Theory and Method: A Behavioral Science View. Reading, Mass.: Addison-Wesley, 1970.

Argyris, Chris — Management and Organizational Development. New York: McGraw Hill, 1971.

Argyris, Chris — Personality and Organization. New York: Harper & Row, 1957.

Balch, Robert W. — "The Police Personality: Fact or Fiction?" The Journal of Criminal Law, Criminology, and Police Science, 63, No. 1 (March 1972): 106-119.

Bales, Robert F. — Personality and Interpersonal Behavior, New York: Holt, Rinehart and Winston, 1970.

Banton, Michael — The Policeman in the Community. New York: Basic Boosk, 1964.

Barkdull, Walter L. — "Probation: Call It Control - and Mean It." Federal Probation, 40, No. 4 (December 1976): 3-8.

Barnlund, Dean C. , and Haiman, Franklyn S. — "A Philosophy and Method of Change." In Small Group Communication, pp. 206-215. Edited by Robert S. Cathcart and Larry A. Samovar. Dubuque, Iowa: William C. Brown Co., 1970.

Baron, Roger; Fleeney, Floyd; and Thornton, Warren. — "Preventing Delinquency Through Diversion." Federal Probation 40, No. 4 (March 1973): 13-18.

Beckhard, Richard — "The Confrontation Meeting." Harvard Business Review 45, No. 2 (1967): 149-153.

Beer, Stafford — Decision and Control. New York: John Wiley and Sons, 1966.

Bennis, Warren — Changing Organizations. New York: McGraw-Hill, 1966.

Bennis, Warren; Benne, Kenneth; and Chin, Robert — The Planning of Change. New York: Holt, Rinehart, and Winston, Inc., 1969.

Bennis, Warren, and Slatter, Philip — The Temporary Society. New York: Harper & Row, 1968.

Bertinot, Libby, and Taylor, Jack E. — "A Basic Plan for Statewide Probation Training." Federal Probation 38, No. 2 (June 1974): 29-31.

Bittner, Egon — "Police Discretion in Emergency Apprehension of Mentally Ill Persons." Social Problems 14 (Winter 1967): 278-292.

Blake, Robert R.: Mouton, Jane S.; and Sloma, Richard L. — "An Actual Case History of Resolving Intergroup Conflict in Union-Management Relations." In Managing Intergroup Conflict in Industry, pp. 155-195. Edited by Robert Blake, Herbert Shepard and Jane Mouton. Houston, Texas: Gulf Publishing Co., 1964.

Blake, Robert R.: Mouton, Jane S.; and Shepard, Herbert A. — "Foundation and Dynamics of Intergroup Behavior." In Managing Intergroup Conflict in Industry, pp. 86-101. Edited by Robert Blake, Herbert Shepard, and Jane Mouton. Houston, Texas: Gulf Publishing Co., 1964.

Blake, Robert R.: Mouton, Jane S. — "The Intergroup Dynamics of Win-Lose Conflict and Problem-Solving Collaboration in Union Management Relations." In Intergroup Relations and Leadership, pp. 94-140. Edited by Muazfer, Sherif. New York: John Wiley and Sons, 1962.

Blake, Robert R.: Mouton, Jane; and Shepard, Herbert. — "An Intergroup Problem-Solving Approach to Mergers." In Managing Intergroup Conflict in Industry, pp. 146-152. Edited by Robert Blake, Herbert Shepard, and Jane Mouton. Houston, Texas: Gulf Publishing Co., 1964.

Blake, Robert R.: Mouton, and Jane S. — "Interventions into Situations of Intergroup Conflicts." In Managing Intergroup Conflict in Industry, pp. 101-113. Edited by Robert Blake, Herbert Shepard, and Jane Mouton, Houston,

Texas: Gulf Publishing Co., 1964.

Blake, Robert R.: Mouton, Jane S.; and Shepard, Herbert — "Problem-Solving: A Third Approach to Agreement." In Managing Intergroup Conflict in Industry, pp. 86-101. Edited by Robert Blake, Herbert Shepard, and Jane Mouton. Houston, Texas: Gulf Publishing Co., 1964.

Blake, Robert R.: Mouton, Jane S.; and Shepard, Herbert — "Strategies for Improving Headquarters - Field Relations.: In Managing Intergroup Conflict in Industry, pp. 114-121. Edited by Robert Blake, Herbert Shepard, and Jane Mouton. Houston, Texas, Gulf Publishing Co., 1964.

Blake, Robert R.: Mouton, Jane S.; and Sloma, Richard C. — "Using Third-Party Judgment to Resolve Intergroup Disputes." In Managing Intergroup Conflict in Industry, pp. 50-57. Edited by Robert Blake, Herbert Shepard and Jane Mouton. Houston, Texas: Gulf Publishing Co., 1964.

Blake, Robert R.: Mouton, Jane S.; and Shepard, Herbert A. — "The Win-Lose Orientation to Intergroup Disagreement." In Managing Intergroup Conflict in Industry, pp. 18-33. Edited by Robert Blake, Herbert Shepard and Jane Mouton. Houston, Texas: Gulf Publishing Co., 1964.

Blau, Peter M., and Scott, Richard W. — Formal Organizations. San Francisco: Chandler Publishing Co., 1962.

Blumstein, Alfred — "Systems Analysis and the Criminal Justice System." The Annuals 374 (Nov. 1967): New York: John Wiley and Sons, 1967.

Boulding, Elise — "Further Reflections on Conflict Management." In Power and Conflict in Organizations, pp. 146-150. Edited by Robert Kahn and Elise Boulding. New York: Basic Books, 1964.

Boulding, Kenneth — "The Individual as a Party to Conflict." In Conflict and Defense, pp. 80-104. Edited by Kenneth Boulding. New York: Harper & Bros., 1962.

Boulding, Kenneth — "TheOrganization as a Party to Conflict." In Con flict and Defense, pp. 145-165. Edited by Kenneth Boulding. New York: Harper & Bros., 1962.

Boulding, Kenneth — "A Pure Theory of Conflict Applied to Organiza-tions, pp. 136-145. Edited by Robert Kahn and Elise Boulding. New York: Basic Books, Inc. 1964

Brandstatter, A. F. — "A Career Concept for Police." The Journal of Crimimal Law, Criminology and Police Science 61, No. 3 (Sept. 1970): 438-445.

Breer, William M. — "Probation Supervision of the Black Offender." Federal Probation 6 (June 1972): 31-36.

Brown, Douglas — The Human Nature of Organizations. New York: American Management Associations, 1973.

Brown, William — "Local Policing - A Three Dimensional Task Analysis." Journal of Criminal Justice 3, No. 1 (Spring 1975): 1-15.

Brunswick-Frenkel, Else — "Further Explorations by a Contributor to 'The Authoritarian Personality'," In Studies in the Scope and Method of 'The Authoritarian Personality', pp. 226-275. Edited by Richard Christie and Marie Jahoda. Glencoe, I11.: The Free Press, 1954.

Buckley, Walter — Modern Systems Research. Chicago: Aldine Publishing Co., 1968.

Burke, Warner W., and Hornstein, Harvey A. — The Social Technology of Organization Develop-ment. La Jolla, California: University Associates, Inc., 1972.

Burns, Tom, and Stalker, G.M. — The Management of Innovation. London: Tavistock Publications, 1961.

Carlson, Helena: Thayer, Robert; and Germann, A.C. — "Social Attitudes and Personality Differences Among Members of Two Kinds of Police Depart-ments." The Journal of Criminal Law, Criminology, and Police Science 62, No. 4 (Dec. 1971): 564-567

Cathcart, Robert S., and Samovar, Larry A. — Small Group Communication: A Reader. Dubuque: Iowa: William C. Brown Co., 1970,

Chang, Dae, and Zastrow, Charles H. — "Police Evaluative Perceptions of Themselves, The General Public and Selected Occupational Groups." Journal of Criminal Justice 4, No. 1 (March 1976): 29-33.

Chaves, Felix J. — "Counseling Offenders of Spanish Heritage." Federal Probation 40, No. 1 (March 1976): 29-33.

Christie, Richard, and Jahoda, Authori- Marie — Studies in the Scope and Method of 'The tarian Personality.' Glencoe, Illinois: The Free Press, 1954.

Churchman, C. — Systems and Management Annual. New York: Mason/Charter Publishers, 1975.

City of New York Commission on Human Rights — "Community Values and Conflict 1967: A Conference Report."

Coch, Lester, and French, Jr., John — "Overcoming Resistance to Change." In Group Dynamics, pp. 336-350. Edited by Dorwin Cartwright and Alvin Zander. New York: Harper & Row, 1968.

Coe, Rodney, M., and Barnhill, Elizabeth A. — "Social Dimensions of Failure in Innovation." Human Organization 26 (Fall, 1967): 149-156.

Cohen, Yona — "Staff Supervision in Probation." Federal Probation 40, No. 3 (Sept. 1976): 17-23.

Cohn, Alvin W. — "Training in the Criminal Justice Nonsystem." Federal Probation 38, No. 2 (June 1974): 32-37.

Colbert, Paul A., and Kirchberg, Susan M. — "Operating a Criminal Justice Unit Within a Narcotics Treatment Program." Federal Probation 37, No. 4 (Dec. 1973): 46-51.

Coleman, J. S. — Community Conflict, Glencoe, I11.: Free Press, 1957.

Conrad, John — "Corrections and Simple Justice." The Journal of Criminology and Police Science 64, No. 2 (June 1973): 208-217.

Coser, Lewis — The Functions of Social Conflict. New York: The Free Press, 1964.

Cumming, Elaine; Cumming, Ian, and Edell, Laura — "Policeman as Philosopher, Guide and Friend." Social Problems 12 (Winter 1965): 276-286.

Cvetkovich, Goerge — "Small Group Dynamics in Extended Judgment Situations.: In Human Judgment and Social Interaction, pp. 315-335. Edited by Leon Rappoport and David Summers. New York: Holt, Rinehart and Winston, 1973.

Davis, James H. — Group Performance. Reading, Mass.: Addison - Wesley, 1969.

Deutsch, K. W. — The Nerves of Government: Models of Political and Control. New York: The Free Press, 1963.

Deutsch, Morton — "Conflicts: Productive and Destructive." Journal of Social Issues, 25 (1969): 7-41.

Deutsch, Morton — "Cooperation and Trust: Some Theoretical Notes." In Nebraska Symposium of Motivation, pp. 275-318 Edited by Marshall R. Jones. Lincoln: University of Nebraska Press, 1962.

Deutsch, Morton — "The Effects of Cooperation and Competition upon Group Process." In Group Dynamics, pp. 461-482. Edited by Dorwin Cartwright and Alvin Zander. New York: Harper & Row, 1968.

Deutsch, Morton — The Resolution of Conflict. New Haven: Yale University Press, 1973.

Diffenbaucher, George I. — "Settling for 'Humanization': Evidence of Dispair or of Facing Reality?" Federal Probation 40, No. 1 (March 1976): 25-28.

Doob, Leonard W. — Resolving Conflict in Africa. New Haven: Yale University Press, 1970.

Dutton, John M., and Walton, Richard E. "Interdepartment Conflict and Cooperation: Two Contrasting Studies." Human Organization 25 (1966): 207-220.

Eastman, George D., and McCain, James A. "Police Managers and Their Perceptions of Higher Education." Journal of Criminal Justice 1, No. 2 (Summer 1973): 113-124.

Elbing, A. D. Behavioral Decisions in Organizations. Glenview, Ill.: Scott, Foresman, 1970.

Ells, Jerry G., and Sermat, Vello "Motivational Determinants of Choice in Chicken and Prisoner's D. lemma." Journal of Conflict Resolution 12 (Sept. 1968): 374-380.

Evan, William M. Organization Theory. New York: John Wiley and Sons, 1976.

Ewald, William R. Environment and Change. Bloomington, Indiana: Indiana University Press, 1966.

Faris, Robert "Interaction Levels and Intrgroup Relations." pp. In Intergroup Relations and Leadership, pp. 24-45. Edited by Muzafer Sherif. New York: Wiley and Sons, 1962.

Fiedler, Fred E. A Theory of Leadership Effectiveness. New York: McGraw-Hill, 1967.

Fisher, Roger "Fractionating Conflict." In Conflict Resolution, pp. 157-169. Edited by Clagett Smith. Notre Dame, Indiana: University of Notre Dame Press, 1971.

Fosdick, Raymond American Police Systems. Montclair, NJ: Patterson Smith, 1969.

Gardner, Neely Group Leadership, Washington, D.C.: National Training and Development Service, 1974.

Gawthrop, Louis C. Administrative Politics and Social Change. New York: St. Norton's Press, 1971.

Glaser, Daniel The Effectiveness of a Prison and Parole System. New York: The Bobbs-Merrill Co., 1964.

Glaser, Edward M. — "Research Frontier: Utilization of Applicable Research and Development Results." Journal of Counseling Psychology, 12 (1965): 201-205.

Goldman, Ralph M. — "A Theory of Conflict Processes and Organizational Offices." Journal of Conflict Resolution 10, No. 3 (Sept. 1966): 328-343.

Golembiewski, Robert — Men, Management and Morality. New York: McGraw-Hill, 1965.

Golembiewski, Robert — Organizing Men and Power. Chicago: Rand McNally, 1966.

Golembiewski, Robert; Gibson, Frank; Cornog, Geoffrey — Public Administration. Chicago: Rand McNally, 1966.

Graziano, Anthony M. Power — "Clinical Innovation and the Mental Health Structure: A Social Case History." American Psychologist 24 (Jan. 1969); 10-18.

Greiner, L.E. — "Patterns of Organizational Change." Harvard Business Review 45, No. 3 (1967): 119-123.

Gross, Edward — "Symbiosis and Consensus As Integrative Factors in Small Groups." In Small Group Communication, pp. 63-71. Edited by Robert S. Cathcart and Larry A. Samovar. Dubuque, Iowa: William C. Brown Co., 1970.

Hage, Jerald, and Aiken, Michael — Social Change in Complex Organizations. New York: Random House, 1970.

Hammond, Kenneth R.; Todd, Frederick J.; and Wilkins, — "Cognitive Conflict Between Persons: Application of the 'Lens Model' Paradigm." Journal of Experimental Social Psychology 2 (1966): 343-360.

Hammond, Kenneth R. — "The Cognitive Conflict Paradigm." In Human Judgment and Social Interaction, pp. 188-205. Edited by Leon Rappoport and David Summers. New York: Holt, Rinehart and Winston, 1973.

Hammond, Kenneth R., and , Brehmer, Berndt — "Quasi-Rationality and Distrust: Implications for International Conflict. In Human Judgment and Social Interaction, pp. 338-391. Edited by Leon Rappoport and David Summers. New York: Holt, Rinehart and Winston, 1973.

Hardman, Dale G. — "Corrections and the Community: A View Through a Crystal Ball." Federal Probation 34, No. 1 (March 1970): 19-26.

Harnack, Victor, and Fest, Thorrel B. — Group Discussion Theory and Technique. New York: Appleton-Century-Crofts, 1964.

Harris, Kay M. — "Criminal Justice: Rehabilitation or Punishment?" Remarks for the Mid-Winter Workshop of the Metropolitan Washington Chapter of the National Association of Social Workers. Washington, D.C., Jan. 1975 (mimeograph), pp. 6-7.

Havelock, Ronald G. — Planning for Innovation. Ann Arbor: Center for Research on Utilization of Scientific Knowledge, University of Michigan, 1970.

Havelock, Ronald G. — Training for Change Agents. Ann Arbor, Michigan: Institute for Social Research, 1973.

Hawley, Claude, and Weintraub, Ruth — Administrative Questions and Political Answers. New York: D. Van Nostrand Co., 1966.

Hodges, Jr., Harold M. — Conflict and Consensus. New York: Harper & Row, 1974.

Horejsi, Charles R. — "Training for the Direct Service Volunteer in Probation." Federal Probation 37, No. 3 (Sept. 1973): 38-41.

Hornstein, Harvey A., and Johnson, David — "The Effects of Process Analysis and Ties to His Group Upon the Negotiator's Attitudes Toward the Outcomes of Negotiations." Journal of Applied Behavioral Science 2 (1966): 449-463.

Horwitz, Murray — "Managing Hostility in the Laboratory and the Refinery." In Power and Conflict in Organizations, pp.

77-94. Edited by Robert Kahn and Elise Boulding. New York: Basic Books, 1964.

Howell, William S., and Smith, Donald K. — Discussion. New York: The Macmillan Co., 1956.

Howlett, Frederick W., and Hurst, Hunter — "A Systems Approach to Comprehensive Criminal Justice Planning." In Classes, Conflict, and Control, pp. 539-550. Edited by Jim Munro. Cincinnati: Anderson Pub. Co., 1976.

Jackson, Wayne P. — "Treatment of the Offender in the United Kingdom." Federal Probation 35, No. 2 (June 1971): 50-57.

Jacobs, Paul — Prelude to Riot. New York: Random House, 1966.

Jacoby, Jacob — "Multiple-Indicant Approach for Studying New Product Adopters." Journal of Applied Psychology 55 (August 1971): 384-388.

Jacoby, Jacob — "Personality and Innovation Proneness." Journal of Marketing Research 8 (May 1971): 244-247.

Jagiello, Robert — "College Education for the Patrolman - Necessity or Irrelevance?" The Journal of Criminal Law, Criminology and Police Science 62, No. 1 (March 1970): 114-121.

Johnson, Deborah, and Gregory, Robert J. — "Police-Community Relations in the United States." The Journal of Criminal Law, Criminology and Police Science 62, No. 1 (March 1971): 94-103.

Johnson, Elmer H. — Crime, Correction and Society. Homewood, Illinois: Dorsey Press, 1964.

Julian, James W. and Perry, Franklyn A. — "Cooperation Contrasted with Intra-Group and Inter-Group Competition." In Small Group Communication, pp. 89-91. Edited by Robert S. Cathcart and Larry A. Samovar. Dubuque, Iowa: William C. Brown Co., 1970.

Kahn, Robert L., and Wolfe, Donald — "Role Conflict in Organizations." In Power and Conflict in Organizations, pp. 115-126. Edited by

Robert Kahn and Elise Boulding. New York:

Katz, Daniel — "Approaches to Managing Conflict." In Power and Conflict in Organizations, pp. 105-114. Edited by Robert Kahn and Elise Boulding. New York: Basic Books, 1964.

Katz, Daniel, and Kahn, Robert — The Social Psychology of Organizations. New York: John Wiley & Sons, 1966.

Keldgord, Robert E., and Norris, Robert O. — "New Directions for Corrections." Federal Probation 36, No. 1 (March 1972): 3-9.

Kellogg, Frederic R. — "Organizing the Criminal Justice System: A Look at 'Operative' Objectives." Federal Probation 40, No. 2 (June 1976): 50-55.

Kerr, Clark — Labor and Management in Industrial Society. New York: Doubleday and Co., 1964.

Kessel, Colin — "Effects of Group Pressure and Commitment on Conflict, Adaptability, and Cognitive Change." In Human Judgment and Social Interaction, pp. 296-303. Edited by Leon Rappoport and David Summers. New York: Holt, Rinehart and Winston, 1973.

Klein, Donald — "Some Notes on the Dynamics of Resistance to Change: The Defender Role." In Concepts for Social Change. Edited by G. Watson. Wash., D.C.: NTL Institute for Applied Behavioral Science, 1967, p. 30.

Klyman, Fred I., and Kruckenberg, Joanna — "A Methodology for Assessing Citizen Perceptions of Police." Journal of Criminal Justice 2, No. 3 (Fall 1974): 219-233.

Knapp, William M., and Podell, Jerome E. — "Mental Patients, Prisoners, and Students with Simulated Partners in a Mixed-Motive Game." Journal of Conflict Resolution 2 (June 1967): 235-241.

Knekel, Fletcher — "Police in Crisis." Look 32, No. 3 (Feb. 6, 1968).

Kuhlman, Carl E.; Miller, Monroe J.; and Gungor, Erol — "Interpersonal Conflict Reduction: The Effects of Language and Meaning." In Human Judgment and Social Interaction, pp. 229-237. Edited by Leon Rappoport and David Summers. New York: Holt, Rinehart and Winston, 1973.

Lafave, Wayne — Arrest: The Decision to Take a Suspect into Custody. Boston: Little, Brown and Co., 1965.

Lawrence, Paul R., and Lorsch, Jay W. — Organization and Environment: Managing Differentiation and Integration. Homewood, Ill,: Richard D. Irwin, 1967.

Lankes, George — "How Should We educate the Police?" The Journal of Criminal Law, Criminology and Police Science 62, No. 1 (March 1971): 587-592.

Lassoon, Kenneth — "The Cop." In The Workers, pp. 193-218. Edited by Kenneth Lassoon. New York: Grossman Pub., 1971.

Leonard, V. A. — The Police of the Twentieth Century. Brooklyn: The Foundation Press, 1964.

Levy, Ruth — "Predicting Police Failures." Journal of Criminal Law, Criminology and Police Science 58, No. 2 (1967): 275.

Likert, Rensis — The Human Organization. New York: McGraw - Hill Book Co., 1967.

Likert, Rensis — New Patterns in Management. New York: McGraw-Hill, 1961.

Likert, Rensis, and Likert, Jane G. — New Ways of Managing Conflict. New York: McGraw-Hill, 1976.

Lorsch, Jay W., and Sheldon, Alan — "The Individual in the Organization: A Systems View." In Managing Group and Intergroup Relations, pp. 161-182. Edited by Jay W. Lorsch and Paul R. Lawrence. Homewood, Ill.: Richard D. Irwin, Inc., 1972.

Luger, Milton, and Lobenthal, Joseph S. — "Cushioning Future Shock in Corrections." Federal Probation 38, No. 2 (June 1974): 18-23.

MacNamara, Donal, and Riedel, Marc — Police: Perspectives, Problems, Prospects. New York: Praeger, 1974.

Macpherson, David P. — "Probation and Corrections in the Seventies." Federal Probation 35, No. 1 (March 1971): 14-17.

Maier, N. R. F. — Problem Solving and Creativity: In Individuals and Groups. Belmont, Calif.: Brooks Cole Publishing Co., 1970.

Maier, Norman R. F. — Problem-Solving Discussions and Conferences. New York: McGraw-Hill, 1963.

Mangum, Claude T. — "The Humanity of Probation Officers." Federal Probation 36, No. 2 (June 1972): 47-50.

Marrow, A. J.; Bowers, David G.; and Seashore, S. E. — Management by Participation. New York: Harper & Row, 1967.

Maslow, Abraham — Eupsychian Management. Homewood, Ill.: The Dorsey Press, 1965.

Mazur, Allan — "A Nonrational Approach to Theories of Conflict and Coalitions." Journal of Conflict Resolution 12 (June 1968): 196-205.

McCarthy, Henry — "Some Situational Factors Improving Cognitive Conflict Reducation and Interpersonal Understanding." Journal of Conflict Resolution 21 (June 1977): 217-234.

McDowell, Charles P. — Police in the Community. Cincinnati: The W. H. Anderson Co., 1975.

McGregor, Douglas — The Human Side of Enterprise New York: McGraw-Hill, 1960.

McManus, G. P.; Griffin, J. I.; Wetteroth, W. J. Boland, M.; and Hines, P.T. — Police Training and Performance Study. Wash., D. C.: U. S. Government Printing Office, 1970, p. 34.

Medeiros, James A., and Schmitt, David E. — Public Bureaucracy. North Scituate, Mass.: Duxbury Press, 1977.

Melcher, Arlyn J. — General Systems and Organization Theory: Methodological Aspects. Kent State, Ohio: Center for Business and Economic Research, Kent State University, 1975.

Meyer, John C., and Taylor, Winthrop E. — "Analyzing the Nature of Police Involvements: A Research Note Concerning the Effects of Forms of Police Mobilization." Journal of Criminal Justice 3 No. 2 (Summer 1975): 141-145.

Milers, R. — "Human Relations or Human Resources." Harvard Business Review 43 (July - August 1965): 148-163.

Mintz, Ellen, and Sandler, Georgetta — "Instituting a Full-Service Orientation to Policing." The Police Chief 16, No. 6 (June 1974): 44-50.

More, Harry W. — Critical Issues in Law Enforcement. Cincinnati: The W. H. Anderson Co., 1972.

Mortensen, David C. — "A Transactional Paradigm of Verbalized Social Conflict." In Perspectives on Communication in Social Conflict, pp. 90-124. Edited by Gerald R. Miller and Herbert W. Simons. Englewood Cliffs, New Jersey: Prentice-Hall, 1974.

]Moscovici, Serge; Lage, Elizabeth; and Naffrechoux, Martine — "Conflict in Three-Person Groups: The Relationship Between Social Inflience and Cognitive Style." In Human Judgment and Social Interaction, pp. 304-314. Edited by Leon Rappoport and David Summers. New York: Holt, Rinehart and Winston, 1973.

Muney, Barbara F., and Deutsch, Morton — "The Effects of Role-Reversal During the Discussion of Opposing Viewpoints." Journal of Conflict Resolution, 2 (September 1968): 345-356.

Munro, Jim L. — "Towards A Theory of Criminal Justice Administration: A General Systems Perspective." In Classes, Conflict, and Control, pp. 135-152. Edited by Jim Munro. Cincinnati: Anderson Publishing Co., 1976.

Myrdal, Gunnar — An American Dilemma. New York: Harper & Row, 1944.

Myrdal, Gunnar — Asian Drama: An Inquiry into the Poverty of Nations. New York: The Twentieth Century Fund, 1968.

Nanus, Burt — "A General Model for Criminal Justice Planning." Journal of Criminal Justice 2, No. 4 (Winter 1974): 345-355.

National Advisory Commission on Criminal Justice Standards and Goals — Corrections. Wash., D.C.: Gov't Printing Office, Jan. 23, 1973.

Natinal Advisory Commission on Criminal Justice Standards and Goals — Criminal Justice System. Wash., D.C.: Gov't Printing Office, Jan. 23, 1973.

National Advisory Commission on Criminal Justice Standards and Goals — Police. Wash., D.C.: Gov't Printing Office, Jan. 23, 1973.

National Planning Association — Causes of Industrial Peace. Wash., D.C.: National Planning Association, 1953.

Negendhi, Anant R. — Modern Organizational Theory. Kent, Ohio: Kent State University Press, 1973.

Negandhi, Anant R. — Organizational Theory in an Open System, New York: Kennikat Press Corp., 1975.

Neilsen, Eric H. — "Understanding and Managing Intergroup Conflict." In Managing Group and Intergroup Relations, pp. 329-343. Edited by Jay W. Lorsch and Paul R. Lawrence. Homewood, Illinois: Richard B. Irwin, 1972.

Newman, Donald — Correction: The Determination of Guilt or Innocence Without Trial. Boston: Little, Brown, and Co., 1966.

Newman, Graeme R.; Articolo, Donald J.; Trilling, Carol — "Authoritarianism, Religiosity and Reactions to Deviance." Journal of Criminal Justice 2, No. 3 (Fall 1974): 249-259.

Niederhoffer, Arthur — Behind the Shield. New York: Doubleday, 1967.

Niederhoffer, Arthur, and and Blumberg, Abraham — The Ambivalent Force: Perspectives on the Police San Francisco: Rinehart Press, 1973.

Nye, Robert D. — Conflict Among Humans. New York: Springer Pub. Co., 1973.

O'Leary, Vincent, and Newman, Donald J. — "Conflict Resolution in Criminal Justice." Journal of Research in Crime and Delinquency 7, No. 2 (July 1970): 99-119.

O'Leary, Vincent, and Ryan, Edward — A Study of Conflict Resolution in Criminal Justice A Publication of the Probation Management Institute, Administered by the National Council on Crime and Delinquency, Oct. 1969.

Palmer, Ted — "An Overview of Matching in the Community Treatment Project." Presented at the Annual Meeting of the Western Psychological Association, San Diego, California, March 30, 1968, pp. 1-21.

Palmer, Ted — "Matching Worker and Client in Corrections." Social Work 18, No. 2 (March 1973): 95-103.

Palmer, Ted — Types of Probation Officers and Types of Youth on Probation: Their Views and Interactions. Youth Studies Center, University of Southern California, 1963.

Palmer, Ted — "Types of Treaters and Types of Juvenile Offend ers." Youth Authority Quarterly 18, No. 3 (Fall 1965): 1-9.

Petelle, John L. — "The Role of Conflict in Discussion." In Small Group Communication, pp. 143-148. Edited by Robert S. Cathcart and Larry A. Samovar. Dubuque, Iowa: William C. Brown, Co., 1970.

Pfiffner, John M., and Sherwood, Frank P. — Administrative Organization. Englewood Cliffs, N.J., Prentice-Hall, 1960.

Phillips, Gerald M., and Erickson, Eugene C. — Interpersonal Dynamics in the Small Group. New York: Random House, 1970.

The President's Commission on Law Enforcement and Administration of Justice — The Challange of Crime in a Free Society. Wash., D.C.: U. S. Gov't Printing Office, 1967.

The President's Commission on Law Enforcement and Administration of Justice — Task Force Report: The Police. Wash., D.C.: U. S. Gov't Printing Office, 1967. pp. 122-124.

Radelet, Louis A. — The Police and The Community: Studies. Beverly Hills: Glencoe Press, 1973.

Rapoport, Anatol — "Critiques of Game Theory." Behavioral Science 4 (1959): 49-68.

Rapoport, Anatol — Fights, Games and Debates. Ann Arbor, Mich.: University of Michigan Press, 1961.

Rapoport, Anatol — Strategy and Conscience. New York: Harper & Row, 1964.

Rappoport, Leon, and Summers, David A. — Human Judgment and Social Interaction. New York: Holt, Rinehart and Winston, 1973.

Raymond, Jonathan S.; Miller, Jerome S.; and Sensenig, John — "A Source of Potential Social Conflict: Police versus Addict Value Structures." International Journal of Criminology and Penology 3, No. 3 (Aug. 1975): 267-278.

Regoli, Robert M. — "An Empirical Assessment of Niederhofter's Police Cynicism Scale." Journal of Criminal Justice 4, No. 3 (1976): 231-241.

Reiss, Albert J. — The Police and the Public. New Haven: Yale University Press, 1971.

Remington, Frank J.; Newman, Donald J.; Kimball, Edward L.; Melli, Maryold; and Goldstein, Herman. — Criminal Justice Administration. Indianapolis: Bobbs-Merrill, 1969.

Robinson, James A. — "Further Problems of Research on International Relations." In Intergroup Relations and Leadership, pp. 205-209. Edited by Muzafer Sherif. New York: Wiley and Sons, 1962.

Robinson, John P.; Rusk, Jerrold, G.; Head, Kendra, B. — Measures of Political Attitudes, Ann Arbor, Michigan: Survey Research Center, 1968.

Rogers, Everett M., and Rogers, Rekha Agarwala — Communication in Organizations. New York: Free Press, 1976.

Rogers, Everett M. — Diffusion of Innovations. New York: The Free Press of Glencoe, Inc., 1962.

Rokeach, Milton — Beliefs, Attitudes and Values. San Francisco: Jossey-Bass, 1970.

Rokeach, Milton — "The Nature and Meaning of Dogmatism." Psychological Review 61, No 3 (1954): 194-204.

Rosenberg, Morris — "Faith in People and Success Orientation." In The Language of Social Research, pp. 158-161. Edited by Paul Lazarsfeld and Morris Rosenberg. New York: The Free Press, 1955.

Rubinstein, Jr. — City Police. New York: Farrar, Strauss and Giroux, 1973.

Sandford, Merritt R. — "Individual Conflict and Organizational Interaction."

In Power and Conflict in Organizations, pp. 94-104. Edited by Robert Kahn and Elise Boulding. New York: Basic Books, 1964.

Scheier, Ivan H. — "The Professional and the Voluteer in Probation: An Emerging Relationship." Federal Probation 34, No. 2 (June 1970): 12-18.

Schein, Edgar — Organizational Psychology. Englewood Cliffs, N.J. Prentice-Hall, 1970.

Schelling, Thoms C. — "Game Theory and The Study of Ethical Systems." Journal of Conflict Resolutions 12, No. 1 (March 1968): 34-44.

Schon, Donald — Technology and Change. New York: Dell, 1967.

Schwartz, Ira M. "Volunteers and Professionals: A Team in the Correctional Process." Federal Probation 35, No. 3 (Sept. 1971): 46-50.

Seiler, John A. "Diagnosing Interdepartmental Conflict." In Managing Group and Intergroup Relations, pp. 310-324. Edited by Jay W. Lorsch and Paul R. Lawrence. Homewood, Ill.: Richard D. Irwin, 1972.

Shapiro, Stewart B. Management of Conflict. Los Angeles: Institute of Industrial Relations, University of California, 1973.

Shepard, Herbert A. "Responses to Situations of Competition and Conflict." In Power and Conflict in Organizations, pp. 127-135. Edited by Robert Kahn and Elise Boulding. New York: Basic Books, 1964.

Sherif, Muzafer "Intergroup Relations and Leadership." In Intergroup Relations and Leadership, pp. 3-21. Edited by Muzafer Sherif. New York: Wiley and Sons, 1962.

Sherif, Muzafer, and Sherif, Carolyn W. "Attitudes Formation and Change." In An Outline of Social Psychology, pp. 538-578. Edited by Muzafer and Carolyn Sherif. New York: Harper and Bros., 1956.

Sherif, Muzafer, and Sherif, Carolyn W. "Intergroup Relations." In An Outline of Social Psychology, pp. 280-332. Edited by Muzafer and Carolyn Sherif. New York: Harper and Bros., 1956.

Sherman, Lawrence; Milton, Catherine; and Kelly, Thomas Team Policing. Wash., D.C.: Police Foundation, 1973.

Simmel, Georg Conflict. Trans. by Kurt H. Wolff. New York: The Free Press, 1955.

Simons, Herbert W. "The Carrot and Stick as Handmaidens of Persuasion in Conflict Situations." In Perspectives on Communication in Social Control, pp. 178-184. Edited by Gerald W. Miller and Herbert W. Simons,

Simons, Herbert W. "Prologue." In Perspectives on Communication in Social Control, pp. 3-8. Edited by Gerald W. Miller and Herbert W. Simons. Englewood Cliffs, New Jersey: Prentice-Hall, 1974.

Sirota, David, and Greenwood, Michael J. "Understand Your Overseas Work Force." "Harvard Business Review 49, (Jan.-Feb. 1971): 53-60.

Sherif, Muzafer, and Sherif, Carolyn W. "Attitudes Formation and Change." In An Outline of Social Psychology, pp. 538-578. Edited by Muzafer and Carolyn Sherif. New York: Harper and Bros., 1956.

Skoler, Daniel L. "Correctional Unification: Rhetoric, Reality, and Potential." Federal Probation 40, No. 1 (March 1976): 14-20.

Skolnick, Jerome H. Justice Without Trial. New York: John Wiley and Sons, 1967.

Stein, Harold Public Adminstration and Policy Development. New York. Harcourt, Brace and Co., 1952.

Steiner, Gary A. The Creative Organization. Chicago: The University of Chicago Press, 1965.

Steinfeld, George J. "A Cognitive-Behavioral Analysis of Institutional Conflict and a Humanistic Solution." International Journal of Criminology and Penology 3, No. 4 (Nov. 1975): 323-344.

Stogdill, Ralph M. "Intragroup-Intergroup Theory and Research." In Intergroup Relations and Leadership, pp. 48-65. Edited by Muzafer Sherif. New York: Wiley and Sons, 1962.

Stufflebaum, Daniel "The Use and Abuse of Evaluation in Title III." Theory into Practice 6 (1967): 126-133.

Summers, David A. "Conflict, Compromise, and Belief Change in a Decision-Making Task." Journal of Conflict Resolution 12, No. 2 (June 1968): 215-221

Swank, Calivn J., and Parsons, James C. — "Police Organizations and the Art of Effecting Change." International Journal of Criminology and Penology 2, No. 3 (Aug. 1974): 289-294.

Takagi, Paul — "Administrative and Professional Conflicts in Modern Corrections." The Journal of Criminal Law and Criminology 64, No. 3 (Sept. 1973): 313-319.

Tamm, Quinn — "Equal Justice-Under Law." The Police Chief 33, No. 11 (Nov. 1966), p. 6.

Tannenbaum, A. S. — Control in Organizations. New York: McGraw Hill, 1968.

Taylor, James C. — Technology and Planned Organizational Change. Ann Arbor, Mich.: Institute for Social Research, The University of Michigan, 1971.

Thibaut, John — "The Development of Contractural Norms in Bargaining: Replication and Variation." Journal of Conflict Resolution 12, No. 1 (March 1968): 102-112.

Thomas, Kenneth W. — "Issues in Management of Conflict." In Management of Conflict, pp. 5-22. Edited by Stewart Shapiro. Los Angeles: Institute of Industrial Relations, University of Calif., March 13, 1973.

Thompson, James — "Supreme Court and the Police: 1968." Journal of Criminal Law, Criminology and Police Science, 57, No. 4 (Dec. 1966): 425.

Thompson, Victor A. — Bureaucracy and Innovation. University, Alabama: University of Alabama Press, 1976.

Tiffany, Laurence; McIntyre, Donald; and Rothenberg, Daniel — Detection of Crime: Stopping and Questionning, Search and Seizure, Encouragement and Entrapment. Boston: Little, Brown and Co., 1967.

Toch, Hans — "The Care and Feeding of Typologies and Labels." Federal Probation 34, No. 3 (Sept. 1970): 15-19.

Toch, Hans — Police, Prisons and the Problem of Violence. Rockville, Maryland: National Institute of Mental Health, U.S. Dept. of Health, Education, and Welfare, 1977.

Toch, Hans; Grant, Douglas J.; Galvin, Raymond T. — Agents of Change: A Study in Police Reform. New York: John Wiley and Sons, 1975.

Todd, Frederick J.; Hammond, Kenneth R.; Wilkins, Marilyn M. — "Differential Effects of Ambiguous and Exact Feedback on Two-Person Conflict and Compromise." Journal of Conflict Resolution 10, No. 1 (March 1966): 99-97.

Treger, Harvey — "Breakthrough in Preventive Corrections: A Police-Social Work Team Model." Federal Probation 36, No. 4 (Dec. 1972): 53-58.

Trojanowicz, Robert — "The Policeman's Occupational Personality." The Journal of Criminal Law, Criminology and Police Science 62, No. 4 (Dec. 1971): 551-559.

Turner, William — The Police Establishment. New York: G. P. Putnam's, 1968.

Vollmer, August — The Police and Modern Society. Montclair, N.J.: Patterson Smith, 1972.

VonBertalanffy, Ludwig — General System Theory, New York: George Braziller, Inc., 1968.

Walton, Richard E. — "Interpersonal Confrontation and Basic Third Party Functions: A Case Study." Journal of Applied Behavioral Science 4, No. 3 (1967): 327-350.

Walton, Richard E. — Interpersonal Peacemaking: Confrontations and Third Party Consultation. Reading, Mass.: Addison-Wesley Pub. Co., 1969.

Walton, Richard E. — "Legal-Justice, Power Bargaining, and Social Science Intervention: Mechanisms for Settling Disputes." Institute for Research in the Behavioral, Economic and Management Sciences, Institute Paper No. 194, March 1968.

Walton, Richard E. — "Third Party Roles in Interdepartmental Conflict." Industrial Relations 7, No. 1 (October 1967): 29-43.

Walton, Richard E., and Dutton, John M. — "Interdepartmental Conflict and Its Management: A General Model and Review." Krannert Graduate School of Industrial Administration, Purdue University, March 1968.

Ward, Richard — "The Police Role: A Case of Diversity." The Journal of Criminal Law, Criminology and Police Science 62, No. 1 (March 1971): 580-586.

Warren, Marguerite Q. — "Classification of Offenders As An Aid to Efficient Management and Effective Treatment." The Journal of Criminal Law, Criminology and Police Science 62, No. 2 (June 1971): 239-258.

Watson, Goodwin — Change in School Systems. Wash., D.C.: NTL Institute for Applied Behavioral Science, 1967.

Watson, Goodwin — "Resistance to Change." In Police Community Relations, pp. 555-561. Edited by Alvin Cohn and Emilio Viano. New York: J. B. Lippincott, 1976.

Watson, Nelson, and — Police and Their Opinions. Wash., D.C.: International Association of Chiefs of Police, 1969.

Weick, Karl E. — The Social Psychology of Organizing. Reading, Mass.: Addison-Wesley Pub. Co., 1969.

Weinder, Normal L. — "The Effect of Education on Police Attitudes." Journal of Criminal Justice 2, No. 4 (Winter 1974): 317-328.

Werthman, Carl, and — Gang Members and the Police. U.S. Dept. of Health, Education and Welfare, Grant No. 62224.

Westley, William — "The Escalation of Violence Through Legitima-
tion."

The Annals 364 (March 1966): 126.

Wilson, James Q. — "Innovation in Organization: Notes Toward a Theory." In Approaches to Organizational Design, pp. 193-218. Edited by James D. Thompson. Pittsburgh: University of Pittsburgh Press, 1966.

Wilson, James Q. — Varieties of Police Behavior. Cambridge: Harvard University Press, 1968.

Wilson, P. R., and Chappell, D. "The Effects of Police Withdrawal from Traffic Control: A Comparative Study." The Journal of Criminal Law, Criminology and Police Science 62, No. 1 (March 1971): 567-572.

Zaleznik, Abraham and Moment, David. The Dynamics of Interpersonal Behavior. New York: John Wiley and Sons, 1964.

Zaleznik, Abraham; Dalton, Gene W.; and Barnes, Louis B. Orientation and Conflict in Career. Boston: Harvard University Graduate School of Business Administration Division of Research, 1970.

Zaltman, Gerald; Duncan, Robert; and Holbek, Jonny. Innovations and Organizations. New York: John Wiley and Sons, 1973.